HISTORY AND
THE CHRISTIAN HISTORIAN

History and the Christian Historian

Edited by

Ronald A. Wells

WILLIAM B. EERDMANS PUBLISHING COMPANY
GRAND RAPIDS, MICHIGAN / CAMBRIDGE, U.K.

© 1998 Wm. B. Eerdmans Publishing Co.

255 Jefferson Ave. S.E., Grand Rapids, Michigan 49503 /

P.O. Box 163, Cambridge CB3 9PU U.K.

Printed in the United States of America

03 02 01 00 99 98   7 6 5 4 3 2 1

Library of Congress Cataloging-in-Publication Data

History and the Christian historian / edited by Ronald A. Wells.

p.   cm.

Includes bibliographical references.

ISBN 0-8028-4536-3 (alk. paper)

1. History (Theology)   I. Wells, Ronald, 1941- .

BR115.H5H534   1998

261.5 — dc21   98-29922

CIP

Contents

CONTENTS

II. DISCRETE THEMES AND SUBJECTS

III. APPLICATIONS FOR TEACHING HISTORY

Introduction

This book arises out of a concern of historians who are Christians. We ask: what case can be made for connecting our historical work and our religious convictions? We note that it is now acceptable, arguably necessary, for a historian to situate him/herself in a historical discourse. The standpoint of the historian must, in one way or another, be noted as part of the historical interpretation. This represents a historical sea change. It has affected all of us, as much those whose training came before the change, as those who came of age as scholars during the change. The abandonment of "that noble dream" of doing history as "reality as it actually was" did not come easily. While some of us, especially those writing in this volume, welcomed the change with qualifications, there were others who lamented that history written from an acknowledged perspective would lead to a crisis of historical understanding. If all history was but a "take" on the past, it is asked, by what standard can we choose between professionally acceptable and unacceptable work? Such concerns are not trivial. As Christian historians we mark our identities by the "reality" that God exists and that God came among us in the historical person known to us as Jesus. Thus we have an important stake in the epistemological crisis that the legitimation of "standpoint" has engendered.

There is no going back to the positivist ideology that energized historical research over the past century. The day is gone forever when

1

historians could assert that all scholars of good will would see more or less the same historical reality if enough research were done. We now accept what, I believe, we always knew but did not have the insight or the courage to say aloud: that historical voices were never acontextual voices from nowhere but contextual voices from somewhere; that historians are people from somewhere too, and that our presuppositions influence, to one degree or another, the questions we ask of the past and the interpretative structures to construct and interpret the past. If the historical task is negotiating the space between past contexts and our own, it serves the cause of truth-seeking if we all come clean about the roles we play. As Hans-Georg Gadamer has reminded us, this task of interpretation — hermeneutics if you will — is not just the stuff of historical work but "the original characteristic of the being of human life itself."[1]

Once we see that historical accounts or interpretations are "constructions of reality," not "reality" itself, we cannot rest assured that we have come to the finality of truth, either in the testimonies of historical actors or in our own representations of them. This approach is often called the "sociology of knowledge" approach because of its insistence that all knowledge is socially constructed.[2] This requires of all historians a "hermeneutics of suspicion" because, since all texts are "constructed," they need to be "deconstructed" to interpret them. Now some practitioners of the old way gasp, and insist that such a set of understandings will leave us in a state of constant revision, never to arrive at truthful conclusions. However, we cannot see how our understandings are so new or so threatening. We think that this is what, in fact, historians have always done, i.e., to pursue what, to them, are compelling questions that connect the past and the present, and then make statements that approximate reality, knowing full well that another historian, asking different questions, will give another, revisionist interpretation. Nonetheless, some historians persist in resisting this line of thought. Indeed, in a session at a major historical meeting a few years ago a prominent historian from a major university said that s/he had no idea what his/her presuppositions were, and that s/he asked no questions of the past that did not arise from historical texts or artifacts. One cannot tell if

---

1. Hans-Georg Gadamer, *Truth and Method* (New York: Crossroad, 1989), 259.

2. This way of thinking was begun in this century by classic sociological thinkers like Karl Mannheim. The most accessible extant work in this tradition is Peter Berger and Thomas Luckmann, *The Social Construction of Reality* (New York: Penguin Books, 1966).

such objections are devious or naive; but, put charitably, the scholar in question perhaps was trying to push the session to reexamine where a thoroughgoing perspectivalism might lead. That is actually an important concern to which we shall return below.

The issues raised by the essays in this book try to connect with a larger and longer conversation, both in terms of Christian discourse specifically and of historical discourse generally. The relationship of Christianity and history has been discussed in many useful, sometimes elegant, books. Over the past generation or two we note the good and helpful work of, for example, Herbert Butterfield, Christopher Dawson, Van Harvey, and C. T. McIntire.[3] There were also some useful collections of essays, e.g., by George Marsden and Frank Roberts[4] and by C. T. McIntire and Ronald Wells.[5] This book stands on the shoulders of those efforts, but a comparison of the last two named collections and this one will demonstrate how much the conversation in the field has changed.

This book also drafts off the force created by the recent resurgence of religious history.[6] Some of the people writing in this book have participated in the revision of American history that saw religion take an important place in historical discourse. They have done a great deal to recover religion from relative neglect. Religion is no longer a derivative matter, but an important reality in its own right to be studied. By rehabilitating religion *in* history these and other scholars have opened

---

3. Herbert Butterfield, *Christianity and History* (London: G. Bell and Sons, 1949); H. Christopher Dawson, *The Dynamics of World History* (London: Sheed and Ward, 1957); Van Harvey, *The Historian and the Believer* (New York: Macmillan, 1967); C. T. McIntire, *God, History and Historians* (New York: Oxford University Press, 1977).

4. Frank Roberts and George Marsden, eds., *A Christian View of History?* (Grand Rapids: Eerdmans, 1976).

5. C. T. McIntire and Ronald Wells, eds., *History and Historical Understanding* (Grand Rapids: Eerdmans, 1984).

6. George M. Marsden, *Fundamentalism and American Culture* (New York: Oxford University Press, 1980); idem, *The Soul of the American University* (New York: Oxford University Press, 1993); Mark A. Noll, *Princeton and the Republic, 1768-1822* (Princeton: Princeton University Press, 1989); Nathan Hatch, *The Democratization of American Christianity* (New Haven: Yale University Press, 1989); Margaret Bendroth, *Fundamentalism and Gender* (New Haven: Yale University Press, 1993); Joel Carpenter, *Revive Us Again: The Reawakening of American Fundamentalism* (New York: Oxford University Press, 1997); D. G. Hart, *Defending the Faith: J. Gresham Machen and the Crisis of Conservative Protestantism in Modern America* (Baltimore: Johns Hopkins University Press, 1994).

the way for religious discussion *about* history. In our time, when writing history from a standpoint is increasingly acceptable, we are grateful for this opportunity to contribute our own — Christian — views to the historical conversation.

While in the chapters to follow we offer our views in full and open Christian disclosure, we do so in a way consistent with our membership in the academy. Historians in academic life proceed with care and civility. We do not present our views in triumph nor do we play some sort of interpretative trump card. For us, a Christian perspective is more about our angle of vision than about the actual subject matter of history. After all, we see what most other honest scholars see. In some cases, though, our different questions or angles of vision allow or cause us to ask or to try to see what others do not. Even so, our membership in the academy requires that we present that insight in a proximate, not an ultimate, way. While the core truth of reality may exist — somewhere "out there" or in the mind of God — we sure do not know it finally or ultimately. While we have something to contribute, it is not something entirely different from our non-Christian fellow historians. Therefore, two points need to be made at the same time: we believe that God is with us and in us, and that makes a difference for our historical study [this should encourage fellow Christians, colleagues and students alike]; we accept our role in the academy to be cooperative and dialogical [this should reassure some secular colleagues who perhaps feared that our contributions would be imperial].

Historians reading this book, colleagues and students alike, may now see where and how this volume fits into Christian discourse. But, they may rightly wonder where and how this book connects with current trends in the historical profession. In answer, we suggest that our perspectival concerns are in accord with, for example, the views expressed in one of the more influential books to appear in recent years, *Telling the Truth About History*, by Joyce Appleby, Lynn Hunt, and Margaret Jacob. With them we note that "history has been shaken right down to its scientific and cultural foundations at the very time those foundations themselves are being contested."[7]

Joyce Appleby (at this writing, president of the American Historical Association) and her colleagues came to the historical profession as

---

7. Joyce Appleby, Lynn Hunt, and Margaret Jacob, *Telling the Truth About History* (New York: Norton, 1994), 2.

outsiders. Being women made a difference. As they say, "for outsiders, skepticism and relativism offer modes of inquiry essential to redressing the wrongs of exclusion."[8] Prior historical narratives often excluded women, minorities, and working-class people from the historical narrative and from the history profession as well. For Appleby, Hunt, and Jacob (hereafter AHJ) it is important to take notice of a larger structural nexus. There was, from the late 1950s onwards, a substantial democratization both of the academy and also of how the academy functioned: the opening up of higher education to nearly all who wanted it; the rise of skepticism and relativism as modes of inquiry; the dethroning of science as the model for historical method. These trends were interrelated in that they promoted democratic change in both the structure of the academy and in the epistemological assumptions on which it operated. As AHJ write, "We routinely, even angrily, ask: Whose history? Whose science? Whose interests are being served by those ideas and those stories? The challenge is out to all claims to universality. . . ."[9]

It is vital, however, both for the integrity of this book and for the practice of history itself to follow along with AHJ as they make the counterpoint to the point of the previous paragraph. While they forthrightly insist that a hermeneutic of suspicion is necessary if history is to be more inclusive, they equally insist that these modes of inquiry can be destructive as well. From historians who have drunk too deeply at the waters of postmodern deconstruction there comes an attack on knowledge itself. Thus, a good part of what AHJ do in *Telling the Truth About History* is as much a defense of our ability to know the past at all as it is an assault on privileged views about science, the nation, and the public history of powerful groups. Historians defending the old, canonical "metanarrative" will not like what AHJ do to that historical world; but far more devastating is their critique of the postmodern philosophy of those who try to do history after the mode of Foucault and Derrida.

These three colleagues, in summary, offer a very winsome conclusion to their analysis of recent historiography. They call for a democratic practice of history that "encourages skepticism about dominant views, but at the same time trusts in the reality of the past and its knowability."[10] Such a view is good for the study of history and good for civil society.

8. Ibid.
9. Ibid., 3.
10. Ibid., 11.

Since all histories are constructions, to some degree, all honest historians will want to listen to other voices. No representation of the past, or the conjunction of past and present, escapes the contingent nature of the standpoint from which it was written. This attitude informs what AHJ call "practical realism," i.e., that it is very important to balance the two imperatives in the argument, that the past is *both* partial *and* knowable.[11] To finish this discussion about *Telling the Truth About History* we say that it is satisfying for Christian historians to find ourselves in such broad agreement with the president of the American Historical Association and her coauthors in this matter of celebrating standpoint but not denigrating the reality of past truth.

I would like to respond in advance to the two sets of concerns, pointing in different directions, that this presentation is likely to engender: non-Christians who may ask if religious convictions can really mean something for our historical work are asked to give us a hearing in these essays; Christians who may ask if our historical work will be substantially — some would say antithetically — different from that of secular scholars are also asked to give us a hearing before they express their possible disappointment at our cautious and partial answers. If there is a common understanding among the thirteen scholars writing here it is that we are indeed, in a way, double-minded. On the one hand we are historians with research degrees from credible institutions. We know what history is, how to study it, and write about it. We are civil in our discourse and dialogical in intent. On the other hand we insist that our standpoint — that God exists "in reality" and that we "know" God through Jesus — has an impact on how we think about our historical tasks. While we accept, of course, the criticism of some historians that a Christian standpoint is different in kind than ones rooted in, e.g., race, class, and gender,[12] we insist that we are not afflicted with "false consciousness" if our Christian perspectives have impact on our historical work.

The essays in this book were commisioned by the editor. I asked people in my various networks if they would like to participate in a book on Christianity and historiography, and if they had something fresh and interesting to say. These essays are the best available to me, and I present them with pleasure. While I cannot claim that they are a representative

11. Ibid., 247-70.
12. See Carolyn J. Mooney, "Devout Professors on the Offensive," *Chronicle of Higher Education*, May 4, 1994, A18.

sample of what Christian historians are doing in history, I am sure that the subjects raised are not ones in which Christian concerns are privileged, but ones which all historians can find interesting. The essays cluster themselves roughly into three groups: the first four speak specifically to the question of perspective and epistemology; the next six take up specific themes or address discrete areas of historiographical concern; the last three are more applied and are directed toward the teaching of history.

We begin with a group that looks at various aspects of the whole matter of standpoint or perspective. George Marsden's essay sets the tone for the rest of the book in asking what possible difference all this might make. A senior scholar who has given much time to, and taken much heat for, arguing these issues in public, Marsden gives us some ideas he first mooted in his much-discussed book, *The Outrageous Idea of Christian Scholarship*. Marsden eschews triumphalism and is the soul of moderation in giving assurances that Christian historians will indeed be Christians but also will play by the rules of the academy, neither quoting Bible verses nor claiming special providences. Shirley Mullen then gives a patient and discursive account of the historian's encounter with post-modernism. She offers an interesting conclusion about the various meanings of "witness." Next, C. Stephen Evans is a philosopher who engages issues that historians themselves have not so successfully addressed. He discusses the ways in which many historians and philosophers have discounted religious truth. He offers an alternative viewpoint to this conventional wisdom. The section concludes with a diffident essay by Daryl Hart that discusses the role of an organization — the Conference on Faith and History — in its attempt to do what this volume invites, i.e., relating Christianity to historical study.

The second group of essays addresses themes or discrete areas of historiographical concern. We begin with Margaret Lamberts Bendroth's inquiry into what can be said about relating Christian concerns to women's history. Because the distance between the two is often so great, Bendroth says, a map will be necessary for many on the journey. Her essay provides that map. Mark Noll takes a different tack, of looking into the crises in historical study and how an allied field, the study of missions, might be helpful to historians. Bill J. Leonard then asks the controversial question about who owns history. He gives us a fascinating glimpse into the competition for that ownership in writing about America's largest Protestant denomination. Richard Pointer next takes us through the dynamically changing field of American Puritan studies, and he suggests the intriguing ways in which interdisciplinary cultural studies can enrich historical analysis. Robert Swierenga shows the neglect that religion has received in writing the history of rural America. He suggests ways in which that field might be revived. Finally, Ronald Wells takes on the conflicted history of, and historiography about, Northern Ireland, suggesting the ways in which religious insights might decode that conflicted history and historiography.

The third group of essays bringd the theories of the first section and the examples of the second section back to earth, that is, "earth" seen as the need to teach history to undergraduates. Jerry Summers retraces some of the ground explored by Shirley Mullen, but the purpose here is to relate faith and history for the classroom. Our engagement with postmodernism (for we all are a bit postmodern now) will have curricular and pedagogical implications. Summers offers a framework for that engagement. G. Marcille Frederick next asks what it would mean in our teaching for professors to articulate a democratic standpoint of justice and peace. With the help of the historian Hayden White, Frederick suggests ways in which narratives employed in teaching can be used responsibly and justly. Finally, Edwin Van Kley invites students and other readers to consider what "multiculturalism" actually amounts to when looked at historically. In Van Kley's take on it, the new viewpoint is not so new after all and is something that even the most conventionally minded among us can embrace without giving up all we have previously known.

In the end, we present these essays to three groups: to historians, Christian and non-Christian alike, for discussion; to students, to bring them into the conversation; to the general reader, to disclose the vitally interesting stuff that historians talk about. They are essays in Christian historiography, but, like Christianity itself, they are not meant to be kept among ourselves. We look forward to the engagement that these essays will cause.

Ronald A. Wells

I. Perspective and Theory

What Difference Might Christian Perspectives Make?

GEORGE M. MARSDEN

A few years ago the Institute for the Study of American Evangelical-ism held a conference at Wheaton College to which a small group of scholars were invited to discuss the question of advocacy in scholarship, especially as related to religious faith. The scholars were mostly historians and represented a variety of outlooks. My paper happened to be the first up for discussion and in it I said the usual things I have been saying about why various Christian perspectives should be treated like other perspectives in the mainstream academy. I also emphasized that Christian scholars need not violate the legitimate rules of the academic game. Rather, as in a court of law, it does no good in the mainstream academy to try to settle an issue by an appeal to a special revelation. We must, instead, argue for our perspectives according to standards of argument and evidence accessible to people from a wide variety of other viewpoints. So in such settings Christians will not be quoting Bible verses or alleging special providences as means of historical explanation.[1]

---

1. The conference was held in 1994 and the paper, "Christian Advocacy and the Rules of the Academic Game," has been published with the other conference papers in *Religious Advocacy and American History*, ed. Bruce Kuklick and D. G. Hart (Grand Rapids: William B. Eerdmans, 1997). A revised version of that paper also appears as chapter three of *The Outrageous Idea of Christian Scholarship* (New York: Oxford University Press, 1997). Substantial portions of the present paper are adapted

11

What I had to say seemed to me to be so conciliatory, and in my view so thoroughly sensible, that I expected a warm reception with perhaps some helpful reflections on how these moderate points might be stated a bit more clearly. I did receive a warm reception, but not of the sort I expected. Rather I ran into a firestorm of opposition from two historians who, up to that time, I thought had always been somewhat sympathetic. These were Bruce Kuklick and Paul Boyer. Subsequently each has stated his views publicly. Kuklick, for instance, says the following in a review of *The Soul of the American University:*

> It is hard to believe that Marsden actually means what he says, and it occurs to me that he has not thought through clearly the claims that he makes. Does he think that at his university, Notre Dame, they teach a Roman Catholic chemistry? Or that Aryan biology would be sanctioned at his former university, Duke?
>
> This carries over into the social sciences and history as well. Would Calvin College actually devote itself to Presbyterian anthropology or worry that Episcopal psychology should get a hearing? Should historians of the Reformation be primarily identified as Protestant, French, or female? As I have said, there are serious issues to be confronted here. But the perspectivalism that Marsden appears to defend demeans his vision of the university.[2]

Paul Boyer expressed his reservations in an address to the Conference on Faith and History two years ago. Boyer is genuinely puzzled as to what the fuss over Christian perspectives is about if historians are going to be so well behaved as I suggest, not quoting Bible verses to settle arguments or invoking special providences. I have argued that since most scholars today acknowledge that social location makes a difference to scholarship, more or less the same principles should apply to serious Christians as to women, African Americans, or native Americans. Such places to stand and the commitments they involve may change scholarly

from chapters four and five of *The Outrageous Idea* and are used here with the permission of Oxford University Press.

2. Bruce Kuklick, review of Marsden, *The Soul of the American University* in *Method and Theory in the Study of Religion* 8:1 (1996): 82. For a fuller account of the initial exchange and for related papers from that conference see *Religious Advocacy and American History,* Bruce Kuklick and D. G. Hart, eds. (Grand Rapids: Wm. B. Eerdmans, 1997).

perspectives, at least in some important ways. Boyer responds by pointing out that social location does not *necessarily* make a difference in scholarship. African Americans, he suggests, might be more prone to see slavery as a holocaust, rather than as just a tragedy; but there is no reason why whites might not also see it as a holocaust. So black insights on slavery are not unattainable by whites — if they are sufficiently sympathetic in imagination. Nor do twentieth-century women necessarily have deeper insights than some men might on the experiences of eighteenth-century women. If, in fact, social locations do produce special sensitivities, he goes on, those sensitivities are likely to have the downside of lessening other important sensitivities. So, rather than emphasizing the differences that social or religious location may make, says Boyer, we should try to minimize them, learning from all perspectives. In this way we can help avoid the undesirable balkanization of scholarship, which is the bane of the profession.[3]

These are serious criticisms which I want to answer in two sorts of ways. First I want to suggest two sets of preliminary principles that I think clear the road of most such general objections. Second, I want to provide some examples of ways in which Christian perspectives can make positive contributions to scholarship and therefore (in answer to Boyer's last point) ought to be encouraged and cultivated.

I have divided the preliminary principles into two sets. First are three things that Christian perspectives do *not* mean. Then three positive types of things they do mean.

Three Things Christian Perspectives Do Not Mean

First, Christian perspectives on academic topics will not change everything, but will change some things. In this respect they are like feminist perspectives. So it is no objection to the project of looking for the relationships between faith and learning to say that regarding some technical areas they make no apparent difference. It may be that there is no Christian or Muslim mathematics, no Jewish view of photosynthe-

---

3. Paul Boyer, "Invisible Saints? Religion in American History Textbooks, Survey Course, and Historical Scholarship," Address to the Conference on Faith and History, October 7, 1994. I am grateful to Boyer, who has been a congenial critic and correspondent, for furnishing a copy of his text for this presentation.

sis, and so forth. But it just does not follow that religious perspectives are therefore irrelevant to all scholarship. When one gets beyond the technical to the larger questions of significance, religious perspectives often do make a difference. There may not be a Roman Catholic chemistry, but there is a Roman Catholic view of nature. Certainly there is a Roman Catholic view of economic justice. And while there may not be one "Presbyterian" view of anthropology, there are important Christian views of human nature. The fact remains that in some important areas of great significance there may be a big difference. So we should talk about those.

Second, for Christianity to make a difference it does not mean that the perspective must be uniquely Christian. This mistake is at the heart of Paul Boyer's first objection. One would hardly argue that because virtually any question or scholarly agenda that might be proposed by a Marxist scholar could be posed by a non-Marxist that therefore a distinctive Marxism was not shaping the Marxist's scholarship. The fact is that the whole set of questions that shapes a Marxist's scholarship is likely to be quite different from the non-Marxist's. Even the unlikely case of a complete coincidence of questions would not negate the point that Marxism was indeed shaping the Marxist's scholarship. Or think of the feminist analogy. Just because a non-feminist may for other reasons come to the same conclusion that a feminist does, it does not make the feminist's view any less feminist. For instance, fundamentalists and feminists both disapprove of pornography. Just because some secularists or peoples of other religious faiths may happen to agree with aspects of a Roman Catholic view of economic justice or of the environment does not mean that there are not distinctly Christian reasons for Catholics to hold such views.

I think that what leads to this type of objection is that we Christians sometimes speak of "distinctly" Christian scholarship. What we mean, or ought to mean, is that our scholarship is grounded in distinctly Christian principles. What people *suppose* us to mean is that we expect our scholarship to be unique. We need to make that clear.

A third and related point is that there are no set formulae for *the* Christian perspective. Rather, there are many types of Christians and so many sets of questions that Christians are (or should be) likely to ask. So the examples I give are not presented as definitive examples of how Christians ought to think, but rather as examples of how people might think differently about some things if they made a conscious effort to relate faith and learning.

Three Pervasive Types of Influence

Once these typical objections are cleared out of the way, it is important to see how pervasive the influence of Christian views can be — even when we are not explicitly talking about them. These influences are most commonly seen in three ways. First, our Christian commitments shape our selection of topic. What is worth studying? This is particularly important for historians, who confront almost an infinite number of choices. Our priorities and values shape these choices. So we should be reflecting on how our Christian commitments do so.

Second, our Christian perspectives will influence the questions we ask about the subject. Christian scholars are likely to be interested in a different set of issues than are other scholars and to see different things. For instance, Nathan Hatch's much acclaimed *Democratization of American Religion* is built on insights growing out of decades of an insider's reflections on the relationship of evangelicalism to democratic culture. Dale Van Kley's groundbreaking studies of the religious origins of the French Revolution have offered much-discussed challenges to interpretations that could see only secular causes for an event with such secularizing results.[4]

Professor Harry Stout of Yale has reflected perceptively on the subtle yet substantive influences of particular theological commitments. Speaking of his work in American Puritan studies, Stout observed that it certainly does not require being a Christian to take the Puritans' own beliefs seriously. In fact, two of the giants in the field who have done the most for rehabilitating respect for Puritan theology have been Perry Miller and his student, Edmund S. Morgan, both self-proclaimed atheists. Despite Stout's immense admiration for these historians, he found his own work on Puritanism moving in some importantly different directions, reflecting his spiritual autobiography. Even historians so sympathetic to the Puritans as Miller and Morgan had been interested primarily in the origins of the American nation. Miller had talked about the New England "Mind" on the supposition that human ideas are

---

4. Nathan O. Hatch, *The Democratization of American Christianity* (New Haven: Yale University Press, 1989). Van Kley's culminating synthesis after three decades of research and publication on this topic is *The Religious Origins of the French Revolution: From Calvin to the Civil Constitution, 1560-1791* (New Haven: Yale University Press, 1996).

15

essentially what history is. Stout, on the other hand, was more interested in the Puritan church than in the American nation and he was more interested in "faith" as a basic factor in human history, rather than "Mind." That meant that not only were Puritan theological debates of interest, but so were "other more interior themes of piety, spirituality, meditation, devotion, or conversion — all of which minimized conflicts and represented the stable bedrock on which an enduring Puritan religiosity was built."[5]

The third pervasive type of influence has to do with determining which of the theories that are current we are likely to accept. For instance, Christian scholars who accept the authority of ancient texts are unlikely to accept radical postmodern deconstruction of the authority of all texts or that humans are, in effect, the only creators of reality.

Christian perspectives inevitably influence our choices in each of these three ways and so inevitably make a difference. I think, however, that our reflections on these differences have generally been underdeveloped. We learn self-censorship in graduate school. I see the case as similar to that of feminism. Forty years ago gender made a difference in scholarship, but few reflected on it. Today we have all benefited from such reflections. So we need similar consciousness-raising concerning the implications of our religious perspectives. This is especially important for the generation now coming out of graduate school.

Some Examples

If we engage in some hard thinking on these topics, we should be able to find some areas in which Christian perspectives can legitimately make a positive difference in our scholarship. Let me give some brief examples.

We can start with the doctrine of creation, the affirmation that God is the creator of heaven and earth. This claim of Christianity and kindred religions has momentous scholarly implications. In fact, one way to describe the history of modern Western thought is as a rejection of the doctrine of creation and its systematic exclusion as a consideration in academic study, outside of theology itself.

Scientific naturalism is, of course, a very useful methodological

5. Harry S. Stout, "Theological Commitment and American Religious History," *Theological Education* (Spring 1989): 44-59.

stance, which Christians employ all the time in the technical aspects of their scholarship. Scientific naturalism, however, like the liberal culture of which it is a part, is not ideologically neutral. It defines natural science as dealing only with natural causes.

Many people think of exclusively naturalistic methodologies primarily with regard to the natural sciences, where they indeed may have bearing on larger speculations; but it is actually in the humanities and the social sciences where they have far more pervasive implications. The exclusion of theism in these fields means that humans and their cultures have to be regarded as though they were nothing more than the products of natural evolutionary processes. With God eliminated a priori, there is no other approach that makes sense.

If Christian scholars who believe in creation question this arbitrary dogma that scholars may not view humans as more than products of purely natural forces, it will have important implications in the humanities, the social sciences, and in the study of religion itself. For instance, if considerations about God are a priori eliminated from consideration, then the accounts of human morality that make the best sense are those that posit that they have evolved as survival mechanisms. Moral standards are constructed simply to serve various cultural interests. It follows, then, that no moral standards are absolute. Rather, they are to be valued only insofar as one approves of the cultural functions they perform. Yet there is no independent standard for evaluating cultural functions. All we are left with is our own interests and our own preferences. Some sort of moral relativism seems the only consistent option.

Christian scholars' own work may involve analysis of how humans construct moral systems to serve cultural functions. But they will put that analysis in an entirely different framework. Ultimately, they will insist, principles of morality originate with God. God has provided humans with a moral law which, however imperfectly we may understand it, should be our guide. Cultural constructions of morality are thus not in principle equal. Some are closer to what God commands and some are further away. One may need to be modest in making judgments on many fine points. On the other hand, Christians should see themselves as working within a universe of God-created laws in which some acts are simply wrong.

We must acknowledge, of course, that Christians often disagree among themselves regarding the moral implications of the Christian faith. One group of Christians may insist that Christians may in no circumstances participate in warfare and that they must do all they can to seek disarmament. Others may be equally insistent that in some circumstances warfare is justified and that unqualified Christian pacifism would be the surest way to invite warfare. Nevertheless, these two groups would be in agreement that Christians should be peacemakers, even though they might disagree deeply regarding how that is best accomplished. Both groups of Christians in this debate, furthermore, would be agreed that there are normative standards of God's will that they should seek to follow and that Christ's command to be peacemakers is an important reason to work for peace. Yet their applications of these principles might be exactly the opposite. Even in cases in which Christians may flatly disagree on what is the proper moral principle, however, they at least agree that there are principles higher than the preferences of us or our group.

Whatever Christians' particular applications of their moral principles, such questions provide important openings for dialogue with those in the pluralistic academy. Most of those who deny the relevance of theism to academic inquiry nonetheless hold very strong opinions about what is right and wrong. They may very strongly advocate, for instance, equal treatment for women and minorities. Yet, given the evolutionary naturalism to which they have limited themselves, they have no adequate basis for the absolutist moral claims they are likely to make.

The *Chronicle of Higher Education* carried an account that wonderfully illustrates the moral dilemmas of contemporary academia. The author is an anthropologist, a profession that long has been dominated by the dogma of cultural relativism. The problem over which she was agonizing was how to regard that dogma in the light of practices such as the mutilation of women in female circumcision or of racial genocide in countries she was studying. Her problem was that she was trained to ask the standard contemporary academician's question, "What authority do we Westerners have to impose our own concept of universal rights on the rest of humanity?" To that question she could find no good answer. Nonetheless, her deep aversion to the practices forced her to conclude that "when there is a choice between defending human rights and defending cultural relativism, anthropologists should choose to promote human rights."[6]

6. Carolyn Fluehr-Lobban, "Cultural Relativism and Universal Rights," *Chronicle of Higher Education* (June 9, 1995): B1-2.

A similar moral impasse among some of the most progressive of contemporary academics is well illustrated in a symposium on "Freedom and Interpretation," sponsored by Amnesty International. The participants were asked to consider how they could defend human "rights" in the light of "the deconstruction of the self for the liberal tradition" from which the concept of "rights" arose.[7]

In a purely naturalistic universe without God there is no compelling way to resolve this dilemma. Contemporary academia is in a moral stalemate. Cultural relativism is essential to dismantling the many Western traditions that postmodern scholars do not like, but there is no consistent way to keep it from dissolving the moral traditions they themselves affirm. In purely evolutionary theory there is hardly a convincing basis for treating all persons as equals or for special concerns for the weak and the disadvantaged.[8] Christian theism, on the other hand, can provide grounds for supporting moral intuitions that many academics find themselves having, despite a lack of any adequate intellectual basis. Without theism, in a world where all moral systems are seen simply as constructions of interested groups, it is difficult to see any way of defending the moral claims of one group versus those of another. Ultimately, as Nietzsche long ago recognized and many postmoderns have reaffirmed, power becomes the only adequate arbiter of contested moral claims. According to Christianity, on the other hand, we should love our neighbors and even our enemies, since we are all creatures of the same loving creator. Without such a principle, it is difficult to see how contemporary academics can defend such common beliefs as that all humans should be treated as sisters or brothers. Often all they have as a basis for

7. Barbara Johnson, editor's introduction, *Freedom and Interpretation: The Oxford Amnesty Lectures 1992* (New York: Basic Books, 1993), 2.

8. I realize, of course, that there are many attempts to construct such an evolutionary morality and that relativism may foster tolerance and even some egalitarianism. Nonetheless, none has a convincing principle with which to dissuade humans from their natural self-interest. The sort of Christian critique I have in mind is Dennis O'Brien's comment in a review of Robert Wright, *The Moral Animal: Why We Are the Way We Are: The New Science of Evolutionary Psychology*, in *Commonweal* (June 2, 1995): 26, when he observes: "But the notion that this brand of 'determinism' is the key to compassion is perverse. The best that can emerge from thoroughgoing determinism would be a 'morality' of excuses (victims are blameless) never a morality (you have a moral responsibility not to blame victims!). I do not see how there can be a moral compulsion to forgive the victim, when there is no moral agent to whom one can appeal."

such beliefs are the vestiges of nineteenth-century romanticism (sometimes refracted through socialism) which they could never defend on adequate intellectual grounds.

This is, of course, not to argue that Christianity does not have its own intellectual problems or moral dilemmas. Certainly it does (even if Christians may see these problems as less troubling than the alternatives). For the moment, however, the point is simply to illustrate that if one puts the doctrine of a creator into one's intellectual picture it should substantially change some important parts of one's intellectual outlook.

Another characteristic assumption of our age that a Christian perspective might challenge is what we can call "The Transcendent Self." Christian scholars, at least those with more traditional theological perspectives, should be critical of this absolutization of humanity. With God the creator out of the way as a serious component of Western thought, views of human capacities have become immensely inflated. Christians, of course, long have emphasized human significance and the value of humans who may seem least significant. Yet such affirmations have been in the context of recognizing human limits. As Pascal suggests, humans are the crown of creation and the scum of the earth. Whatever the particulars in their views of human nature, Christians have been traditionally united in proclaiming that the heart of human sinfulness is the illusion that we can be our own gods, a law unto ourselves, creating and controlling our own reality.

Such traditions, which originate in the Hebrew Scriptures, ought to transform religiously committed scholars into dissenters from many theories taken for granted in current academia. It should make them critical of viewpoints, especially strong in the arts and literature, that emphasize human freedom and creativity as the supreme values. Although of immense worth, these human gifts will reach their highest expressions when exercised within a sense of the limits of the individual in relationship to communities, the created order, and ultimately to God. Individuals who act as though they are a law unto themselves or who proclaim there is no law are prone to destroy those around them. Granted, excessive religious zeal is a danger as well. That does not change the fact that current philosophies that absolutize the self pose a real danger.

Denials of anything higher than human achievement pay their dividends in popular and celebrity culture, another area ripe for critique by scholars who see more to life than the self. Here again, as on

MTV, creativity knows no limits, but not because the artistic goals are so high. Cynicism has become a cliché. Similarly, the world of advertising and mass culture has no shame in exploiting the ideals of unlimited freedom that cashes out as sensuality and self-indulgence. As Jaroslav Pelikan has observed, "a generation is made victim of their own sexual desires."[9] Scholars from all sorts of traditions might critique such cultural trends, but scholars with theological perspective are more likely to see them as part of a larger pattern of self worship that has almost a cultic quality.

The Augustinian theme of the human tendency to absolutize the relative can also be an important motif in Christian scholarship that critiques other idols of the age. For instance, a fruitful classroom theme for Christian scholars since at least mid-century has been to identify the various "isms" that contend for our allegiances: nationalism, socialism, Marxism, liberalism, individualism, conservatism, scientism, subjectivism, objectivism, romanticism, sexism, feminism, racism, relativism, intellectualism, anti-intellectualism, populism, elitism, materialism, consumerism, and so forth. This may seem like a cliché of Christian triumphalism unless each of these "isms" is also taken seriously as representing some important value or insight, which it tends to absolutize. It distorts reality because it takes something that is good, or at least very attractive, in human experiences and subordinates all else to it. Christians need to be alert to these tendencies in human nature and culture and to teach students how to respond with discrimination to the spirits of the age.

Particularly they need to be alerted to the tendencies of Christians themselves to absolutize the culturally relative, often in the name of Christ. Christian scholars who study the church or Christianity itself should recognize how Christian faith constantly becomes entangled with the cultural forces of the age. Not only do various "isms" reshape the church, but so do more impersonal forces such as those of the market, demands of modern media, technologies, or other forces associated with modernization. Accommodations to such forces are not always bad and some are necessary, but they are usually dangerous. The best education involves not only being critical, but self-critical. For that, the Christian perspective on the human condition, and the deceptiveness of the human heart, provides an excellent place to stand.

9. Jaroslav Pelikan, review of Jo Ann McNamara, *Sisters in Arms: Catholic Nuns through Two Millennia* in *New Republic* (October 14, 1996): 39.

It is for that reason that I want to emphasize in closing that one of the themes of Christian scholarship should be humility. Christians must stand for the truth as they understand God to have revealed it. Yet they also must see themselves as personal representatives of Christ on earth. Rather than thereby inflating their egos, they must see this role as one of humility and servanthood. Its evidences will be seen in the loving ways we treat others. In this respect I know of no better example than the late George Rawlyk, who until his death in 1995 was probably the leading figure promoting evangelical scholarship in Canada. Through countless acts of concern for other people, regardless of their status, he illustrated how being a Christian scholar is first of all a spiritual condition.

Ultimately people are convinced not simply by arguments, although sound scholarship is essential. They are convinced also by the character of the people who present arguments. We all can remember revered teachers whom we believed largely because of the integrity of what they represented personally. So Christian scholars should, without compromising their scholarship, present themselves as models of genuine servanthood within adverse academic communities.

In *The Structure of Scientific Revolutions,* Thomas Kuhn remarks on the difficulty of conversion from one paradigm to another. When it does happen, it is not so much that people in one paradigm fully understand the arguments of those in the other paradigm as they admire what they are doing. "They can say: I don't know how the proponents of the new view succeed, but I must learn whatever they are doing, it is clearly right."[10] Christian scholars, not only in their thinking but their doing, should be building communities that merit such admiration.

10. Thomas S. Kuhn, *The Structure of Scientific Revolutions,* second edition, enlarged (Chicago: University of Chicago Press, 1970), 203.

Between "Romance" and "True History": Historical Narrative and Truth Telling in a Postmodern Age

SHIRLEY A. MULLEN

In Book I, Part III, Section VII of his *Treatise on Human Nature*, David Hume is setting forth his ideas about the nature of beliefs. To illustrate one of his points about belief, he turns to our thinking about the past as if our thinking about the past is so clear to us that it can serve to guide our thinking in areas where our thinking is not so clear.

> If one person sits down to read a book as a romance, and another as a true history, they plainly receive the same ideas, and in the same order; nor does the incredibility of the one, and the belief of the other hinder them from putting the very same sense upon their author. His words produce the same ideas in both; tho' his testimony has not the same influence on them. The latter has a more lively conception of all the incidents. He enters deeper into the concerns of the person: represents to himself their actions, and characters, and friendships, and enmities: He even goes so far as to form a notion of their features, and air, and person. While the former, who gives no credit to the testimony of the author, has a more faint and languid conception of all these particulars; and except on account of the style and ingenuity of the composition, can receive little entertainment from it.[1]

---

1. David Hume, *Treatise on Human Nature*, ed. P. Nidditch, 2nd ed. (Oxford: Clarendon Press, 1978), 97-98.

We will not stop at this point to consider Hume's characterization of the nature of belief. Nor will we pause to debate whether or not he has been entirely fair in his assessment of the impact of fictional literature. Certainly not everyone would agree with Hume's ranking of the impact of "true history" over "romance." But that is another discussion. What I would like to call our attention to is Hume's assumption that the power and impact of historical literature derives from the belief that there is a clear difference between works of history and works of fiction, and that this difference is linked to the fact that works of history are "true" in a way that novels are not. He takes for granted in the illustration that the reader's beliefs—if he reads as "true history"—will be confident and strong—not the loose reveries of the "castle builder."

In this discussion, I believe that Hume has captured something of the common sense view of what makes the difference between historical literature and fictional literature. History is true in a way that fictional literature is not. Whenever we use a novel as a source in a history class—students' first observation in discussing the novel as a source is that it is "not true." Or I think of the plaintive cry of one of our majors in Senior Seminar after a discussion of historical narrative that had involved reading Eric Hobsbawm's *Invention of Tradition*—"But if we're not getting at truth, then what is history?" And then there is the response of the third-year history grad student who, when asked what she understood herself to be doing that made history unique within the genre of narrative literature, replied simply that "History is about real people."

These observations invite further comment, but I offer them here solely to support my contention that Hume's comments do, in fact, ring true with something widely shared at least in Western "common sense" —that history is significantly different from fictional literature and that this difference is linked to its being "true" in a way that literature is not. It is precisely these convictions—that history is significantly different from literature—and that this difference is linked to history's value and reliability as a discipline, and to its claim to be pursuing truth about the past—that seem to be threatened by much of the discussion today that goes on under the rubric of postmodernism. To the extent that our understanding of the identity and value of historical study as a discipline is linked to a strong sense of difference between fictional literature and history, then as this sense of difference is undermined —as it is being undermined in these days—so is the sense of one's identity and value as an historian. This concern is shared by many in the historical profession.

Dorothy Ross, in discussing Peter Novick's *That Noble Dream,* asks why historians want to reformulate ideas of objectivity. She then proceeds to answer her own question. "My guess is they want to retain the connotations of the term that allow them to differentiate history from fiction. . . . Or that allow them to differentiate historiography from merely subjective opinion. . . . Or that allow them to legitimate the particular kind of contextual and genetic analysis that historians do but that social scientists and literary critics do not do."[2] There is a sense that the clarity and the credibility of our task as historians is linked to our being able to be, and to be viewed as being, "objective" or "true" in a way that fictional narrative is not. As David Harlan describes the situation, "Now, after a hundred-year absence, literature has returned to history, unfurling her circus silks of metaphor and allegory, . . . demanding that historians accept her mocking presence right at the heart of what they had once considered was their own autonomous and truly scientific discipline. The return of literature has plunged historical studies into an extended epistemological crisis. It has questioned our belief in a fixed and deter- minable past, compromised the possibility of historical representation, and undermined our ability to locate ourselves in time. The result of all of this has been to reduce historical knowledge to a tissue of remnants and fabrications concealing, it is said, an essential absence."[3]

The concern is also one that might well trouble Christian histori- ans, in particular, for these issues go to the root not only of how we understand our profession as historians, but also of our profession (in a different sense of that word) of faith as Christian believers — for our faith is integrally linked to questions of historicity. Whether we confess our faith in terms of the Apostles' Creed, or in terms of personal expe- rience — our confession of faith is linked to the affirmation that certain things have actually happened in the past and have significant and de- terminate meaning for our lives today.

In this chapter, I will attempt to do three things: first, to summarize the challenge raised by postmodernism for the traditional modern un- derstanding of the nature of the historian's task; second, to identify four

2. Dorothy Ross, "Afterward," *American Historical Review* (1991): 705.

3. David Harlan, "Intellectual History and the Return of Literature," *American Historical Review* (1989): 581.

response patterns from within the historical profession to the challenges of postmodernism; and third, to suggest several alternative lines of response that seek to both recognize the insights to be gained from the postmodern critique, and honor the strategic and principled concern to preserve an understanding of the peculiar nature and value of historical narrative and the historian's task.

I. The Postmodern Challenge

First, what is the challenge raised by postmodernism for the historian's task? In particular, in what ways has postmodernism challenged the traditional division between history and literature? Postmodernism raises crucial questions about the meaningfulness of the historian's self-understanding as someone who seeks to tell "true" stories about the past. That was the way that a recent guide to young history students described the task of historians — "Ever since Herodotus," the author said, "historians have tried to tell true stories about the human past."[4] This traditional sense of "truth" is quite different from that expressed by Joan Scott in a recent discussion — "By 'history,' I mean not what happened, not what 'truth' is 'out there' to be discovered and transmitted, but what we *know* about the past, what the rules and conventions are that govern the production and acceptance of the knowledge we designate as history. My first premise is that history is not purely referential but is rather constructed by historians. Written history both reflects and creates relations of power."[5] It is interesting that, as Gilderhus reaches the end of his book, he notes that "the full implications of this body of thought (postmodernism) for history have not become clear, they appear to question such fundamentals as reason, objectivity, and the knowability of the past, suggesting essentially that historical narratives differ hardly at all from fiction."[6] Gilderhus ends the book, modifying his original notion of the historian's task by the more tempered and rather vague pronouncement that, "If historians can agree on little else, at least they should

4. Mark Gilderhus, *History and Historians: A Historiographical Introduction*, 3rd ed. (Englewood Cliffs, N.J.: Prentice-Hall, 1987), 6.
5. Joan Scott, "History in Crisis? The Others' Side of the Story," *American Historical Review* (1989): 681.
6. Gilderhus, *History and Historians*, 134.

rejoice in the knowledge that they have many true stories to tell about the human past."[7]

Not only is there questioning of the meaning of the use of "truth" as historians have traditionally used the term — but there is also a sense that even if there were a Truth about the past out there to be grasped, historians would not be able to find it. Postmodernism challenges the moral and epistemological appropriateness of the stance from which historians — at least since the nineteenth century — have sought to study the past. We have all been taught that the goal of the historian is to recognize and to seek to rise above the biases, and the parochialism, of one's own class, gender, religious, and national perspective. We have been trained to believe that, for something to be historically established — as for something to be scientifically established — it must be a truth that is available to all. In the words of Herbert Butterfield, "Now I, personally, would never regard a thing as 'historically established' — that is to say as genuinely demonstrated by historical evidence — unless the case for it can be made out in a coercive and inescapable manner to any student of the past — Protestant or Catholic, Christian or non-Christian, Frenchman or Englishman, and Whig and Tory."[8]

Postmodernism has emphasized the inevitability of one's seeing from a particular perspective. The ideal of objectivity has been portrayed by postmodernism as an unattainable ideal that has served to privilege the accounts produced by those in power — usually some combination of white, male, European, political, or diplomatic historians. Postmodernism challenges the notion that the historian, like the scientist, and unlike the writer of fictional literature, should, or can, meaningfully work with the ideal of objectivity. There is no such thing as seeing the past from "nowhere" or as "anybody" or "everybody" sees.

Third, the postmodernist challenge to the uniqueness of the historian's task is linked to postmodernism's understanding of the relationship of language to the world. Traditionally, the historian has understood herself to be using words to describe and to make sense of a world that is "out there" as opposed to the writer of fiction who is creating a world.

---

7. Ibid., 135.

8. Herbert Butterfield, "Does Belief in Christianity Validly Affect the Modern Historian?" in *Herbert Butterfield — Writings on Christianity and History*, ed. C. T. McIntire (New York: Oxford University Press, 1979), 134.

According to the postmodernist, all narratives — not just the narratives of fiction — are creating worlds and realities and cultures — not reflecting them. That is the nature of language. For the postmodernist, the historian cannot assume that written sources are mirrors of "reality" — for the sources may be the creators as much as the mirrors of their historical context. The "indeterminacy" of the subject in literary sources has been raised by a literature professor as one of the difficulties for historians in knowing what to make of fictional writings for historical analysis,[9] but if one assumes that all use of language is creative and manipulative, then this indeterminacy of the subject to which the text refers really becomes a problem for all texts used by the historian — not just texts that are explicitly understood to be fictional. Historians become then, not studiers of the past, but studiers of the language of the past. We learn what it is possible for people to have understood and thought by the language that was available to them.[10] We also learn how people came to terms with new circumstances and shaped these new realities by the language with which they described it. It is this sort of study that Lynn Hunt is undertaking in *Politics, Culture, and Class in the French Revolution*.[11] Such exploration still does not, according to a postmodernist vision, get us closer to the "reality" of the past — for even if we were to understand the language of the past as creating a world rather than reflecting it — our attempt to grasp that world through our study of the language of another time and place would still be fraught by the lack of transparency and the lack of determinacy in language itself.

That leads to the fourth challenge. For, not only does language create, rather than reflect, our "realities," but those "realities" created by language will themselves be elusive because of the nature of the language from which they were created. Language, according to the postmodernist, is not "firm" and univocal in its meaning. It is infinitely malleable — and the meaning of language is as much a product of the "hearer" as of the "speaker" — of the reader as of the author.

If we must assume that all texts are creators of reality, rather than

9. Philip Stewart, "This Is Not a Book Review: On Historical Uses of Literature," *Journal of Modern History* (1994): 522.

10. See, for example, J. G. A. Pocock's *Virtue, Commerce and History* (New York: Cambridge University Press, 1985), though I would not characterize Pocock himself as a postmodernist.

11. Lynn Hunt, *Politics, Culture, and Class in the French Revolution* (Berkeley: University of California Press, 1984).

reflectors of reality, then there is no way that historians can rely on any texts to point beyond themselves to some reality in the past about which they purport to speak. And this is the very conclusion that Stephen Greenblatt reaches in his discussion of European interpretations of the New World. The sources, as he boldly asserts, tell us about the sixteenth-century explorers rather than about the realities of the New World. Of course, this assertion raises all sorts of interesting questions. If texts are as opaque as Greenblatt asserts, how would we ever know if they speak of any reality at all, and why should we assume that Greenblatt's assertions about sixteenth-century Europeans are any more to be trusted as "reality" about the sixteenth-century Europeans than their portrayals of the New World are to be trusted to be accurate portrayals of the New World?[12] It certainly may be true that texts about the "New World" may say as much about the "Old World" as about the "New World" — but one can only make sense of this assertion if one has a view of language that is much more determinate than that of many postmodernists. Thus, not only has the feasibility of the historian's goal of telling true stories about the past been challenged by postmodernism, but also the legitimacy of the historian's traditional understanding of the nature of sources and their corresponding "rules of evidence."

II. Responses from the Community of Historians

As historians have encountered the challenges raised by postmodernism — in particular, this blurring of the boundaries between history and literature, they seem to have produced four main types of response.

The first response is simply to resist the blurring of the boundaries between history and literature — in fact to resist much of what would go under the category of postmodernist history — on the grounds that it is destroying the discipline of history and the goods in our society that the traditional study of history has supposedly honored and helped to perpetuate. This is the response of someone like Gertrude Himmelfarb, who sees postmodernism, and much of social history as well, as con-

---

12. Stephen Greenblatt, *Marvelous Possessions: The Wonder of the New World* (Chicago: University of Chicago Press, 1991). For another example of this sort of thinking, see David Prochaska, "History as Literature, Literature as History: Cagayous of Algiers," *American Historical Review* (1996): 671-711.

tributing to the undermining of such values as individual freedom, individual responsibility, rational discourse in the present, and to the failure to do justice to the reality of the past — and to those who lived out their lives in the midst of that reality. Himmelfarb sees in much of the new history the "danger of . . . a new kind of condescension, a condescension toward those contemporaries who left few records of their 'consciousness' and are at the mercy of the historian who can 'invent,' 'imagine,' 'create,' or 'construct' a consciousness that is suspiciously in accord with the historian's own consciousness."[13] The emphasis in this response is really to focus on the "goods" that seem to be threatened by the new approach to history — both the values that traditional historical study is seen to foster, but also the value of the "past" itself — rather than explicitly to refute any of the assertions of postmodernism, or even to recognize the concerns within the profession and within society that might make postmodernism attractive.

A second response is to embrace the collapsing of these boundaries between history and literature and to celebrate the new-found freedom for creativity and exploration that is offered by the postmodern vision. I would take this to be the view of Keith Jenkins in his new work *On "What is History?"*[14] and of David Harlan in "Intellectual History and the Return of Literature."[15] In this approach, one does not worry too much about the big picture of historical "Truth." One enjoys the discourse — and the particular truths that, according to Harlan, are still possible even without the large general truths. The distinctness of history as a discipline, to the extent that it is a concern at all, seems more to be assumed than argued for. Harlan, in responding to David Hollinger's remarks about his article, comments almost laughingly that Hollinger seems to think that he, Harlan, has mistaken historical writing for storytelling.[16] But the supposed confusion is treated by Harlan as an assertion so unreasonable as to need no reply.

A third response to the challenge of postmodernism is to acknowledge the value of the questions of postmodernism, but to argue that these

13. Gertrude Himmelfarb, "Some Reflections on the New History," *American Historical Review* (1989): 668. See also Himmelfarb, *The New History and the Old* (Cambridge, Mass.: Belknap Press, 1987).

14. Keith Jenkins, *On "What is History?"* (New York: Routledge, 1995).

15. D. Harlan, "Intellectual History and the Return of Literature," 581-609.

16. D. Harlan, "Reply to David Hollinger," *American Historical Review* (1989): 622.

questions and the blurring of the boundaries between literature and history threaten neither the identity, nor the value, nor importantly, the methods and practice of historical study. Indeed, the new questions and the new ways of looking at things can help us to do better what we have been trying to do all along. According to this response, historians have every reason to continue their enterprise of critical scholarship — of seeking truth about the past and of striving for objectivity. The concerns of postmodernism may make us more careful in our work, and more conscious of our limitations, but they need not change our fundamental understanding of the historian's task. For, according to this approach, it is the very seeking and striving after truth and a place of "objectivity" — not the achievement of these ideals — that has characterized the historian's task. It is these ideals that have elicited confidence in the value of the historian's task — and it is the results of the activities done in the name of these ideals (as well as public confidence in the results of these activities) that have made historical study valuable as a weapon in the pursuit of social justice and redress of past grievances. It is the results of historical study pursued according to the rules of "modern critical scholarship" that have, according to this third response, exposed past injustices, and that have occasioned rethinking of our memories in ways that have enabled us to imagine new possibilities for the future. It is the fruits of traditional critical scholarship that have enlarged our understanding of the past — along gender lines, ethnic lines, class lines, etc. Traditional critical scholarship has enabled new groups to tell new stories. It has brought about the exposure of past injustice in such a way that it has served as a catalyst for change in the present. Furthermore, it is the confidence in history as a discipline whose pursuit of truth is different from the goals of literature that has gained credibility and legitimacy for these new fields of historical knowledge and understanding. One of the clearest examples of this type of response comes in the work *Telling the Truth About History* by three historians who are women — Joyce Appleby, Lynn Hunt, and Margaret Jacob.[17] They view their own careers within the profession as evidence of the self-correcting capability of the traditional historical profession.

In this response, there is no sustained effort to establish epistemological grounds for our confidence in the truths of historical scholarship.

17. Joyce Appleby, Lynn Hunt, and Margaret Jacob, *Telling the Truth About History* (New York: Norton, 1994).

The argument is rather that what historians do has worked. It has done what a democratic society would want the study of history to do — provided a framework and a method where everyone can have a voice, and where everyone's voice can be heard. The "rules" can be made to work for everyone.[18] As in the case of the second response, those in this third category are not afraid of the blurring of distinctions between literature and history. But those in this category are less focused on the "delights" and freedom offered to the historian by postmodernism and more concerned to establish that traditional historical scholarship, with its present goals and practices, can hold its own, and can benefit from the insights and concerns of postmodernism. They believe that the goals of the historian — truth, objectivity — and the questions of the historian are sufficient to mark history off as a distinct discipline within our society, and as one of value. Furthermore, they believe that the methods and goals of critical historical scholarship are able to meet the moral challenge that is implicit in the postmodern critique — that, in short, the tools of modern critical scholarship are empowering for all groups. These tools are themselves the means whereby traditionally marginalized groups can challenge dominant power structures and the intellectual paradigms that support those structures. In short, this response would see critical historical scholarship as having within itself the possibility of self-correction, or transcending its own short-sightedness. It can accomplish, using its traditional methods, the very goals that postmodernism is seeking to accomplish.

A fourth response is to acknowledge the challenge of postmodernism to the ideals of objectivity; to acknowledge the blurring of literary and historical studies — but to argue that the identity and credibility of history as a discipline has not rested on its purported objectivity — or sharply distinct kind of truth-telling. Whereas the third response is a response directed to the moral and political charges of postmodernism, this fourth response is directed to the epistemological sensitivities of historians — the charge that they cannot do what they have taken themselves to be doing. According to this response, the ideal of objectivity

18. I take this to be very close to what Allan Megill calls "critical pluralism" in his article, "Recounting the Past: 'Description,' Explanation, and Narrative in Historiography," *American Historical Review* (1989): 653. See also Megill, "'Grand Narrative' and the Discipline of History" in *A New Philosophy of History*, ed. Ankersmit and Kellner (Chicago: University of Chicago Press, 1995), 151-73.

has never done the work that it has been presumed to have been doing within the profession. It is this line of argument that J. H. Hexter pursues in his response to Peter Novick's *That Noble Dream.* According to Hexter, historians have never (or at least not for a long time) labored under the illusion of arriving at objective truth about the past. It has not been this ideal — or its supposed realization that has motivated historians or identified their particular concerns as scholars. What has marked the discipline is not the ideal of objectivity, but a method, or a set of practices understood by the profession.[19] Nancy Partner refers to this set of practices as a "protocol." In her words, "A stable and clear distinction between fiction and non-fiction is the product of a strict protocol of literary historicity imposed by the force of a strong cultural demand."[20]

The general tenor of the responses in this category do not seem overly concerned about the challenge that postmodernism poses for the discipline of history, though Nancy Partner — whose commentary I would put in this response category — would no doubt take issue with this general posture of disciplinary confidence. According to Partner, the real challenge today to the profession is not at the epistemological level, but rather at the level of "protocol" — at what practices we will allow to be considered historical. In particular, she is concerned at the blurring of fact and fiction in narratives that would be understood to be historical by the public (e.g., popular movies that mix history and fiction). According to Partner, "The danger inherent in capricious, opportunistic violations of the protocol of historicity is really not that millions of people will absolutely come to believe this or that, but that millions of people will come to be cynical, disabused and wary, to believe nothing and thus feel no connection with the polity at all."[21] So, for Partner, it is the clarifying of the conventions of historical practice, rather than an adjustment of the ideals that is called for. Implicit in her argument is her sense that it is not the reaching of the ideal of objectivity that has made the historical discipline distinct, but a sense of trustworthiness that historians are attempting to do what everyone understands them to be doing — telling true stories about the past.

---

19. See J. Hexter, "Carl Becker, Professor Novick, and Me; or Cheer Up, Professor N," *American Historical Review* (1991): 675-82.

20. N. Partner, "Historicity in an Age of Reality-Fictions," in *A New Philosophy of History,* 35.

21. Ibid., 39.

III. Reflections on the Situation

It seems clear that, despite the challenges of postmodernism to historical studies — challenges that, on the one hand, bring literary studies closer to historical studies, and on the other, make it harder for historians to move in the direction of the natural sciences — historians are continuing to do their work. Some of this dogged persistence may simply be for lack of options. But the responses would suggest that the postmodern challenges have not undermined that last bastion of the historian's defensive repertoire — common sense.

As I survey all four responses, I am struck by how very much they all rely, not on carefully reasoned arguments about the epistemological nature of historical narrative, but on common sense. Common sense is no stranger to the historian. Long before we were confronted with the challenges of postmodernism to the unique character of historical narrative or to the practices of modern source criticism, historians have had to deal with what I take to be the even more fundamental problem of what in the world we are writing about: What is this thing called the past? We cannot see it or touch it. We cannot reason to it. It is not the necessary conclusion to an argument. And yet we take it to be there. Indeed, we cannot escape it. In the words of Milan Kundera, "The future is an apathetic void of no interest to anyone. The past is full of life, eager to irritate us, provoke us and insult us, tempt us to destroy or repaint it. The only reason people want to be masters of the future is to change the past. They are fighting for access to the laboratories where photographs are retouched and biographies and histories rewritten."[22]

We cannot not believe the past. It is difficult to disagree with Elizabeth Anscombe in her article, "The Reality of the Past," in which, though she puzzles about the meaning of statements about the past, she takes it as given that we could not doubt that the past is there, and that in some way it makes sense to say that "Nothing that happened in the future could make it not still true that the things that happened in the past did happen as they happened, even though nobody could know it."[23]

22. Milan Kundera, *The Book of Laughter and Forgetting* (New York: Alfred A. Knopf, 1980), 22.

23. G. E. M. Anscombe, "The Reality of the Past," *Metaphysics and the Philosophy of Mind — The Collected Papers of G. E. M. Anscombe* (Minneapolis: University of Minnesota, 1981), 116.

So, we historians have leaped the hurdle of ontological skepticism about the past. Even the most epistemologically skeptical of postmodernist historians seem to take the existence of a real past for granted.[24] We have done this on the basis of common sense. Common sense also undergirds, as I have already suggested, the assertions and convictions of all the responses to the postmodern challenges to the uniqueness and value of the historian's task. We believe that we are doing something different than the writer of fiction is doing. Whether one puts it in terms of one's goals or one's method or one's questions, or one's accountability to a community, there is a common sense that the historian's task is not the same as that of the author or critic of fiction. The historian is limited by artifacts or evidence in ways that writers of fiction are not. And we are assumed by the larger world, also on the basis of common sense, to be doing something quite different from the writer of fiction.

I would suggest that, in addition to common sense, there are several other places that we might look in order to help us clarify the identity and legitimacy of history as a discipline — a discipline different from literature and different because it does deliver a kind of truth that literature does not. Certainly there will be the tendency to continue to look to the scientific aspect of our studies to set us apart from literature. This is no doubt understandable — given the fact that science is still seen as the most reliable authority in our culture at large. Science — at least at the practical level — continues to yield results that offer humans (at least at first glance) greater predictive capability and more control over their lives.

To the extent that we may want to continue to associate ourselves with science and its methods to ground our identity as separate from literature, we may want to consider an enlarged and more complicated understanding of the operations of science such as is presented in Steven Shapin's recent book, *A Social History of Truth — Civility and Science in Seventeenth-Century England* (Chicago: University of Chicago Press, 1994). Shapin challenges the notion that the beliefs we have arrived at in modern science — those things we hold to be true — have been arrived at in ways that are radically different from the ways in which beliefs were arrived at in the world that might be described as "premodern." Specifically, he suggests that individual scientists have arrived at their beliefs in much the same way as people have always arrived at their fundamental beliefs about the world — not through moving by various

24. See Harlan, "Reply to David Hollinger," 622.

35

stages of experimentation from skepticism to certainty, but through much more traditional means such as reliance on trust in the community, and reliance on the character of one's colleagues. He grants that the "community" of the scientific world is a larger and much more impersonal community than the community of trust in the premodern world. Furthermore, he grants that the trust in these scientific communities is based on expertise and competence, not on personal knowledge of someone's character and trustworthiness. Nevertheless, Shapin qualifies even these two points by noting that on a daily level, within particular laboratories, the older criteria of trust in the character of particular persons continues to play a much larger role in our willingness to rely on someone's conclusions, and to rely on the authority of those conclusions as an untested basis from which to proceed with one's own work.

Our attention is thus called to the persistent role of authority, tradition, trust, community, and character in shaping our beliefs about the world — even in the midst of an age that purports to defend its beliefs on the basis of experimentation by experts. We cannot fully disengage our work as scholars from our context and from our character. These are matters that are coming to be appreciated by the historical community at large, and ought to be appreciated by Christian historians as well. It is clear from our discussion of various responses to postmodernism that our reliability as a discipline rests, in part at least, on our being a community of mutual accountability to rules of evidence, a community that is sensitive to concerns of social justice, a community that is perceived to be trustworthy.

If Herbert Butterfield were alive today, he would perhaps be less likely to feel the need to draw such a sharp line between the concerns of the historian as practitioner of scientific or technical history and as discerner of significant meaning in history. Though he sought to preserve these lines between scientific historical truth, which is open to all, and one's own sense of the meaning of history, he acknowledged the blurriness of these lines. "There may be some justice in the claim that history is a 'science,' but if so, it is a science dominated by the fact that its particular kind of truth can only be attained by imaginative self-giving in human sympathy. . . . Historical understanding depends upon this compassion, this urge to see even the outcasts as human beings who could fall in love or be hurt. . . ."[25]

25. Butterfield, "The Christian and Academic History," in *Writings,* 179-80.

In conclusion, I would suggest that there are several other directions in which we as historians might look, besides the world of the natural scientist, for help in coming to a clearer understanding for ourselves of the nature of our task — and for help in defending our claim to be a truth-telling discipline — separate from literature — even in a postmodern age. I suspect, in fact, that we have much to gain from looking in other directions besides the world of the natural scientist — for it is not at all clear that the methods of the natural sciences can accommodate all of the realities with which historians want to deal. To the extent that historians seek to contain their concerns within the realm of the natural scientist, they may have to narrow their questions or deal with a much more constricted sense of what is important about human activity in the past. The historian must become small and less interesting to fit into the model of the scientist. (I am not claiming here that scientists are less interesting or smaller than historians, but simply that historians will be smaller historians if they try to be scientists.) Witness the efforts by Carl Hempl and others to make historical explanation fit the model of scientific explanation. There is much of interest to historians — motive, meaning, etc. — that cannot be touched with the methods of science.

Furthermore, these other directions, perhaps more than the methods of the natural scientist, allow us to receive and to benefit from the insights of the postmodern critique. And there are important insights to be gained from taking seriously the concerns of the postmodernist. We are all far more biased in our seeing than we like to think. Our seeing of the world is always affected by what we want to be true — and by what we have been brought up to think to be true. We do use language (consciously and subconsciously) in ways that hide power struggles in the name of truth. Furthermore, language is slippery. And this slipperiness, in combination with our blindness, does obscure our ability to see clearly in both our dealing with the past and with the present. In one sense, none of these insights should be surprising to historians or to Christians. We as historians and as Christians, of all people, should be acquainted with human fallenness.

As Christians and as historians, we want ways of understanding our truth-telling that, on the one hand, preserve the possibility of speaking of a world "out there" — that save us from the perils of relativism and extreme subjectivism — but, on the other hand, also allow us to recognize that truth is more than a thing out there to be found — that it is connected with our desire to know the truth, and that it is connected with our desire to be changed by the truth — and allow us to recognize that, in a fallen world, the concerns of truth will always be intertwined with the concerns of power. That is the nature of our world.

Finally, I offer three metaphors that would seem to be worth further probing in the days ahead as we seek to come to terms with the challenges of postmodernism. First, we might draw more fully on the image of historian as detective or lawyer — that is, metaphors that link our activities to the truths of legal procedure rather than to the truths of science.[26] In the courtroom, we are confronted with all of the epistemological limitations that confront the historian in seeking to reconstruct the past from present evidence, with all the limitations of texts, and with all the tendencies of humans to consciously and subconsciously shape truth for their own advantage. Nevertheless, we continue to believe that a jury can be convinced of a verdict. And we believe that the verdict does represent something about the truth of the situation in question rather than simply the mindset of the jury. (One could argue that the consequences of not believing this are just too socially devastating, at least in a democratic society. But I suspect the belief is more confident than that.)

Second, we might draw more fully on reflections from the fields of ethics and aesthetics. For they too are realms that must wrestle with how to establish their claim to be dealing with truths or realities that cannot be tested by experiment. I am particularly interested here in metaphors of vision and perception employed heavily by people like Lawrence Blum, Iris Murdoch, Simone Weil, and Martha Nussbaum. The appeal of such metaphors is that they do allow for belief that there is something "out there" and they allow for discussion about what is out there. The pursuit of Truth thus remains a sensible enterprise. But these metaphors also allow for the fact that good and wise human beings often do not have the same view of things, even where the "facts" are fairly clear. These metaphors provide a framework where one does not have to cast one's opponent as being evil or stupid. But neither does one have to settle for a passive relativism. Metaphors of vision leave room for the recognition associated with postmodernism that where we stand, our background, our locatedness does affect what we see. And yet these metaphors provide a means for moving beyond uncritical pluralistic relativism. We can always invite

26. Robin Winks, *The Historian as Detective: The Historian on Evidence* (New York: Harper & Row, 1969).

others to see what we see. We are invited to see an ever larger vision of the world, without having to trade in our own sense of things. Metaphors of vision also recognize the role of desire in our coming to truth. Though we have never known quite what to do with this, there has long been a strand of recognition in our culture that desire and choice play a role in our seeing. (Pascal speaks to this in his thought that there is enough light for those who desire to see, but enough darkness for those who are of a "contrary disposition.") Admittedly, these metaphors often assume a blurred distinction between fact and fiction. Nussbaum and Murdoch, especially, see literature as an avenue for seeing truth about the world, but this very association may allow historians to acknowledge the linkages between the narratives of history and the narratives of fiction and yet also allow the historian room to present his own seeing of the difference between various kinds of narrative.

Third, we might pay more attention to a metaphor linked both with courtroom metaphors and with vision metaphors — but one that has an explicit place within the Christian tradition — metaphors of "witness." Witnesses are called upon to report what they have seen. They may give reasons for having reached particular conclusions about what they have seen. But there is always room for others' freedom to believe or not to believe their testimony. There is space for doubt as well as for belief. And the credibility of a witness will be judged by others. It will be affected by the perceived character of the witness. It will be affected by past experience with the witness. It will be affected by the extent to which others testify to the same truth, or to which others' testimonies provide corroborating evidence. At no point can the witness claim the certainty of logical necessity for her testimony, but that is not to say that there is no place to stand between the certainty of logical necessity and the uncertainty of fiction.

Reflections on the metaphors of witness (as well as metaphors of vision and perception) seem to honor the postmodern insights that knowledge cannot be divorced from context, or from interpretations, or from language, or ultimately from the use that we choose to make of our knowledge. In certain ways, I suspect that these metaphors — though admittedly not without problems of their own — might come closer to a biblical understanding of the nature of knowledge. In scripture, knowledge and truth are intimately connected to persons, to context, and to action. Our knowing, our "seeing clearly" in scripture is linked at various times to obedience, to the state of our "heart," and perhaps most mysteriously of all to our loves (Paul's prayer that "love may abound yet more and more in knowledge and in all judgment that we may approve things that are excellent"). As believers, we have seen God in our lives and we witness to that seeing, inviting others to see what we've seen — respecting their freedom and leaving them space to come to see the same truth. As historians, we believe we have seen certain truths about the past. We believe we have had certain insights. In the same way, we might invite others to see the same truth — recognizing that our character, our trustworthiness, our honesty in dealing with sources (as that is judged by our colleagues) is as important in our reliability as a witness to the past, as it is in our witness to the truth of the gospel. Just as we know the value of the community of believers to correct our seeings in the realm of faith, so we need the community of historians to enlarge our seeings and our understandings of the past. And, though we may not be able to claim the certainty of the natural sciences — in separating ourselves from the narratives of fiction — it does seem that there is enough clarity about our situation to continue doing our work — to know when we sit down whether we ought to read a book as a work of "romance" or as a work of "true history."

Critical Historical Judgment and Biblical Faith

C. STEPHEN EVANS

Historical accounting, by almost universal modern consent, involves that the narrative satisfactorily rendering a sequence believed to have taken place must consist of events, and reasons for their occurrence, whose connections may be rendered without recourse to supernatural agency.[1]

Hans Frei

In *The Eclipse of Biblical Narrative,* Hans Frei tells the story of how what he terms the "realistic character of Biblical narrative" came to be "ignored, or — even more fascinating — its presence and distinctiveness came to be denied for lack of a 'method' to isolate it." As Frei tells the tale, the realistic or "history-like" character of biblical narrative is an obvious feature of the text, so much so that it is "acknowledged by all hands to be there."[2] Nevertheless, because commentators tended to assume that mean-

---

1. Hans Frei, *The Eclipse of Biblical Narrative* (New Haven: Yale University Press, 1974), 14.
2. Frei, *The Eclipse of Biblical Narrative,* 10.

This chapter is a revised version of an article that first appeared in *Faith and Philosophy* 11, no. 2 (1994), and is used here by permission. Much of this material appears in reworked form in *The Historical Christ and the Jesus of Faith* (Oxford: Clarendon Press, 1996).

ing consists of ostensive reference, the history-like character of the narrative could only be coherently understood if the narrative was actually historical. However, the many supernatural elements in the narrative made it increasingly difficult and finally impossible to believe in the historical truth of the narrative, for "it is taken for granted that modern historians will look with a jaundiced eye on appeal to miracle as an explanatory account of events."[3] In the end, Frei maintains, the history-like character of the narrative was either ignored or denied. Since commentators could recognize the history-like character of the text only by thinking of it as actual history, they increasingly ignored that character. On Frei's account, the alternative overlooked was that of "realistic narrative," the type of narrative embodied in the modern realistic novel.

Now Frei is certainly correct to claim that a narrative may have a history-like or realistic character without being historical. Modern realistic fiction is a concrete demonstration of that. So he is correct to say that the question of whether a narrative has a history-like character and thus a "literal" meaning must be distinguished from the question of whether a narrative is historically reliable. However, as Frei certainly recognized, a narrative intended as history and not fiction is also "history-like." Having established that a narrative is history-like, it may also be valuable and important to establish whether it is intended as history, and if it is, whether the historical narrative is a reliable one.

In this essay I wish to discuss the assumption that seems to make it necessary for many people to regard the narratives found in the New Testament concerning Jesus of Nazareth as fundamentally historically untrue: the assumption that critical historical judgment rules out taking seriously accounts of events that involve miracles or supernatural agency. If miracles can occur as part of history, and if it is possible to have good historical evidence that miracles have occurred, then there seems to be no good a priori reason for denying the intended historical character of the New Testament narrative. If the narrative is history-like, one possible explanation of this fact is that it was written as history. Of course the deistic and humanistic dismissal of the narrative as untrue remains an option. However, I wish to show that those who are in some way committed to the truthfulness of the New Testament narrative are not forced by this commitment to deny its narrative character as history. The possibility remains that it is true history.

3. Frei, *The Eclipse of Biblical Narrative,* 14.

I. The Significance of the Incarnational Narrative

Since the narrative of Jesus' life, death, and resurrection, as contained in the four Gospels, is of supreme importance for Christian faith, I shall focus my attention in the remainder on this particular narrative.[4] Part of the evidence that Frei is right in his contention about the eclipse of the realistic character of the New Testament narrative is that many readers may find it hard to understand why the historical truth of the narrative should be so important. Surely, they may say, what is really important is the moral ideal represented by the life and teachings of Jesus, regardless of the historicity of the story. Alternatively, they may say that we can "demythologize" the narrative and extract from it some moral or existential truth. Or, they may affirm, with Joseph Campbell, that the narrative can and should simply be read as myth that may or may not have some historical basis but communicates in a powerful way the basic metaphysical/psychological truth about the human condition, task, and destiny.[5] Surely, it is something like this that is important, not the factual, historical truth of the narrative.

4. Of course many biblical critics would insist that what we have in the Gospels is not a single narrative but multiple narratives whose unity cannot be presupposed. In one sense this is undoubtedly correct; we do indeed have four Gospels and no doubt each tells a tale that differs significantly from the others in various respects. Nor do I see any particular reason to deny that each of the Gospels may embody different traditions that were preserved, orally or in written form. However, the church has always assumed that these different narratives were all attempts to tell one story, the story of Jesus of Nazareth, even if the story was told for different purposes and from different points of view. Furthermore, the church has assumed that it was legitimate to blend these diverse narratives in order to recover this story, however difficult it may be to "harmonize" some of the details. I shall therefore speak of the incarnational narrative (singular) without thereby denying that this narrative is derived from multiple narratives, or implying that the narrative can be legitimately rendered in only one way. A true story can still be told in different ways.

One should recognize that in speaking of this narrative, I give primacy to the account the church accepted of the New Testament. That is, the reading of the New Testament that seems most relevant is the reading that was actually given by the church, the one that was actually formative for Christian faith. It is not simply a matter of developing an account from scratch on some supposedly scientific basis, but of testing the reading developed by the church.

5. See Joseph Campbell, *The Hero With a Thousand Faces*, 2nd ed. (Princeton: Princeton University Press, 1968).

43

I cannot really demonstrate that reading the Bible in such ways is "wrong"; I am not even sure exactly what that would mean. However, I would like to say something about why the historical character of the narrative has always been regarded as crucial for orthodox Christianity. The narrative in question is of course not simply the narrative as it might be "scientifically" reconstructed by biblical scholars, but the narrative as developed from the New Testament by the church.

From the traditional Christian perspective, the historical narrative in the New Testament is not "mere" history, but it is fully history. The Christian rejects the divorce of fact and value, the real and the good, that is so characteristic of modernity. The Christian holds that the Bible contains a record of God's revelation of himself in history. Nor is this revelation simply an historical communication of timeless truths. Rather, the revelation consists of God's actions in history. Jesus is not merely a symbol pointing to some eternal truth about God, but God incarnate, making possible the redemption of the human race, and ultimately of the whole created order, through his life, death, and resurrection. The narrative is not simply an illustration of metaphysical truth, but is itself the record of how God has accomplished salvation. If God has not accomplished salvation in history in this manner, then the New Testament account is untrue in a fundamental sense.

I shall assume in what follows that this New Testament narrative contains supernatural and miraculous elements that are essential to the story and ineradicable from it. The fundamental miracle is simply the presence of Jesus himself as God incarnate. The claim is that Jesus was and is not merely human, even though he was and is fully human. Jesus is the Word, the One who is one with God, the One through whom all things were made.[6] Jesus is one with the Father; he has the authority to forgive sins.[7] His authority and divinity are manifested by his teachings, and ultimately attested by the miracles he performed, including especially the supreme miracle of his being raised from the dead by the Father. To remove references to supernatural agency from this story is to transform it into a different story altogether.

6. See John 1:1-3.
7. See John 10:30 and Matthew 9:6.

II. The Assumptions of the "Critical Historian"

Why precisely do "modern historians" or those who wish to emulate them find it impossible to take seriously as history a narrative with such supernatural elements? Why, to use Frei's words, should it be "taken for granted that modern historians will look with a jaundiced eye on appeal to miracle as an explanatory account of events"? Though it is often assumed and frequently asserted that a "modern, critical" approach to the narrative must exclude the supernatural, attempts to explicitly argue for such a view are more rare. Perhaps the best-known attempt to make such an argument has been provided by Ernst Troeltsch, the important turn of the century German theologian. Among contemporary theologians, Van Harvey, who makes no secret of his debt to Troeltsch, has repeated and reformulated Troeltsch's position.[8] I shall give an exposition of the views of Troeltsch and Harvey, and in so doing critically examine the reasons they give for their view that taking miracles and supernatural agency seriously involves a "pre-critical" view of history.[9]

Both Troeltsch and Harvey are quite clear that the problem with traditional Christian approaches to the gospel narrative does not arise from particular historical findings, but from the *method* to which the modern historian is committed.[10] Thus, the issues to be faced do not concern the

8. The fullest statement of Van Harvey's position is found in his book *The Historian and the Believer* (New York: Macmillan, 1966). A more contemporary statement of his position is found in an essay, "New Testament Scholarship and Christian Belief," in *Jesus: History and Myth* (Buffalo, NY: Prometheus Books, 1986), 193-200. A concise statement of Troeltsch's views can be found in his essay, "Historiography," Vol. 6 of *Encyclopedia of Religion and Ethics,* ed. James Hastings (New York: Charles Scribner's Sons, 1922), 716-23. Harvey himself cites Troeltsch's *Gesammelte Schriften,* vol. II (Tübingen: J. C. B. Mohr, 1913), 729-53, repeatedly in *The Historian and the Believer.*

9. Some of the arguments that follow are similar to arguments developed by William J. Abraham in his fine book *Divine Revelation and the Limits of Historical Criticism* (Oxford: Oxford University Press, 1982). Abraham argues that critical historical judgment does not always preclude an acceptance of miracles. However, Abraham goes further than I am willing to in accepting the validity of the principles of Troeltsch that I wish to criticize, and then arguing that the religious believer can give a "rebuttal" that overcomes the negative conclusions that historical research would otherwise give rise to. In what follows I wish to challenge the prima facie validity of those very principles.

10. Harvey, *The Historian and the Believer,* 4-5.

evidence for or against some particular miracle; rather they concern the general principles historians should follow. As is so often the case, this discussion of "methodology" is really a discussion of philosophical issues, and hence requires no special training as a biblical scholar to understand.

Both Troeltsch and Harvey make several crucial assumptions that are questionable, but which I shall not examine in this essay. Both assume, I think, an internalist, evidentialist account of all historical knowledge. That is, both assume that if I am to know something about the past, I must know it on the basis of evidence of which I am aware or at least of which I could become aware. This ignores the possibility that at least some historical knowledge or justified beliefs may be the result of reliable, belief-producing mechanisms. On a "reliabilist" account of historical knowledge, beliefs formed by such mechanisms might constitute knowledge even if I am not aware of the evidence for the belief.[11] This possibility has real relevance to the case of historical religious knowledge, since some theologians, such as John Calvin, have attributed our knowledge of the truth of the biblical narrative to the internal operation of the Holy Spirit, and while this could be construed evidentially, it might also be understood in a reliabilist manner.

Secondly, Harvey and Troeltsch seem to assume a kind of "ethic of belief" or "morality of knowledge" that implies that we have intellectual duties not to hold historical beliefs without the right kind of evidence. The topic of what are our intellectual duties is a fascinating one, but I shall not discuss it in this paper, except to point out that in most cases we don't have voluntary control over our beliefs, and thus our duties can't be construed simply as duties to acquire or refrain from holding certain beliefs, but more plausibly as duties to cultivate certain kinds of intellectual habits. For this paper, I will provisionally accept the general idea that with respect to historical beliefs, we have some intellectual duties to cultivate the kinds of habits a good historian would have, whatever those might turn out to be, and the assumption that our historical knowledge is best understood as based on evidence. Though I don't believe Harvey has in fact clearly laid out a plausible ethic of belief to back up his charge that holding Christian beliefs in the face of

11. For a good account of the difference between internalist "evidentialist" epistemologies and "reliabilist" externalist epistemologies see William Alston, *Epistemic Justification: Essays in the Theory of Knowledge* (Ithaca, NY: Cornell University Press, 1989).

modern critical history involves intellectual dishonesty, this is an issue I shall have to leave for another occasion.

According to Troeltsch, there are three principles of critical historical investigation that cause problems for the traditional Christian. There is first the *principle of criticism*.[12] Essentially, this is a claim that historical judgments are always provisional, corrigible, and approximative. Such judgments are always more or less probable, based on the evidence available for them. Secondly, there is the *principle of analogy*.[13] This principle is a kind of assumption of uniformity, in that it is assumed that our present experience is not radically different from the experiences of humans in the past. The same kinds of causal laws and natural processes operative today were operative in the past. Thirdly, there is the *principle of correlation*.[14] This is essentially an assumption about causality, that holds that one must always understand an historical event in the context of its natural antecedents and consequences. Historical events must be understood in terms of their natural historical contexts.

Van Harvey essentially takes over Troeltsch's three principles, reinterprets them so as to eliminate certain obvious objections, and places them in the context of more contemporary discussions of evidence and epistemology. Harvey's own account of the "morality of knowledge" involves four aspects: (1) the radical autonomy of the historian, (2) the responsibility of the historian to employ arguments and statements that can be rationally assessed, (3) the need of the historian to exercise "sound and balanced judgment,"[15] and (4) the need to use "critically interpreted experience as the background against which sound judgments are made about the past."[16] When expressed in summary form, the last three of

12. Troeltsch does not cite this principle in a clear form in his essay "Historiography" but it is perhaps implicit in his claim that modern historians "take a purely scientific attitude to facts." See p. 718. Van Harvey cites Troeltsch's *Gesammelte Schriften* II: 729-53, as the basis of his discussion of the principle of criticism.

13. Troeltsch states this idea on p. 718 of "Historiography": "On the analogy of the events known to us we seek by conjecture and sympathetic understanding to explain and reconstruct the past."

14. In "Historiography" this idea is stated on p. 718: "The sole task of history in its specifically theoretical aspect is to explain every movement, process, state, and nexus of things by reference to the web of its causal relations."

15. Harvey, *The Historian and the Believer*, 39-64.

16. Harvey, *The Historian and the Believer*. The quote is from p. 38. The discussion of this principle occupies much of pp. 68-99.

these sound platitudinous, but when developed by Harvey they are filled in with a "Troeltsch-like" content that gives them more critical punch.

Harvey himself says the first three of his principles go together as a kind of "package," while the fourth is logically more distinct.[17] I agree with this claim; in fact, it appears to me that suitably interpreted versions of the first three principles, without the fourth, would probably not get Harvey the conclusions he wishes. Nevertheless, all of his principles bristle with difficulties. I shall try to show that each of the first three principles is ambiguous in the following way; each has what I shall call a platitudinous interpretation, which gives the principle its plausibility, but which has no controversial implications for traditional Christian beliefs. Each allows for a more radical reading, which does conflict with traditional Christian beliefs about the supernatural. However, I will argue that the principles Harvey espouses are implausible as principles binding on all reasonable historians when interpreted in this more radical way.

1. The *autonomy* of the historian is understood by Harvey in terms of the Enlightenment ideal as articulated by Kant: "Dare to use your own reason." This is understood as the rejection of all authority; the only authority that exists for the critical historian is the authority that he confers on his sources. Harvey quotes Collingwood with approval: "In so far as an historian accepts the testimony of an authority and treats it as historical truth . . . he obviously forfeits the name of historian." Harvey himself says, "If the historian permits his authorities to stand uncriticized, he abdicates his role as critical historian. He is no longer a seeker of knowledge but a mediator of past belief; not a thinker but a transmitter of tradition." All this is justified by appealing to the historically conditioned nature of witnesses and authorities: "What a witness thinks he sees is in large part filtered through the prism of his own individual mode of perception and conception which, in turn, is heavily influenced by the modes of thought of the culture of which he is a part. Men are historical creatures, and their judgments reflect the 'world' that they bring with them and to which they appeal in support of those judgments."[18]

Ironically, Harvey seems to think that "critical historians" are immune from this historical predicament and thus stand apart from the common run of humankind. He doesn't see that the "critical historian" he puts forward as an ideal may similarly be a product of historical

17. Harvey, *The Historian and the Believer*, 38.
18. Harvey, *The Historian and the Believer*, 40, 42.

circumstances. Thus he is uncritical of the assumptions of this "enlightened" thinker. As we shall see when we examine Harvey's fourth principle, the "modern, critical" historian is hardly innocent of philosophical assumptions that may reflect his historical situation, and which color the way he views ancient witnesses.

Harvey would probably defend himself here by noting the dangers of historical relativism; Harvey rightly deplores this relativism and affirms the possibility of "self-transcendence" on the part of the historian.[19] Thus, reliable historical knowledge is possible, he thinks. However, Harvey does not seem to notice that if "self-transcendence" is possible on the part of historians, it is likely that the people historians study must be capable of this self-transcendence as well.

Understood in one sense, the claim that historians must be "autonomous" seems quite uncontroversial. If someone is making an historical investigation, then she must decide what sources are reliable, what inferences to draw from the available evidence, and so on. The historian must certainly recognize general truths about the human condition, such as that humans are sometimes mistaken and deceived, and that sources are sometimes untrustworthy. It would be unreasonable for an historian to take a particular source as an absolute, unchallengeable authority. Rather, the authority of a source is the sort of thing that is open to question, and for which evidence is often appropriately sought.

However, it appears to me that Harvey does not wish to interpret his principle of autonomy simply as entailing such innocent platitudes. Rather, he seems to think that the autonomous historian is one who necessarily takes a superior and suspicious attitude toward all historical sources. People who leave us narratives about the past seem to be generally incapable of getting things right; their accounts are always colored by the biases that derive from their historical situation. This is especially true of people of ancient times, with the notable exception of the Greeks. Harvey here reflects a standard attitude of "modern man," one that is especially clear in his hero Troeltsch, who speaks quite disparagingly of ancient peoples in whom "there is not the slightest trace of a desire for real knowledge or of a critical spirit."[20] We learn from the accounts of such people by reading *through* their stories and reconstructing what really happened on the basis of our superior understanding of the situation.

19. Harvey, *The Historian and the Believer*, 221.
20. Troeltsch, "Historiography," 717.

This concept of autonomy seems overblown to me, as does the exaggerated sense of superiority to ancient peoples. In fact, autonomy in this sense trips over the same kind of problem that plagues classical foundationalism in epistemology generally. Classical foundationalism says I should not believe a proposition unless I have objectively certain evidence for that proposition. The problem immediately arises, of course, as to whether I have evidence for my evidence. To stop a regress, it appears that I must have some evidence that either requires no evidence or that I am willing to accept without evidence. If I don't have enough evidence of the former sort, then it appears I am stuck with the latter.

Harvey says I can accept no authority without critical examination of that authority that gives me a basis for certifying that authority as reliable. However, if I can accept no authority without first critical examination, then how can I possibly gain any reliable basis for my critical examination? Surely some authorities must be accepted (some "witnesses") in order to put into question others. I can't for example rely on things like the number and independence of witnesses unless I can put some basic credence in testimony.

Actually, it appears to me that Harvey is mistaken in the picture he accepts (perhaps unconsciously) of the historian as a godlike being who *bestows* authority on certain fortunate sources. I doubt that it is possible for historians to bestow authority or confer it. Surely, the normal procedure is for an historian to *recognize* an authority as reliable. In many cases it is through evidence that the historian comes to recognize this reliability, but it is unlikely that such reliability could ever be recognized if the historian did not generally accept a lot of evidence as trustworthy without any special evidence. It is true that knowledge of the historical circumstances of an historical source may give an historian insight into ways that sources may be unreliable, and thus sometimes the historian is rightly suspicious of sources. But this suspicion must be balanced by suspicion of the historian towards her own biases. A source may see things wrongly because of bias, but it is also possible that a source sees things rightly, but the historian may be blocked from realizing this because of *her* bias. Blanket, wholesale skepticism about the accounts of ancient peoples is surely as unreasonable as gullible acceptance of all accounts. Whether an account is fanciful and whether an ancient author had a sense of what it means to tell a true story are matters to be determined by the nature of the text itself, and the evidence we have that bears on its story, and not simply determined on the basis of speculative claims about the supposed "mind" of ancient peoples.

2. The second and third principles of Harvey seem to me to be essentially linked together. Harvey says that the historian is committed to "publically assessable evidence" for claims made and that "good judgment" must be employed in assessing that evidence.[21]

As stated these principles look perfectly formal, and also perfectly platitudinous. To flesh out his principles, Harvey borrows a model from early work by Stephen Toulmin. An historical conclusion is founded on data which are linked with the conclusion on the basis of a warrant.[22] Warrants are essentially licensed argument-forms. Conclusions can be challenged by denying the relevance or applicability of the data and warrants to the conclusion or by challenging the warrant itself. These challenges, called rebuttals, are in turn met by giving reasons to accept the warrants, which are called backings.

However, all of this still looks perfectly formal and even platitudinous. It seems unlikely that inferences to supernatural explanations can be excluded by such formal machinery. Why, for example, should the following kind of warrant be excluded: "Since exceptions to laws of nature can only be attributed to the work of God, any event involving such an exception must involve divine agency"? If I accept this principle, then if my data involves an event that I have good reason to believe is an exception to a law of nature, such as a resurrection of a person from the dead, then I would have rational warrant for believing that God was part of the cause of the event.

Perhaps to exclude such a case, Harvey might want to understand the "publically assessable" part of his principles as requiring warrants that are acceptable to all historians, including secular historians. A warrant principle such as the one above would then be excluded as not "public" since it is not accepted by those committed to the assumptions that are embedded in modern-day thinking, assumptions that are in practice naturalistic. In such a case, the principles of Harvey cease to be purely formal and platitudinous, but it is not at all clear that the principles are now obligatory for all reasonable historians. Why, the religious believer may ask, should the unbeliever have the authority to decide which warrants are proper and which are not?

21. Harvey, *The Historian and the Believer*, 38.
22. Harvey, *The Historian and the Believer*, 49-54.

If Harvey attempts to argue that the only warrants acceptable as licensing reasonable inferences are ones that are acceptable to all historians, then I am afraid that proper warrants may be hard to come by. For historians typically disagree about such things as what conclusions are supported by a particular body of data. Once more it seems that something akin to a classical foundationalist epistemology has seeped into Harvey's thought, if he takes this line, for the requirement that warrants be acceptable to all historians seems strikingly akin to the characteristic foundationalist principle that the foundations of our knowledge generally must be acceptable to "all sane, rational beings."

Actually, it is not clear that Harvey would claim that legitimate warrants must be acceptable to all historians. He is much concerned to refute historical skepticism, which he sees as a refuge to the traditional theologian who wishes to evade Harvey's relentless attack. As Harvey sees it, the person who is generally skeptical about knowledge of the past can use this skepticism in the following way: since we don't ever really know what happened in the past, the religious believer is as entitled to her unjustified beliefs as anyone else.[23] Harvey argues that historical skepticism is usually the result of setting up one kind of warrant as an ideal, and despairing when historical judgments cannot all be grounded in that way. Instead, Harvey says one must look at the actual warrants used by historians, and not try to impose some uniform ideal.[24] However, if that is so, why should not Christian historians, and others open to supernatural explanations, employ the forms of warrant that seem reasonable to them? Personal explanations, that is, explanations that attribute an event to the actions of persons acting for reasons, are commonly given by sensible, rational people. If God exists, and if God is personal, then there is no obvious reason why such explanations should be rejected in advance, particularly if we can know something about God and God's character such that one might understand some of the reasons God might have for performing certain kinds of actions.

3. Because of the above arguments, I believe that the crucial principle of the group that Harvey advances is the fourth one: the need to use "critically interpreted experience" in order to understand the past. It is here that the influence of Troeltsch can be seen most clearly.

23. Harvey discusses this type of strategy in pp. 204-42 in *The Historian and the Believer.*
24. Harvey, *The Historian and the Believer,* 47-48.

Harvey's first three principles seem to flesh out to some extent Troeltsch's first principle, the "principle of criticism." His fourth principle seems to embody both of Troeltsch's other two principles, the principle of correlation (the idea that past events must be understood with reference to a natural causal network) and the principle of analogy (the idea that human experience has a certain uniformity such that present-day conclusions can be extended to the past). That is, Harvey seems to understand "critically interpreted experience" in a particular way. Understood in one way, the claim that the historian should employ critically interpreted experience once more sounds quite innocent and unobjectionable. However, Harvey understands this principle to imply that historians must apply his first three criteria in a way that is "informed by the new way of looking at the world created by the sciences."[25] Concretely, this means that on the basis of our present experience of the natural world as governed by scientific laws, we rule out all causes other than natural causes.

He characterizes this requirement in a number of ways. The new thinking that is required of the historian is thinking which is rooted in "what we now call the common-sense view of the world"; autonomous thinking is "thinking in terms of the new world-picture"; rational assessment is "appealing to the known structures of present experience."[26]

Harvey does not accept the positivistic ideal that historical knowledge consists of or even is grounded in laws of nature; he agrees that our warrants for historical beliefs are more like "truisms" or probabilistic generalizations than true laws.[27] Nevertheless, Harvey argues that "history presupposes all the sciences" in the sense that certain events and certain explanations are ruled out as impossible. Thus, the laws of natural science play a negative function by ruling out certain things, even if they do not positively justify our historical assertions. Nor does the new physics change this situation: "Nature, to be sure, may be far more refractory to mathematical description at the subatomic level than hitherto believed, but this does not warrant a return to the credulity once characteristic of a majority of the human race."[28]

Harvey says that miracles may be logically possible, but to be a

25. Harvey, *The Historian and the Believer*, 68.
26. Harvey, *The Historian and the Believer*, 68.
27. Harvey, *The Historian and the Believer*, 82.
28. Harvey, *The Historian and the Believer*, 76, 77.

serious candidate as an historical explanation something must be a "relevant possibility, a likely candidate to account for certain data." Since an alleged miracle "contradicts our present knowledge in a specific scientific field" it is always in tension with well-established warrants. Hence "the burden of evidence and argument suddenly falls on the one who alleges the report to be true" and Harvey thinks that it is extremely difficult to meet this obligation.[29]

However, all of these claims made by Harvey seem philosophical in character, and all of them, like most philosophical claims, seem eminently disputable. It is not clear, therefore, why a historian who did not share Harvey's philosophical biases would be disqualified as a "critical historian." Since Harvey's claims about miracles seem to be at the root of his contentions, they deserve careful examination.

III. Miracles

We cannot possibly examine all of the different claims Harvey makes concerning miracles, and of course the philosophical literature on this issue dating back to David Hume's classical essay is vast. Nevertheless, we cannot assess his claims about the standpoint of the "critical" historian without at least a cursory analysis of his claims about miracles. I will limit my reflection to the following claims that one might take as at least implicit in various places in Harvey: (1) Miracles (understood as exceptions to laws of nature) cannot occur.[30] (2) If a miracle should occur, one

29. Harvey, *The Historian and the Believer*, 86-87.
30. The understanding of miracles as involving exceptions to laws of nature goes back at least to Hume, who defined a miracle as a "transgression of a law of nature by a particular volition of the Deity, or by the interposition of some invisible agent." See Hume's *An Enquiry Concerning Human Understanding* (Indianapolis: Hackett Publishing Co., 1977), 77n. Richard Swinburne, in his *The Concept of Miracle* (London: MacMillan, 1970), 11, also defines miracles in such a way that being a violation of a law of nature is a necessary condition for being a miracle. There have been many attempts to develop a concept of miracle that does not require this notion of an exception to a law of nature, usually on the part of theologians who believe that miracles in the Humean sense cannot be believed. For example, John Hick does this in *Philosophy of Religion*, 4th ed. (Englewood Cliffs, NJ: Prentice-Hall, 1990), 37-38. It seems evident to me that critics like Harvey presuppose the Humean type of definition. Since I think that miracles in this sense are possible and can be rationally believed, I do not object to this definition in principle, though I think that

could never have enough evidence to believe that it did occur; some non-miraculous explanation would always be more probable.[31] (3) An historian cannot appeal to miracle as a rational explanation, because we have no way of assessing the evidence for a miracle.[32] One might of course think that these claims are not completely consistent with each other, but we can charitably interpret them as "fall-back" claims. That is, (1) is a claim that miracles cannot occur, and (2) can be read as a claim that even if (1) is mistaken, the evidence for a miracle would never be sufficient to warrant belief. (3) seems inconsistent with (2), since to know that evidence is insufficient it looks like we should be able to evaluate it, but perhaps (3) can be read as a claim that if we lack ways of assessing the value of evidence, the evidence cannot be sufficient to warrant belief. I will examine each of these claims in turn.

1. The first objection to miracles seems to be metaphysical in nature. Harvey seems to claim at certain places that miracles simply cannot occur; at least I think this is implied by his claim that our knowl-

---

the term "exception" is to be preferred to the term "violation" with its unfortunate and misleading normative connotations. Of course the modern concept of a law of nature was not known in ancient times, and so the definition is anachronistic when applied to the biblical writers. However, I think essentially the same idea can be conveyed using the concepts of natural powers and natural regularities, concepts that certainly were available to the biblical writers. Using this terminology, a miracle can be defined as an event that involves an exception to a natural regularity, one that exceeds the natural powers of natural beings, and that therefore must be attributed to the work of God. People in ancient times, though they lacked the modern concept of scientific laws, were quite well aware that in the normal course of things, it was not possible for a virgin to become pregnant or for a man dead for three days to rise from the grave.

Whether Harvey really wishes to deny that miracles in this sense are possible is unclear. I will consider in the next section his claim that miracles are logically possible, though evidentially weak; if that is his considered view, then he really does not hold the view I attack in this section. However, the stronger claim, that miracles are impossible, is suggested at many points in his work, in the claim that certain things are ruled out by the natural sciences as impossible. For example, on p. 81 of *The Historian and the Believer,* he says that it is simply impossible for us to entertain a story about a hero who, having stepped off a cliff, ascends bodily into the heavens, because we, unlike the "savages" who may have believed the story, understand the scientific principles that determine why bodies fall.

31. This is, I believe, the gist of Harvey's discussion of miracles on pp. 85-89 in *The Historian and the Believer.*

32. Harvey, *The Historian and the Believer,* 229.

edge of the laws of the natural sciences rules out certain events and certain explanations of events as "impossible."[33] Presumably he has in mind here events and explanations that involve exceptions to natural scientific laws. Exactly what sense of "impossibility" he has in mind here is not completely clear, since he later seems to admit that miracles are logically possible.[34] Perhaps he means that miracles are physically or naturally impossible.

How is this assertion that miracles are physically impossible to be understood? If it means only that miracles are events that could not occur in the normal course of nature, because they involve happenings that exceed the powers of "unaided" natural realities, then this claim seems one that can be accepted by all parties. However, being physically impossible or naturally impossible will not then imply that a miracle is impossible *simpliciter,* at least for the religious believer, because the believer will say that in the case of a miracle there is a causal power at work distinct from the powers of the natural objects.

So, presumably the claim that miracles are naturally or physically impossible must be taken in some stronger sense, as entailing that a miracle would involve an exception to a law of nature to which there can be no exceptions. The laws of nature must hold universally. But how could Harvey (or anyone) know that the laws of nature are exceptionless? If Christianity is true (or any form of theism), then the natural world, including the laws of that world, exist because of God's creative activity. Many theists believe that if God chose to do so, he could alter the normal course of nature. This could be stated by saying that God could choose to "override" those laws, but that would be a misleading way to put it. Since those laws only hold because of God, and indeed may be thought of simply as God's "normal" pattern of creative activity, to bring about a miracle there is nothing truly independent of God for God to "override." God may simply alter the way he normally causes a particular bit of nature to function.

Some philosophers have argued that the very concept of a law of

33. Harvey, *The Historian and the Believer,* 77.

34. Actually, again it is frustratingly unclear whether Harvey actually affirms the logical possibility of miracles. What he appears to say is that the affirmation that miracles are logically possible does not really help the defender of miracles, since the real problem is that one cannot have good evidence for miracles. See Harvey, *The Historian and the Believer,* 85-87.

nature implies that there cannot be exceptions to such laws.[35] On this view the claim that there cannot be an exception to a law of nature is a conceptual truth, for a law of nature is simply a description of a universal pattern. If the pattern is not universal, then we do not have a true law of nature. Thus, if a miracle is an exception to a law of nature, then we know a priori that there cannot be a miracle.

This argument commits the same sin that critics of the ontological argument for God's existence allege infects Anselm's attempted proof, namely, trying to decide what is true in the real world by the manner in which we define our terms. Surely we cannot decide whether or not there are any exceptions to the normal regularities of nature by how we choose to define such concepts as "law of nature." If someone insists that a true law of nature must be exceptionless, then the theist who believes in miracles may concede that terms may be defined as one likes, and simply point out that one can then simply redefine the term "miracle" accordingly. If laws of nature must be exceptionless, then we need a concept such as "quasi-laws of nature," which refers to natural regularities which hold except in those rare cases where God chooses to work a miracle. It will then be a factual question whether or not the regularities we observe in nature are "laws" in the strict sense insisted upon, and therefore there are no miracles, or whether there are miracles, and the natural regularities we observe are therefore merely "quasi-laws." It is hard to see how an historian qua historian can pronounce upon such a philosophical issue, where the truth seems to depend on the questions as to whether the laws (or quasi-laws) of nature depend on God or not, and if so, whether or not God might ever have reasons to make exceptions to such laws.

Sometimes theological reasons are given for alleging that there cannot be exceptions to laws of nature. However, it is hard to see why such theologically grounded reasons should be binding on the critical historian qua historian. In any case the theological reasons usually given appear flimsy to me. It is sometimes claimed that a miracle as an exception to a law of nature misrepresents the relationship of God to nature by picturing a miraculous event as caused by an intrusion into nature from "outside." God, however, is always at work in the natural order, upholding it by his creative power. Perhaps some ways of talking

---

35. For a good example of this type of argument, see Alistair McKinnon, "'Miracle' and 'Paradox,'" *American Philosophical Quarterly* 4 (October 1967): 308-14.

about miracles do suggest that God is normally not actively present in the natural order, but that is certainly not a necessary implication of belief in miracles. All that is needed is a distinction between God's "normal" creative activity in upholding the processes of nature and a special act in which God wills a particular end, and such a distinction can clearly be made without implying that God is deistically absent from creation.

Sometimes it is argued that a miracle would be a sign of inconsistency on God's part; God "would not violate the laws he has made." However, natural laws are not normative ethical or legal principles that it would be wrong for God to violate. Nor does it seem that it would be inconsistent of God to perform some special action for a special reason on a special occasion. It is the sign of a brilliant stylist, and not an imperfection, for a writer to make an exception to a literary rule that she normally follows, and that a lesser writer may feel the need to slavishly obey. Nor is a miracle rightly seen as an attempt by God to step in and "fix" something that has gone wrong with the natural processes; a miracle may in fact be something God has intended to do from all eternity, a special event that symbolically "fits" the natural order. Thus, C. S. Lewis sees the death and resurrection of Christ as an event that is anticipated and figuratively expressed in the whole cycle of nature, where to produce life, a seed must be buried and "die."[36] A miracle may be a culminating and fulfilling event that symbolically expresses the character of the God who upholds all of nature.

The upshot of all this is that I see no good reason why a critical historian should believe that miracles cannot occur. It may well be, of course, that many modern historians, and even many modern theologians, believe this. However, if they do believe it, they do not believe it for reasons that have anything to do with history, but for philosophical reasons. The only good philosophical reasons I can see for holding such a view would be reasons for believing that God does not exist, or that, if God does exist, God would never have reason to perform a miracle. I doubt very much myself that anyone has good grounds for believing either of these things; at best they are philosophically controversial positions, certainly not views that historians must hold to be good historians, and they are views that Christians have very good reasons not to hold.

36. C. S. Lewis, *Miracles* (New York: Macmillan, 1947), 116-20.

2. Perhaps Harvey will fare better with epistemological rather than metaphysical objections to belief in miracles. As noted above, he claims that even if a miracle were to occur, we could still never have sufficient evidence for the miracle. At the very least anyone who claims a miracle has occurred bears a heavy burden of proof, and Harvey thinks that it will be extremely difficult to satisfy this obligation.[37] This type of argument is, of course, a standard one, going back to Hume's famous objections to miracles, which are also epistemological in character.

Here my discussion must be even more sketchy than in the last section, since the philosophical literature dealing with Hume-type arguments against belief in miracles is enormous. Here again Harvey does not really develop his argument, but seems to assume that it is simply obvious that miracles require an enormous amount of evidence, and that it is difficult if not impossible to provide such evidence.

Hume's own main argument against miracles revolves around the concept of probability. Essentially, he claims that since a miracle involves a "violation" of a law of nature, miracles are highly unlikely events. Laws of nature for Hume are descriptions of the normal course of experience. Hume himself says that a "firm and unalterable experience" has established these laws, and that our experience is uniformly against miracles. Strictly speaking, this is a question-begging claim; if we really knew that our experience of natural regularities was "unalterable" then we would know that miracles could not occur, and we would be back to the metaphysical-type argument just considered. However, such a claim would contradict Hume's own claims about the nature of experience and our knowledge of laws of nature, so we should probably regard this as a slip on his part. Nor are we entitled to say that our experience is completely uniform that miracles have not occurred, since that begs the question at issue, which is whether anyone has experienced a miracle. So probably what Hume means is that in the overwhelming majority of cases, our experience is that nature is uniform. Since he thinks we estimate probability on the basis of past experience, it follows that the prior probability of a miracle is extremely low. For Hume, this means that the evidence on behalf of a miracle would have to be extremely powerful to warrant belief in the miracle, evidence of such force that "its falsehood would be more miraculous, than the fact, which it endeavors to establish."[38]

---

37. Harvey, *The Historian and the Believer*, 87.
38. Hume, *An Enquiry Concerning Human Understanding*, 76, 77.

I believe the first thing to say in response to Hume's argument is simply that extremely improbable events can occur, and that it is possible to have strong evidence for their occurrence. So even if Hume is right in his claim that the prior probability of a miracle is always exceptionally low, it does not follow that belief in a miracle would always be unreasonable, though it would follow that we would need strong evidence to reasonably believe in a miracle. However, it is not at all obvious that Hume's claim about the probability of miracles is correct.

Estimates of prior probability are very tricky, since they are usually made relative to some body of background knowledge. If we know that a box contains 9,999 white marbles and one black marble, then we know the probability of drawing a black marble on any particular draw is rather low. On the other hand, if we draw a great many marbles, then the probability of drawing a black marble sometime or other becomes increasingly high. Similarly, if miracles are very rare events, then the probability of a miracle at any particular place and time may be very low, while the probability of a miracle occurring at some time or other may be very high.

The number of people in the world who are Olympic swimmers is quite small compared with the total population of the world. Hence, if all we know about a particular person is that she is a member of the human race, the probability that she will be an Olympic swimmer is extremely small. If we know that this person attends a college known for producing many Olympic swimmers, the probability is somewhat higher, and if we know the person is a member of the swim team at that college, the probability may actually become quite high. If we see the person swim in a pool and by consulting our watches determine that she is swimming at a world-class rate of speed, the probability may become still higher. The point is that in estimating probability, we bring to bear all the relevant knowledge we have, and not just our knowledge of the frequency with which events of the type occur. The difficulty with estimating the prior probability of a miracle lies in determining what relevant background knowledge we have.

Clearly, it would be relevant if someone had some knowledge or well-founded beliefs about the existence of God and God's character and purposes. If I know that God does not exist, or that if he does, he is the sort of being who would not act in a way that would involve an exception to a law of nature, then I have good grounds for estimating the prior probability of a miracle as very low. On the other hand, if I believe that God exists, miracles would be somewhat more probable. If I believe that God loves and has concern for his creation, and especially for the human race, and that this creation, particularly the human race, has gone terribly wrong, then it seems to me that it is not too improbable to believe that God would take some action to restore that creation and that fallen humanity. A miracle that was part of a plausible narrative, perhaps including other miracles, that involves such a restoration would be much more probable than a miracle that was an isolated occurrence, serving no discernible divine purpose. Exactly what the prior probability of a miracle like the resurrection of Jesus may be if this is correct may be very difficult to say, since we have no way of quantifying such matters, but it seems reasonable to me to affirm that Hume is wrong in his dogmatic claim that the probability must be vanishingly low.

I believe that it must be possible for observers to recognize and give credible testimony that an exception to what is thought to be a law of nature has occurred. If this were not possible, then it would be impossible to test laws of nature, and almost all philosophers of science and working scientists agree that such testability is an important characteristic of genuine scientific laws. If we followed Hume's policy, we would in effect always reject an observation of an apparent counterinstance to a law of nature, on the grounds that its prior probability is too low, but this would make scientific progress impossible.

So it must be possible to believe on reasonable grounds that an exception to what is currently accepted as a law of nature has occurred. The opponent of miracles will probably object at this point that though such a case might be an exception to what is accepted as a law of nature, it may not be an exception to the true laws of nature.[39] Presumably, in the case of a scientific advance in understanding, it is just this situation that obtains. Event E appears to be an exception to accepted law of nature L_1, which then leads us to revise L_1 in favor of L_2.

Certainly, in the case where we have a counterinstance to an accepted law of nature, it is possible that we do not have an exception

39. An argument to this effect can be found in Patrick Nowell-Smith, "Miracles," *New Essays in Philosophical Theology,* ed. Antony Flew and Alasdair MacIntyre (New York: Macmillan, 1955), 243-53. Nowell-Smith argues that our inability to say that some future natural law will not explain the event in effect makes it impossible to define the concept of the supernatural as something to be distinguished from the natural order.

to a genuine law of nature. I believe that Richard Swinburne is correct in his contention that we decide whether or not this is the situation by determining whether the counterinstance is a repeatable or unrepeatable instance.[40] In a case where the counterinstance is repeated when the circumstances are similar, then the reasonable conclusion to draw is that the accepted law of nature should be revised to accommodate the counterinstance. However, in a case where the counterinstance seems to be a "one-time" occurrence, then it would not appear reasonable to revise the accepted law of nature, and it would seem we have a genuine candidate for a miracle.

Of course the judgment about which kind of case we have is a fallible one. Thus, we might judge an event to be an unrepeatable counterinstance and thus an exception to a law of nature, when in fact it is not. However, the possibility of error goes both ways. It is also possible a genuine miracle might occur and be unrecognized. Unless we know a priori that miracles are impossible or extremely improbable, we have no basis for asserting that it will always be more probable that the event could be explained if we had more accurate knowledge of the laws of nature. The mere abstract possibility that an event could be explained by some yet-to-be-discovered law of nature is no reason to believe that it actually can be so explained, any more than the abstract possibility that all of my perceptual experience of the external might be illusory is a reason to believe that the external world does not exist.

3. The third claim of Harvey is that we could not have sufficient evidence for a miracle because we have no way of assessing the force of any putative evidence.[41] Here it seems to me that Harvey is simply mistaken. The evidence for a miracle will consist of the effects of the miracle, and the testimony of those who claimed to observe the miracle and its effects. It would appear to me that this evidence is assessable in the usual manner for historical evidence. In estimating its force, such things as the number of the witnesses, the independence and credibility of the witnesses, and the prior probability of the story must be considered.

Of course in the case of miracles, there is great disagreement about the outcome of this process of weighing the evidence, due in large part, though not exclusively, to the great disagreement about the estimation

40. See Swinburne, *The Concept of Miracle*, 23-32.
41. Harvey, *The Historian and the Believer*, 229.

62

of the background knowledge that shapes the prior probability of the story. This means that there is no algorithm by which such controversies can be settled to the satisfaction of all parties. However, this is a common occurrence in historical studies; historians often have deep and apparently unresolvable controversies about exactly what happened and why. Such disagreements by no means entail that individual parties in such disputes do not have good reasons for holding the views they hold.

IV. Troeltsch's Principles of Correlation and Analogy

Perhaps it is worth briefly looking at two of the principles of Troeltsch to see if they might lend some support to Harvey's rejection of the miraculous as historically credible. Troeltsch held, it will be recalled, that the historian necessarily follows the principles of analogy and correlation. The principle of analogy is a claim that judgments about the past presuppose that our contemporary experience is not radically dissimilar from past experience, and the principle of correlation is a claim that historical understanding involves placing an event in a network of causal antecedents and consequents.

It is difficult to state the principle of analogy in a manner that is both clear and plausible. As proponents of "modern, critical history" like Harvey would be the first to maintain, the worldviews of people of diverse cultures and ages can be profoundly different, and so it is not at all obvious that their experience of the world cannot be profoundly different as well. Nevertheless, if one can state a plausible version of this principle, it is not obvious that it leads to negative conclusions about the possibility of miracles.

Put crudely, I believe that Troeltsch's principle of analogy is supposed to work something like this: Since we don't observe miracles occurring today, we can't reasonably believe they occurred in the past either. Now, as it stands, this inference seems dubious; many religious believers have thought that God would only perform miracles in quite unusual circumstances. If one believed that the incarnation of Jesus was an historical event that made possible the redemption of humanity and the whole created order, one might reasonably believe that miracles might accompany that event even if they do not occur today.

However, even if the inference is sound, the antecedent clause is questionable. That is, Troeltsch — and his followers such as Harvey —

simply assumes that miracles do not occur today. However fashionable such a belief may be among secular intellectuals, it is not shared by millions of people, including many highly educated people. Though I don't see why anyone should accept Troeltsch's principle of analogy, someone might well do so, and reason as follows: Since miracles occur today, it is likely that they occurred in the past as well. Even people who have no direct experience of miracles today might well think that Troeltsch's principle is harmless if they have experiences of God, experiences with a living God who reveals himself as the kind of being who could perform a miracle. Perhaps Troeltsch's principle reveals a kind of sociological truth: people who have no experience of miracles and no experience of the kind of God who could perform miracles find it hard to believe in miracles. Our culture may be such that there are many people who satisfy this description, though I suspect that there are many more who do not, but from this sociological principle no valid inferences can be made about whether miracles truly occur and can be rationally accepted.

Troeltsch's other principle, the principle of correlation, seems ambiguous. If we mean by this principle simply that events must be understood in relation to the actual causal forces and effects that surround them, then it seems plausible enough. However, the religious believer will claim that it is possible that God, who is actively at work in all of creation, is one of those causal powers (as well as being the ultimate creative source of all the other beings exerting causal power). Unless Troeltsch knows a priori that naturalism is true and there is no God, or that God never exercises causal power in the natural world except in accordance with natural laws, then he has no reason to exclude the possibility that the activity of God can be located in the causal network in terms of which an event must be understood.

V. The Sociology of Knowledge and Appeals to Authority

In the end I suspect that Harvey and others who share his view will be unmoved by arguments such as I have put forward. For Harvey, defenses of miracles are difficult to take seriously; such thinking violates "what we now call the common-sense view of the world."[42] Such claims go

42. Harvey, *The Historian and the Believer*, 68.

hand in hand with sweeping claims about what it is possible for the "modern mind" to believe. Defenses of miracles are defenses of a lost cause, roughly akin to putting forward arguments in favor of a flat earth. Those like myself who put forward such arguments are viewed with wonderment; we are living fossils, "pre-critical" thinkers who have somehow survived into the late twentieth century, oblivious to the securely established conclusions of Hume and Kant.

There is a deep irony here, for the mind-set of the "critical" thinker I have just described is anything but critical. In fact, what we have here is an unacknowledged, and perhaps unconscious, appeal to authority, the anonymous authority of the "modern mind." Such an appeal is doubly ironical, for one of the accusations Harvey and his type bring against defenders of the reliability of the biblical narrative is that such defenders uncritically accept the authority of the Bible, though I have been careful in this essay never to appeal to biblical authority. Nevertheless, those who find biblical miracles plausible are somehow unreasonable because they do not accede to the supposed common sense that "we" all are supposed to share.

Though I am not a fan of everything in postmodern writers, one thing that postmodernism has usefully taught us to do when someone talks about "we" is to ask "Who is this 'we'?" Does this "we" include the poor? Does it include women? Does it include non-Westerners and minorities of color within the West? Since traditional religious beliefs, including belief in the supernatural, are more common among the poor, among women, minorities, and in the Christian church in Asia, Africa, and Latin America (though not always more common among the self-appointed advocates of those groups), these questions are quite relevant. Nor of course, for that matter, is there any shortage of white, Western, educated males who believe in the supernatural, if one simply looks around at the actual world. It seems to me that theologians who are truly "critical" will begin to ask critical questions about their own inherited intellectual baggage, and will be much less quick to assume that the taken-for-granted assumptions of many secular Western intellectuals over the past two hundred years form a necessary part of "common sense." Though there is much that is bizarre being put forward under the banner of "postmodernism," surely one thing that this intellectual movement should cause us to do is to reexamine the "modern" intellectual assumptions about the supernatural that we have inherited from the Enlightenment.

Deciding whether belief in miracles is reasonable on the basis of what "most intellectuals" in the West over the past two hundred years have thought is only a bit more reasonable than deciding who to vote for on the basis of who is leading in the opinion polls. Though an appeal to authority can be reasonable, it is not reasonable to appeal to authority to ignore an argument that challenges the grounds upon which an authority's judgment is based. Thus, if the opinions of many Western intellectuals are rooted in dubious philosophical assumptions, an argument that points this out cannot be rebutted simply by appealing to the authority of the intellectuals in question.

Often the names of philosophers are cited by theologians in this connection: Hume, Kant, Marx, Feuerbach, and Nietzsche are frequently invoked. However, if this is to be more than the invocation of sacred mantras the specific arguments of the philosophers in question must be brought into the arena and defended, and this is all too frequently not done. So, when Hans Frei informs us that however dubious Karl Marx's views about the historical Jesus may have been, he was essentially correct in saying that the criticism of historical religion in Germany was a finished task,[43] we must ask whether this is a historical, sociological report or something more than this. If Frei means by this merely that most intellectuals in Germany from this period on ceased to worry very much about the truth of historic Christianity, he may well be correct, but the crucial question is "So what?" Were these intellectuals right to ignore these questions? Were the philosophical assumptions that made it necessary for them to ignore the possibility that the biblical narrative was truly historical, good assumptions? The truly critical thinker, the one with the philosopher's spirit, is willing to ask such questions and ask them in a fresh spirit, without necessarily seeking to answer them "as the age demands," as the past age did, or as the present age tends to do.

I conclude that Van Harvey has by no means given any good reasons why the "critical historian" should rule out the possibility that supernatural, miracle-filled narratives are historically true. If Hans Frei is right in insisting that the New Testament narratives have a "realistic,

---

43. Hans Frei, *The Eclipse of Biblical Narrative*, 224-32. Though it is not completely clear how Frei himself wants us to take his comments here, it is fair to say that at various points Frei does engage in the kind of illegitimate appeal to sociological thinking I criticize here, in which options are dismissed on the grounds that they are not taken seriously anymore by intellectuals of a certain group.

history-like" character, then they should be considered as possibly historical. We may of course reject the historical truth of the biblical narratives; I have given no apologetic argument for the historicity of those narratives. However, those who wish to affirm the biblical narratives as true are not automatically forced to reject their historical character in order to save the truth of the text. It is much too hasty to reject the historicity of a narrative simply on the ground that the narrative contains an account of miracles.

History in Search of Meaning:
The Conference on Faith and History

D. G. HART

Do Christian historians have a particular perspective or share a set of assumptions that make their writing and teaching different from that of their non-believing colleagues? Though many factors led to the founding of the Conference on Faith in History (CFH), the conviction that the faith of the Christian historian sets his or her scholarship apart from that produced by the rest of the profession was probably the greatest reason for organizing the conference almost thirty years ago and has sustained its meetings and publications ever since. According to Charles Miller, the group who met to begin the CFH came up with three qualifications for a Christian historian: a "profound faith in the God and father of our Lord Jesus Christ"; an understanding of "the nature of man, of time, and of the universe"; and a "mastery of the craft and of the art of the historian."[1]

What happens, then, when one of the conference's more accomplished members publishes a book on a significant epoch in the history of American Christianity that according to some church leaders not only falls well short of demonstrating a Christian philosophy of history but also appears to question the hand of God in the development of American evangelicalism? This is what happened when Harry S. Stout, Yale

---

1. Miller, "The Conference on Faith and History: Reminiscences about Origins and Identity, *Fides et Historia* (hereafter cited as *FEH*) 9 (1976): 60.

University's Jonathan Edwards Professor of American Christianity, published his study of George Whitefield. This book, which linked the revivalist's success in part to his theatrics and business acumen, and which revealed the less sanctified aspects of Whitefield's pilgrimage, caused something of a stir among those English-speaking evangelicals of a Calvinistic persuasion who read the theologically hyper-conservative *Banner of Truth* magazine and that magazine's publisher's many reprints of Puritan and Presbyterian classics. Not only had Stout presented the English revivalist warts and all, but even worse was the implicit assertion that human techniques, sometimes overtly manipulative, not the work of the third person of the Trinity, had been responsible for the many conversions that followed Whitefield's itinerant preaching throughout the colonies and British isles.[2]

An outcry first came in a *Banner of Truth* review of Stout's biography. The portrait of Whitefield that emerged, a "bombast and showman" guilty of "shameless egocentricity," was "barely recognizable" to readers long accustomed to Whitefield as the last Calvinistic revivalist. According to the reviewer, David White, "It is fallacious and absurd to trace the origins of modern campaign evangelicalism, with its expensive publicity, deliberate conditioning by a highly charged musical atmosphere and the manipulation of massed choirs, to the straightforward proclamation of a Whitefield who stood in the best tradition of the Puritans."[3] Iain H. Murray, the editorial director of the Banner of Truth Trust, biographer of Jonathan Edwards, and historian of Anglo-American revivalism in his own right,[4] kept up the attack, using the publication of the papers from an Institute for the Study of American Evangelicals conference on trans-Atlantic evangelicalism in which Stout had a chapter as the occasion for offering his estimate of the new Whitefield. What is lacking in Stout's scholarship, as well as in the "new approach to evangelical history," according to Murray, is a failure to write history from "the standpoint of supernaturalism." In fact, the whole tone of this historiography left Murray wondering what these so-called evangelical

2. Harry S. Stout, *The Divine Dramatist: George Whitefield and the Rise of Modern Evangelicalism* (Grand Rapids: Eerdmans, 1991).

3. Review of *The Divine Dramatist* in *Banner of Truth* 366 (March 1994): 29.

4. See, for instance, Iain H. Murray, *Jonathan Edwards: A New Biography* (Edinburgh: Banner of Truth, 1987) and *Revivals and Revivalism: The Making and Marring of American Evangelicalism, 1750-1858* (Edinburgh: Banner of Truth, 1994).

historians would do to the book of Acts "if they determined to re-interpret its events without reference to God."[5] Stout's response to these charges raised and answered important questions about how believers should practice the craft of history. He explained that "professional" historians "agree to settle for something less than ultimate explanations," and that academic "canons of evidence and interpretation" leave "off the field" notions of providence and the work of the Holy Spirit.[6] Still, the damage had been done. A member of a body whose purpose was to reflect upon the significance of Christian teaching for explaining history was guilty of saying that in good history, that is, history practiced by university professors, such questions did not seem to matter.

While all of this took place outside the workings of the Conference on Faith and History, most of its members would have likely sided with Stout in this debate, in part because they agree with his assessment of the role of faith in the practice of historical scholarship, and also because, remembering the historic warfare between science and theology, they possibly feared the restrictions of church dogma upon the pursuit of historical truth. But, Iain Murray's defense of neo-providentialism and the supernatural in the writing of history are much closer than Stout's critical history to the purposes and contributions of the CFH, at least as argued by some of the society's members. Many writers for *Fides et Historia,* as well as historians who have presented at the conference's meetings, have argued against a "secular" reading of history and have attempted in a variety of ways to articulate a Christian philosophy not just of history but also of historical research and writing.

Pointing out the arguable resemblance between the CFH's purpose and Murray's charges about Stout's biography of Whitefield and Stout's subsequent exchange with Murray cast the aims and purposes of the CFH in a different light, one that reveals the difficult terrain the conference has tried to negotiate by promoting scholarship of the highest caliber that also springs from Christian convictions. What follows, then, are some reflections on these putative similarities between the CFH and the Banner of Truth Trust. In a nutshell, the argument here is that the

5. Murray, "Explaining Evangelical History" [a review of *Evangelicalism: Comparative Studies of Popular Protestantism in North America,* ed. Mark A. Noll et al. (New York: Oxford University Press, 1994)], *Banner of Truth* 370 (July 1994): 13, 8.

6. Stout, "Reviewers Reviewed," *Banner of Truth* 378 (March 1995): 7-10, quotation on 8.

writings sponsored by the conference and produced by its members throughout much of its history have exhibited, even if less Calvinistic, the kind of historiography that Iain Murray wants from other evangelical historians.[7] Yet as laudable as the intentions of the conference have been, it has not yet yielded a fully convincing case for the Christian writing and teaching of history, if neo-providentialism be the test. Consequently, this chapter closes with a few remarks about the perils of attempting to practice that sort of Christian history, at least as the conference has promoted it, and gives reasons, even Christian ones, for siding with Stout against Murray in promoting a different version of Christian history.

Fraternal and Inspired Origins

The origins of the CFH are somewhat murky. Officially, the organization began in November 1967, at a meeting of Christian historians convened at Greenville, Illinois, concerning the "Historical Heritage of American Protestantism." At this meeting, approximately seventy historians of evangelical persuasion decided to make formal what had been an informal occurrence for many years. According to Richard V. Pierard, "from time to time various Christian colleges sponsored history conferences or seminars." Another factor was the leadership of historians at Calvin College and Wheaton College who at the annual meetings of the American Historical Association hosted breakfasts for evangelicals in attendance. Pierard also indicates that the conference grew out of a desire of "committed" Christian historians for "closer cooperation and communication."[8] The historians who gathered at Greenville College built upon this momentum and decided to form the CFH, with John W. Snyder and Robert D. Linder assuming leadership responsibilities until a constitution could be drafted and ratified. That same year the conference sponsored its first formal function, a session at the 1967 AHA annual meetings in Toronto where two scholars presented papers.

What makes the origins of the CFH unclear is to compare Pierard's

---

7. The CFH has had a high degree of Calvinists responsible for its affairs. But its Calvinism has been more of the world-and-life-view variety than the five-points-of-Calvinism brand popular within Banner of Truth circles.

8. Richard V. Pierard, "A Note on the Origins of the Conference on Faith and History," *FEH* 1 (Fall 1968): 23.

first-hand report with the reminiscences of Charles Miller, who remembers the origins of the CFH occurring during the 1959 annual meeting of the AHA at the Conrad Hilton Hotel in Chicago. Wheaton College historian Earle Cairns had organized a breakfast fellowship, which according to Miller was less than auspicious. Diners did not feast upon bacon and eggs provided by the staff at the Conrad Hilton, but rather lined up at the cafeteria of the YMCA Hotel at nearby South Wabash and carried their breakfasts on trays out into the hotel lobby into a reserved room under the steps leading to the second floor. Miller recalled that he bumped his head on the ceiling of those stairs. "We were," he added, "a strange conventicle of hesitant Christians meeting almost in secret." Yet, even though those who gathered doubted whether "committed Christians could be distinguished historians," and were simply "teachers of history in Christian colleges . . . still working in their spare time on their doctorates from undistinguished graduate schools," Miller came away from the meeting exhilarated and hopeful. As those in attendance began to supply Cairns with the names of Christian historians, Miller wrote, "we, who had thought we were the last defenders on the wall of Zion, soon found we were surrounded by so great a cloud of witnesses."[9]

Miller's sense of encouragement was not reflected in the CFH's formal proposed constitution which featured a terse statement of purpose. That threefold purpose was: "To encourage evangelical Christian scholars to explore the relationship of their faith to historical studies; To provide a forum for discussion of philosophies of history and to survey current scholarship and foster research in the general area of faith and history"; and, finally, "To establish more effective means of interaction between historians associated with religiously oriented and nonsectarian institutions of higher learning."[10]

Yet, encouraging fellowship among Christian historians, though not stated explicitly in the constitution, was also one of the important functions of the CFH early on and explains why Miller came away from the Chicago breakfast in 1959 with a sense of hope and identity and why 131 others

9. Miller, "The Conference on Faith and History," 59, 60.
10. An evangelical Christian was someone who could affirm the Holy Scriptures as "the Word of God, the Christian's authoritative guide for faith and conduct," and Jesus Christ as "the Son of God and through his atonement . . . the mediator between God and man." "Proposed Constitution," *FEH* 1 (Fall 1968): 5-6.

joined Miller in affiliating with the conference at its beginning. According to John W. Snyder, the conference's first president, the new organization provided an atmosphere of fellowship and camaraderie. "Formerly," he wrote in the first issue of *Fides et Historia,* "one felt strangely alone and slightly illicit in confessing both to serious pretensions as a historian and to faith in Jesus Christ." But the creation of CFH was a sign that an "increasing number" of historians "found the two conjoinable."[11] The fraternal dimensions of the conference, according to Robert D. Linder, the chair of the publication committee, would also be evident in the pages of its journal which was "not simply another scholarly journal." From Linder's perspective the conference's original purpose was "to provide both scholarly encounter and fraternal opportunities for our membership."[12] So too, while urging attendance at the fall 1969 CFH meeting, Linder reminded readers of *Fides* that the conference was not in competition with either the American Historical Association (AHA) or the American Society of Church History (ASCH). Along with producing reputable scholarship Linder hoped the conference was doing something far more important than enhancing academic prestige, namely, "building bridges of understanding and communication." "The CFH represents scholarship with a purpose," he wrote, "plus a chance for Christian fellowship in the setting of a community of scholars."[13]

Linder's editorial proddings were not the only signs that the CFH provided a setting for Christian fellowship. As he also noted in the first editorial of *Fides et Historia,* the conference was made up of established older scholars, younger historians fresh out of graduate school, as well as "history-conscious ministers and history-oriented social scientists."[14] Indeed, one of Linder's reasons for questioning affiliation with the AHA

11. John Snyder, "Open Letter from the President," *FEH* 1 (Fall 1968): 3.

12. Robert Linder, "Editorial," *FEH* 2 (Fall 1969): 2.

13. Linder, "Editorial Comment: 'Come to Dallas!'" *FEH* 2 (Spring 1970): 2. Linder sounded this theme again when in 1971 the conference debated affiliation with the AHA. He thought such recognition advisable in order to be listed in the AHA's program, but not if it meant having to drop the conference's doctrinal statement or abandoning "our stated purpose of fellowship as well as scholarship." To do so, he warned, "would reduce us to the status of simply another organization of historians; and who needs *another* one to join in this day and age?" Linder, "The Conference on Faith and History and the American Historical Association," *FEH* 3 (Spring 1971): 3.

14. "Editorial," *FEH* 1 (Fall 1968): 1.

was the membership of "non-professionals."[15] Early lists of member and editorial boards confirm Linder's comment. The CFH included a number of evangelical seminary faculty in its ranks, such as John Warwick Montgomery, then at Trinity Evangelical Divinity School, and Paul Woolley of Westminster Seminary, who served for several years on the conference's editorial board. Also noticeably present in the conference at the beginning were members of the neo-evangelical intelligentsia. From the start Carl Henry and Harold Lindsell were members, with the latter also serving on the publications committee at the outset and providing free publicity for the CFH in the pages of his magazine, *Christianity Today*.[16] Henry also appears to have participated actively in conference activities, serving as the keynote speaker at the fall 1971 meeting of the CFH.[17] In fact, the early newsletters of the conference, which originally were part of *Fides et Historia*, show a wide and varied set of interests, with the conference being firmly rooted in the larger constellation of neo-evangelical scholarly activities, including the Evangelical Theological Society, *Christian Scholar's Review*, InterVarsity Christian Fellowship, and the American Scientific Affiliation.[18]

Going through *Fides et Historia* shows that as the conference matured, ties of Christian fraternity unraveled. Except for Frank Roberts' occasional benedictions, such as when he asked for God's blessing upon Joel Carpenter,[19] who gave up book review editorial duties when he became religion director at the Pew Charitable Trusts, the conference has undergone a process of institutionalization that is typical of the life of any organization but was also caused by the professionalization of CFH membership. Even though William C. Ringenberg in 1991, then president of CFH, could speak of the conference as a "family" and the "professional

---

15. Linder, "The Conference on Faith and History and the American Historical Association," 3.

16. "Historians Debate God-and-Country Theme," *Christianity Today* (Nov. 7, 1969): 51-52.

17. "The Tensions between Evangelism and the Christian Demand for Social Justice," *FEH* 4 (Spring 1972): 3-10.

18. On the scholarly initiatives of neo-evangelicalism, see Noll, *Between Faith and Criticism*, ch. 5; George M. Marsden, "The State of Evangelical Christian Scholarship," *Christian Scholar's Review* 17 (1988): 347-60; and D. G. Hart, "The Fundamentalist Origins of the American Scientific Affiliation," *Perspectives on Science and Christian Faith* 43 (1991): 238-48.

19. Frank Roberts, "From the Editor," *FEH* 21 (Spring 1989): 3.

organization with which we most completely identify," the pages of *Fides* suggest an organization dominated more by academic than fraternal concerns, more formal, more professional, less accessible to non-historians, less intimate, less fraternal, and less sure of its identity. While the conference may have functioned as a fellowship group of evangelical historians for the first generation, it has over time become another professional organization, still Christian and evangelical in orientation to be sure, but where academic standards count more than spiritual fellowship.

The turning point, though not dramatic, must have been the CFH's affiliation with the AHA, a decision that oriented the conference more toward the academy and, therefore, made it less accessible to nonprofessional members, such as ministers, seminarians, and interested lay men and women. This shift, it should be added, was only natural in an organization that emerged out of an informal network of like-minded individuals who met together at the AHA and communicated regularly, but had to find some way to accommodate new and younger members outside the initial network. Whereas a member's identity within the conference once consisted of meeting for breakfast at the AHA, it is now possible to be part of the organization and "know" it only from reading *Fides et Historia*. These comments are not meant to be nostalgic. The point is that to sustain themselves organizations ultimately must depend on impersonal tests and criteria, that is, bureaucratic ones that can be determined by mail rather than face to face.

Three Stages of the CFH

While the warmth and camaraderie of the CFH may have declined, at least for its younger members, its purpose of encouraging reflection on the relationship between Christian faith and the practice of historical scholarship and teaching has been constant even if diminished in recent years. For the sake of simplification the conference's history breaks down into three periods. The first, which lasted from 1959 to roughly 1973, was the neo-evangelical phase where evangelical historians who were members of the AHA overlapped with other organizations and networks within the neo-evangelical world, hence the presence of folks like Lindsell, Henry, Montgomery, and Woolley to name a few. The second period runs until 1984, and should be called the Calvin College phase. This was a time when explicit ties to the neo-evangelical networks became much less obvious, when Christian liberal arts college faculty who were members of the AHA dominated the conference, and when the historiography of the CFH was overwhelmingly written by historians in the Reformed tradition. The last period is a time when, I would tentatively suggest, the identity of the conference is less certain and this uncertainty can be seen in the efforts — or better, the lack of them — to produce a Christian understanding of history.

The Neo-Evangelical Phase

One of the first things that stands out about the first period of historiographical reflection in the pages of *Fides* is the larger than life presence of the indefatigable John Warwick Montgomery, then professor of church history at Trinity Evangelical Divinity School. About the time of the conference's founding, Montgomery produced two books on the historical character of Christianity, that argued for the historical reliability of the New Testament and the historical factualness of the major redemptive events in the life of Christ.[20] What is striking is that Montgomery's views elicited nine articles or reviews in the pages of *Fides*.[21] What is no less startling is how many of Montgomery's students

20. John Warwick Montgomery, *Where Is History Going? Essays in Support of the Historical Truth of the Christian Revelation* (Grand Rapids: Zondervan, 1969); and *History and Christianity* (Downers Grove, IL: InterVarsity Press, 1972).

21. The debate over Montgomery ran as follows: Ronald J. VanderMolen, "The Christian Historian: Apologist or Seeker?" *FEH* 3 (Fall 1970): 41-56; William A. Speck, "Herbert Butterfield on the Christian and Historical Study," *FEH* 4 (Fall 1971): 50-70; John Warwick Montgomery and James R. Moore, "The Speck in Butterfield's Eye, A Reply to William A. Speck," *FEH* 4 (Fall 1971): 71-77; Steven A. Hein, "The Christian Historian: Apologist or Seeker? — A Reply to Ronald J. VanderMolen," *FEH* 4 (Spring 1972): 85-93; William A. Speck, "A Reply to John Warwick Montgomery and James R. Moore," *FEH* 5 (Fall 1972 and Spring 1973): 107-8; Ronald VanderMolen, "Where Is History Going? And Historical Scholarship: A Response," *FEH* 5 (Fall 1972 and Spring 1973): 109-12; Earl William Kennedy, "John Warwick Montgomery and the Objectivist Apologetics Movement," *FEH* 5 (Fall 1972 and Spring 1973): 117-21; Timothy Paul Erdel, "Stigma and Dogma: A Reply to Earl William Kennedy on Behalf of John Warwick Montgomery," *FEH* 7 (Fall 1974): 26-32; and Earl William Kennedy, "The Reviewer Reviews the Review of the Reviewer's Review, or: the Inerrancy of John Warwick Montgomery Revisited," *FEH* 7 (Fall 1974): 33-36.

went into print in defense of their professor. In fact, Montgomery coauthored only one article in the exchange, with his assistant, James R. Moore, now better known for his work on Darwin and for his repudiation of Montgomery's style of apologetics. To be sure, the conference was not alone in devoting attention to Montgomery's books. So too did the *Reformed Journal, Christian Scholar's Review,* and the *Journal of the Evangelical Theological Society.*[22] But almost a quarter of a century later it is hard to imagine the current membership of the conference giving so much attention to the historical apologetics of a seminary professor, a difficulty that makes all the more obvious how much the CFH has changed along with evangelical academic culture more generally since 1970.

The crux of the matter had to do with the reliability or epistemic certainty provided by historical studies. Ronald J. VanderMolen, who started the whole debate off, objected to Montgomery's wooden epistemology, which, to VanderMolen, failed to recognize the subjective aspects of Christian faith as well as the interpretive nature of historical scholarship.[23] William A. Speck was unwittingly drawn into the fray when he assessed Herbert Butterfield's efforts to trace the Christian influences upon modern notions of history, efforts that Speck deemed a failure because Butterfield had not recognized that the empirical methods of modern history fed "a secular view of life and reinforce[d] the monopoly of scientific, inductive methods of establishing 'truth.'" But Speck's criticisms of Butterfield were not good enough for Montgomery and Moore who would have nothing to do with the "invidious comparison between technical history and Christian commitment." "Every attempt to drive this wedge," they wrote, "is both to destroy the true character of Christianity as a historical religion and to debilitate the historian's work by removing an incarnational Christianity from his purview, thereby rendering its origins and development maddeningly inexplicable." Obviously, a variety of issues were bound up in this exchange, from the sublime — the nature and meaning of Christianity — to the mundane — the nature and purpose of historical study. But sorting out these matters was as difficult as the title to the last entry in the debate was long; William Earl Kennedy had the last word in an article entitled, "The Reviewer Reviews the Review of the Reviewer's

22. Speck, "A Reply to John Warwick Montgomery," and Kennedy, "John Warwick Montgomery," refer to the literature in other journals or periodicals.
23. VanderMolen, "Christian Historian."

Review." But Kennedy's points about the relationship between the objective and subjective aspects of faith were a long way from the concerns of a Christian historian teaching at Polytechnic State University, who wondered if the way he taught Western Civ. was different from his Marxist colleague across the hall.

Perhaps the desultory nature of this debate revealed that the aims of the conference were considerably different from the uses to which evangelical seminary faculty put the study of history. Or perhaps the decision by conference membership to affiliate with the AHA made Montgomery's apologetics an embarrassment. Whatever the explanation, the closing of this debate seems to have marked a change in the CFH, from an organization open to the interests of the neo-evangelical seminary leadership, to one that would focus on the teaching of history at colleges and universities. Thus, having been sidetracked by the claims of Montgomery, the conference moved back to what appeared to be its original constituency and interests, namely, evangelical historians who primarily taught undergraduates and wanted to explore what difference their faith made for their teaching and writing.[24] This began the second period of the conference's history, one dominated by scholars of a Reformed perspective teaching at Calvin and Wheaton and writing thoughtfully about the Christian aspects of historical knowledge and scholarship.

The Calvin College Phase

The titles of essays and articles in *Fides et Historia* published between 1974 and 1984, especially under the editorship of Ronald A. Wells, substantiate this reading of the conference's history. Some authors explored the historiographical implications of specific historians or theologians, such as "Herman Dooyeweerd on History: An Attempt to Understand Him" (6 [Fall 1973]), or "Toynbee's View of Christianity" (6 [Fall 1973]), or "Jacques Ellul and Francis Schaeffer: Two Views of Western Civilization" (13 [Spring-Summer 1981]), or even the reprint of E. Harris Harbison's "Last Lecture" (11 [Spring 1979]). Then there were an assortment of articles addressing specifically the purposes and methods of the Christian historian, such as the straightforward "What Should Be the Role of the Christian Historian?" (8 [Fall 1975]), "The Christian Historian as Activist"

24. Speck, "Herbert Butterfield," 64.

(9 [Spring 1976]), "History, Objectivity and the Christian Scholar" (10 [Fall 1977]), or "Is There a Christian Approach to the Writing of History?" (12 [Fall 1980]). Mixed in with these historiographical topics were always a large assortment of essays covering a Christian approach to a particular topic or field, such as "The Conference on Faith and History and the Study of Early American History" (11 [Fall 1978]), "The Present State of Research in Early Modern European History" (11 [Fall 1978]), "Christianity, Christian Interpretation and the Origins of the French Revolution" (11 [Spring 1979]), or "Social Science History: A Critique and Appreciation" (14 [Fall-Winter 1981]).

The most representative titles in this period were two collections of essays, many of which first appeared in *Fides.* The first was the book edited by two Calvin College historians, Frank Roberts and George Marsden, entitled *A Christian View of History?* [25] Though this collection was more directly the product of Calvin's history department, it contained many of the authors producing essays on Christian historiography for *Fides* and confirms the dominance of Reformed historians (especially with Dutch names) during this second period. The other collection of essays, again with distinct connections to Calvin College, was *History and Historical Understanding,* coedited by C. T. McIntire and Ronald A. Wells.[26] These two titles function like bookends on the second period and explain the dominance of Calvin College within the CFH throughout this decade.

Though opinions about a Christian understanding of or approach to history were by no means unanimous, several themes emerged from the numerous articles and chapters produced by conference members. One was the commitment to excellent scholarship motivated by active faith. Mark A. Noll summarized this conviction well when he wrote about the four tasks of the Christian historian, namely, to be "speaking in the profession," "speaking to the profession," "speaking to the church," and "speaking in the church."[27] Though he encouraged CFH members to "move beyond [their] current interests into the mainstream of con-

---

25. Frank Roberts and George Marsden, eds., *A Christian View of History?* (Grand Rapids: Eerdmans, 1975).

26. C. T. McIntire and Ronald A. Wells, eds., *History and Historical Understanding* (Grand Rapids: Eerdmans, 1984).

27. Mark A. Noll, "The Conference on Faith and History and the Study of Early American History," *FEH* 11 (Fall 1978): 8-9.

temporary historical research," Noll was also sensitive to the charge that he was condoning "a sell-out to 'the world.'" For this reason Christian historians also needed to look for a "specifically Christian approach" to the use of historical methods. Noll believed the best way to pursue this search was to consider theoretical matters or "philosophical questions with which historians [were] often very uneasy" but were necessary if Christian historians were to employ mainstream historical explanations as "servants" rather than as "lords."[28]

The philosophical questions posed by Noll were a second theme to emerge from CFH reflections on history during this period. Two issues raised by Noll concerned the importance of treating historical actors as responsible agents, and employing only those methods that reflected an openness to divine influence. These issues reflected the restrictions or prohibitions that most conference members used to determine whether a piece of historical research was Christian, namely, any method or explanation that sanctioned determinism (i.e., that humans were merely swept along in the historical flow and had no free agency) or reductionism (i.e., that all events could be explained only by natural causes) was beyond the pale of Christian historiography.[29] So, for instance, in an essay on social history Robert P. Swierenga cautioned against behavioral methodology and social science theories that made "a faith commitment to behavioralism as a philosophy of life." But he believed it possible for Christians to pursue social history so long as they used "current models, theories, and techniques critically and selectively, recognizing the . . . humanistic assumptions and world-views out of which they . . . developed."[30] Charles Miller agreed about the dangers of determinism, "whether naturalistic or Marxian," and added "the perfectibility of human beings" to his list of assumptions impermissible for Christian historians.[31]

Christian historians' opposition to all efforts to deny human responsibility in historical developments or to reduce human decisions to impersonal or mechanistic forces was just the flip side of another com-

28. Ibid., 14–15.
29. C. T. McIntire, "The Focus of Historical Study: A Christian View," *FEH* 14 (Fall 1981): 6–17.
30. Robert Swierenga, "Social Science History: A Critique and Appreciation," *FEH* 14 (Fall 1981): 42–51, quotation from 49.
31. Miller, "Conference on Faith and History," 63.

mon theme in CFH historiographical discussions, namely, that history was not directionless but had purpose and meaning. Indeed, the overriding answer to the question of what constituted a Christian approach to history was the notion that human history had meaning, that this meaning could be figured out, at least, by historians, and that such meaning was determined by God. Sometimes the assumption of meaning could take pietistic forms, such as when Janette Bohi asserted that the Christian historian "has a special insight into God's program for the world by virtue of a personal relationship to the Fountainhead of all knowledge."[32] At other times the search for meaning could draw upon Christian notions of providence, such as Peter Russell's claim that "the view of 'general providence' . . . needs a rigorous re-examination and vigorous reassertion" because it offered "a sense of meaning both to history and to its study."[33] Some contributors to *Fides* also attempted to link the meaning of history to Reformed notions about the history of redemption. W. Stanford Reid, for instance, argued that for the believer history was fundamentally "eschatological." History, he wrote, "is the story of the working out of redemption in the world."[34]

Such discussions of Christian meaning inevitably led to attempts to determine those specific events where God had so directed the course of human affairs to bring about his purpose. A favorite example given to demonstrate God's control of history was the abolition of slavery. According to Reid, Christians were under obligation to serve God in all walks of life, a duty that meant that the kingdom of God would be made manifest in the believer's work and social relationships. William Wilberforce's battle against the slave trade, consequently, stood out as one of the "best" examples of such kingdom work because he "pursued his objective and eventually won . . . only by the grace of God."[35] So too, Richard Lovelace, picking up on Reid's interpretation of the Second Great Awakening, advocated the social transformation that classical pietism and Anglo-American revivalism had encouraged "as a result of

32. Janette Bohi, "The Relevance of Faith and History: A Mandate from God," *FEH* 6 (Fall 1973): 49.

33. Russell, "The Challenge of Writing Christian History," *FEH* 21 (Jan. 1989): 16.

34. W. Stanford Reid, "The Problem of the Christian Interpretation of History," *FEH* 5 (Fall 1972): 100.

35. Reid, "The Kingdom of God: The Key to History," *FEH* 13 (Spring-Summer 1981): 13.

the Gospel's salt and light." Lovelace hoped that the study of history would lead evangelicals back to the kingdom-oriented vision of Edwards, Wesley, and Zinzendorf.[36] Thus, the Christian historian's assumption that history had meaning often turned into an apology for Christian activism in which the Christian historian, like the scorekeeper for the home team, tallied up and cheered on the triumph of the forces of light over those of darkness. For some this activism involved using the past to remedy the social needs of the present, while for others it meant demonstrating the relevance of biblical religion through history.[37]

If the Christian historian's search for meaning could fuel evangelical activism, it could also promote reflection about more cerebral matters such as epistemology. Perhaps the classic explanation in CFH circles of what Christian historical knowledge meant was George M. Marsden's effort to show how faith allowed Christian historians to see the facts of history differently than their non-Christian colleagues. Unlike his graduate school peers who taught history in such a way as to insure that their students voted Democratic, Marsden argued that a Christian historian could recognize the value of history even if it did not always appear to be immediately relevant or practical. Christian faith was one such way of discerning other meaningful "dimensions to reality," dimensions that were "valuable" in themselves. This meant that the Christian historian, sometimes only in a glass darkly, could make out in contours of human history "a larger struggle among real spiritual forces and personalities," not unlike the characters in Tolkien's stories, where the outcome of any particular spiritual battle was unknown but the believer could still be assured that "in the end good will triumph." Thus, while in the technical aspects of historical research and writing believers and nonbelievers would stand on common ground, when it came to seeing "overall patterns" and directions in history the "control beliefs" of the Christian would result in the perception of "a new order in reality."[38]

36. Richard Lovelace, "Response to 'The Kingdom of God: The Key to History,'" *FEH* 13 (Spring-Summer 1981): 19-20.

37. For the former, see Ronald D. Rietveld, "The Christian Historian as Activist," *FEH* 9 (Spring 1977): 25-38; for the latter, see William A. Speck, "What Should Be the Role of Christian Historians?" *FEH* 8 (Fall 1975): 76-81.

38. Marsden, "The Spiritual Vision of History," *FEH* 14 (Fall 1981): 55-66, quotations on 62 and 63. For another discussion of epistemology having more to do with objectivity, see M. Howard Rienstra, "History, Objectivity and the Christian Scholar," *FEH* 10 (Fall 1977): 7-25.

The Phase of Uncertainty

Over the last decade or so, the third and last period in this chronology, historiographical reflections, whether calling for Christian activism or Christian knowledge, have been much harder to find. Instead, the conference appears to have contented itself with being an evangelical and smaller version of the American Society of Church History, at least judging by the topics covered in *Fides* articles. Under the editorships of James Johnson and Frank Roberts, in almost every article a religious theme or subject is readily discernible, even if the church proper (as in word and sacrament) is not the subject. But conference members and those who submit articles appear to be much more reluctant to argue for a Christian way of practicing and understanding history. Perhaps this decline means that the conference has reached a stage of maturity where historiographical ruminations are no longer necessary because everyone knows what it means to be a Christian historian and, in the words of Nike ads, just does it.

But another explanation for the CFH's contemporary silence on the nature of Christian history could be that all of the arguments for the difference that Christianity makes for historical scholarship were, finally, not fully convincing. Perhaps, then, rather than reaching a stage of maturity the conference has come instead to a period of uncertainty or diffidence where, beyond sharing certain convictions and a similar career, it is not so easy to say clearly what makes the history written by Christians any different from non-Christians. Reasons for offering this explanation come not just from reading *Fides et Historia*'s table of contents. One might also look for evidence of this diffidence in a publication which, while not a CFH document, might shed some light on this phase of the organization's history. That publication was Ronald A. Wells' book, *History through the Eyes of Faith*, the history volume in the Christian College Coalition's textbook series on understanding academic subjects from a Christian perspective.[39]

In many respects, Wells' book reads like CFH efforts from the second period that endeavored to understand history from a Christian perspective. Wells had been editor of *Fides* at that time. In the introduction he draws upon the essays by C. T. McIntire and George M. Marsden

39. Wells, *History through the Eyes of Faith: Western Civilization and the Kingdom of God* (San Francisco: Harper & Row, 1989).

that had appeared originally in *Fides* and were reprinted in the book Wells coedited, *History and Historical Understanding.* Accordingly, Wells argued for a Christian way of seeing history that examined the spiritual aspects of the human past and recognized the conflict within Western civilization between the kingdom of God and the kingdom of the world. So, in addition to recognizing time and space as dimensions of reality, "Christians insist that there is a third dimension — spirit — and that a whole view of the world must be three-dimensional." Wells' Christian perspective also came through in his critique of modernity (especially capitalism), an example, he argued, of where the conflict between the kingdoms of God and the world was especially evident. One more example of Wells' effort to write Christian history comes from the epilogue where he summarizes the lives of five Christian individuals, whose stories "disclose the testimony of faithfulness to the kingdom": the Anabaptist, Dirk Willems; the Roman Catholic, Mother Teresa; the low church Anglican, William Wilberforce; the Methodist revivalist, Francis Asbury; and the Reformed statesman and journalist, Abraham Kuyper.[40]

Nevertheless, at other times in the book Wells is not so certain about this Christian dimension of history or if a Christian historian can always discern it. On the one hand, the spiritual dimension that Wells detected was fairly generic and tepid, hardly the robust world-and-life-view that so many Reformed scholars in the Christian Reformed tradition found in the apostle Paul's notion of redemption as recreation. For instance, the lesson that Wells drew from the five lives he used to close the book was "that Christianity as personal faith and worldview, has something profound to say to, and about, Western civilization." But he did not go on to say what precisely that statement meant. On the other hand, Wells went to great pains to avoid assigning praise or blame in the various developments he surveyed — though he couldn't quite resist criticizing the excesses of Calvin's Geneva or capitalism.[41] The historian, he wrote, "cannot insist on the normativity of one view among many." To do so is "to leave aside the historical task and to enter the realm of apologetics, where theological rather than historical points are at issue."[42] One can almost hear echoes of the earlier CFH debates over John Warwick Montgomery in that quotation.

40. Ibid., 238.
41. Ibid., 82, 102, 172.
42. Ibid., 82.

The Search for Christian History

The uncertain prospects for a distinctively Christian historiography within the CFH may not bode well for the future of an organization whose purpose was supposedly to encourage such historiography. But skepticism about the possibility of doing Christian history need not stem from wavering faith or failure of nerve. At this point the debate between Harry Stout and Iain Murray mentioned at the outset is instructive. The kind of restrictions the former wanted to place on historians has a better basis in Christian theology than does the providential history advocated by the latter. The Christian historian who avoids assigning praise and blame may do so not for fear of venturing into theology but because he or she is standing smack-dab-in-the-middle of it. This statement implies that the CFH may have been functioning the most Christianly when it was uncertain about what Christian history looks like, though it might have been helpful if the conference were more self-conscious about its reasons for such uncertainty.

One of the givens in the enterprise of Christian history is the notion that the development of human history has direction, purpose, and meaning. Almost everyone agrees about this, even Stout and Murray. The difficulty comes in trying to identify this meaning. What does it mean to say that God was in control of the 1992 United States' presidential election or what does it mean to say that the kingdom of God is coming, in or despite (depending on your perspective) the 1995 collapse of the New Era Foundation? The point of these questions is obvious. When you go from the sublime of the kingdom of God to the ridiculous of U.S. politics you encounter the difficult situation of trying to make a direct connection between the two, in other words, what God intended.

The kind of Christian historical agnosticism advocated here even extends to events like the First Great Awakening, the incident that sparked the debate between Stout and Murray. The latter thinks that Whitefield's efforts on behalf of the colonial revivals were the work of God. From Murray's perspective Whitefield's revivals benefitted the church, both through the spread of sound theology and through the conversion of vast numbers. But how does Murray know that the Great Awakening was the work of God? Did God tell him? His answer would no doubt be that Whitefield's work conformed to the teaching of Scripture and that mass conversions were a confirmation of God's blessing. But this is not the only Christian perspective on Whitefield's revivals.

Roman Catholics would no doubt take a different view. So too would those within the Protestant fold, such as confessional Lutherans and Reformed. Furthermore, is God only at work in history when things go well, when saints are added to his church? Or does the doctrine of providence teach that God is also at work in the revivals that Murray questions, such as those crusades associated with Charles Finney and countless other not-so-Calvinistic evangelists? In fact, the doctrine of providence teaches that God is at work in everything, both good and not so good. But to determine what God intended by a particular event is another matter altogether. In other words, without the special revelation God gave to the apostles and through the risen Christ, twentieth-century Christians, just like the early church, cannot know the meaning from God's perspective of any historical event, even the crucifixion.[43]

This strong assertion brings us back to the question of whether such a thing as Christian history really exists, at least if providential intervention be the test. Are Christian historians better able to discern the hand of God in history than non-Christians? Are their criteria of evaluation any different even from that of an elder in a local church who has to judge whether or not the person meeting with the council is making a credible profession of faith? And if Christians cannot see into the soul of someone else to tell definitively whether God has intervened, are Christian historians any better able to do so with political, economic, or cultural events? One supposes, therefore, that discerning the actions of providence is not the appropriate test for a Christian historiography.

In the end, Christian history is nice work if you can get it. It would be marvelous if, because of faith or regeneration, Christian historians were able to divine what God was up to in all subjects of research and teaching. But Christian theology says we cannot discern God's hand in that way. It also reminds us that we need to trust that God is in control of human history even if we cannot always see that control, that God providentially orders and governs human affairs. No matter how much the historical profession says that history moves from antiquity to modernity, the Bible tells Christians, whether historians or not, that the real direction of history is from the first to the last Adam. Only with a sense

43. On the importance of special revelation for interpreting the meaning and direction of redemptive history, see Richard B. Gaffin, Jr., "The New Testament as Canon," in *Inerrancy and Hermeneutic: A Tradition, A Challenge, A Debate,* ed. Harvie M. Conn (Grand Rapids: Baker Book House, 1988), ch. 10.

of history that culminates in Christ and the establishment of the new heavens and new earth will we finally have a Christian history. The problem for CFH members is that of trying to connect the metanarrative of redemption to the narratives of the United States, ethnic groups, or Western civilization, stories all of which are fascinating and part of God's providence, but that may distract from the grander history of salvation.

Charles Miller once said about the CFH that he was disappointed that it was not the Conference on Faith, Theology, and History, so crucial was theology to the work of a Christian historian. "The Christian historian," he wrote, "must be one in three and three in one — a professing Christian, a thinking theologian, and a practicing historian."[44] Had the conference heeded Miller's words it might have had a better rejoinder to the likes of Iain Murray or John Warwick Montgomery. But, as its history shows, questioning the possibility of Christian history with theological reflection would have undermined the very existence of the Conference on Faith and History.

44. Miller, "Conference on Faith and History," 63.

II. Discrete Themes and Subjects

Men, Women, and God:
Some Historiographical Issues

MARGARET LAMBERTS BENDROTH

Writing women's history is like refocusing a camera. Twirling the historiographical lens even a little bit can make some previously invisible objects — like women in the historical record — suddenly sharp and clear. But the same adjustment taken too far can blur other parts of the picture, sacrificing important details that give meaning and context to the new objects in the foreground. The trick is to find just the right camera setting, one that catches all of the important details in the picture without turning anyone into a fuzzy, unidentifiable blur. Few people would argue against including women in history, but not everyone can agree on where to include them or how their inclusion should change the story as a whole. The problem for women's history is to recast an old familiar photograph in a provocative new light, rich with telling detail, harmonizing background and subjects into a coherent whole.

This itself, most women's historians would agree, is a feminist act. Simply writing women into history challenges not only the established stories of the past, but the entire task of writing history in the first place. Earlier generations of historians, who set themselves to writing "objective" history, tried to take on the role of the cameras themselves, as unbiased, scientific recorders of past events. Feminist historians have been bluntly critical of this approach, which they argue has systematically excluded or derided women. Objectivity, they argue, has all too often been a cloak for concealing intellectual or personal agendas, giving historians far too much power to decide who or what was "important" in the past. Alternatively then, subjective, personal engagement has become a hallmark of women's history and of feminist scholarship in general. Feminist historians have been willing to flaunt their biases openly, purposefully aiming the camera toward the most favorable light. They have also prodded their male colleagues to do the same, arguing that such honesty will lead to more "truth" in history than the so-called "value-free" approach of scientific history.

Recently, these developments have become enormously important to Christian historians. In his recent book, *The Outrageous Idea of Christian Scholarship*, George Marsden has made an explicit comparison between feminist and Christian approaches to scholarly work, arguing for tolerance of religiously-based viewpoints on the basis of acceptance already granted for the work of feminist (as well as Marxist, African American, and gay) intellectuals in the academy. If these other scholars can interpret the world through their own particular intellectual or social lens, Marsden argues, Christians who are willing to play by the same "rules of the academy" should receive a similar hearing.[1]

How valid is this comparison? Certainly feminist scholars have faced some of the same suspicions about their intellectual integrity as Christian scholars often do. Gerda Lerner comments, "as long as historians stay within the confines of androcentric [objective] thought while viewing women in history, they are not generally subject to attack and distortion. They may even receive a pat on the back for 'scholarly impartiality.' But when we begin to practice woman-centered scholarship, stepping outside of androcentric question-setting and value judgments, then we are likely to be . . . attacked for injecting 'political' judgments into supposedly value-free scholarship."[2]

Still, the distance between feminist and Christian history may seem almost insurmountable, a fair judgment given the general lack of interest by both sides toward each other to this point.[3] Religion is a difficult

1. George Marsden, *The Outrageous Idea of Christian Scholarship* (New York: Oxford University Press, 1996).

2. Lerner's comments are found in Ellen DuBois, Mari Jo Buhle, Temma Kaplan, Gerda Lerner, and Carroll Smith-Rosenberg, "Politics and Culture in Women's History: A Symposium," *Feminist Studies* 6 (1980): 53-54.

3. See, for example, Elizabeth Fox-Genovese, "Advocacy and the Writing of Women's History," in *Religious Advocacy in American History,* ed. D. G. Hart and Bruce Kuklick (Grand Rapids: Eerdmans, 1997), 96-111.

subject for the majority of feminist historians, for many of the same reasons that feminism is problematic for some evangelical Christian scholars. But, at the very least for the sake of Marsden's argument, Christian historians should be all the more curious about women's history, and the ways that it has dealt with issues of objectivity and inclusion. The main purpose of this essay, in fact, is to provide a brief "map" of feminist scholarship in history and to invite Christian scholars toward more serious consideration of the issues it has raised.

First, however, a brief explanation: the definition of what is "feminist" is diverse and often contradictory. For the sake of clarity, I have not attempted to be exhaustive, and have drawn most of my examples from my own field of American history, hoping to tantalize readers toward their own investigation with a few suggestive, though painfully limited, footnotes.

Feminism and Women's History

One central tenet of feminism is that "the personal is political"; in other words, the events of everyday life relate directly toward the task of human liberation, sometimes setting it back, sometimes moving it slowly forward. Nothing happens in a vacuum. For a long time, historians assumed that women weren't as historically "significant" as men; for the most part they stayed home, cared for the children, and lived quietly apart from the masculine hustle and bustle of wars, elections, and crop cycles. Thus, one of the tasks of women's history has been to resurrect forgotten lives, even if it is just for the sake of remembering them. Natural scientist Cindy Cowden observes that "reductionist science is inadequate to understand organisms, whether they are spiders, starfish or women; . . . we can only understand organisms by seeing with a loving eye."[4]

When women's history is done well, it brings these two realms of experience, the personal and the political, together. It mediates between two opposing goals: (1) creating a more nuanced, accurate account of the human past by bringing to light the unique particularities of women's experience, and (2) writing with "mythic power," that is, saying something about the human condition as a whole, in a way that attacks and

4. Quoted in Shulamit Reinharz, *Feminist Methods in Social Research* (New York: Oxford University Press, 1992), 3.

dismantles injustices based on gender.[5] The challenge is to avoid lapsing into either agenda, to be neither too much a scribe nor too much a prophet.

Of course, not all feminist history is done well, and historiographical debates in women's history have tended to center around this fundamental tension. On the one hand, women's history has been dismissed for being too much about women — a solipsistic exercise of preaching to converts, ultimately irrelevant to larger historical narratives — or it has been criticized for not saying enough about women and the historical roots of gender inequality, for not really having a political edge. The best women's history is very much about men — it places women's lives within a historical context constructed by members of both sexes, and it also illuminates some of the intricacies of gender relationships for women and men living in the present.

From History to "Herstory"

Scholarship on women, when it first emerged in the early 1960s, was deeply egalitarian. Its goal was to bring to light as much information on women as possible — as much if not more than the profession had already accumulated about the opposite sex. But although this meant that the field of study was theoretically unlimited, the liberal egalitarian politics that drove this scholarly effort severely limited its subject matter: female "firsts" and "pioneers" of various types, especially the heroines of the suffrage movement, usually occupied center stage. When men did appear, they were often in marginal roles, opposing suffrage or setting up various obstacles on the path toward gender equality.[6] Some feminist critics took issue with this heroic approach to women's history as fundamentally ahistorical and apolitical; it did not really challenge the "grand narrative" of American history, the myth of political and economic progress that historians had already constructed around men.

5. Linda Gordon, "What's New in Women's History?" in *Feminist Studies/Critical Studies*, ed. Teresa de Lauretis (Bloomington: Indiana University Press, 1986), 22.

6. See, e.g., Eleanor Flexner, *A Century of Struggle: The Woman's Rights Movement in the United States* (Cambridge: Harvard University Press, 1959); Aileen S. Kraditor, *The Ideas of the Woman Suffrage Movement, 1890-1920* (New York: Columbia University Press, 1965).

In a way, the search for heroines let men off too easily. Survey textbooks could still (and logically had to) relegate women to a separate chapter or sidebar praising their "contribution" to some important event. Its scholarly method was, as historian Linda Kerber writes, largely "descriptive and anecdotal" and suffused with a "Whiggish progressivism" that suggested that "the central theme in women's history was an inexorable march toward the suffrage." Others have dubbed it, simply, "add women and stir."[7]

But more radical critiques were on the way. By the early 1970s, women's historians, informed by the methodologies and insights of the new social history, had moved beyond the heroic paradigm to construct what is often referred to as "herstory."[8] The new model abandoned the "simple-minded search for heroines" or a narrow and uncritical use of the "male oppression model," and made women the subjects, not passive objects, of historical processes.[9] The story of the suffrage movement, for example, became less important than the cultural situation that made the vote so hard to achieve in the first place. And new questions emerged: "How did the masses of women experience their lives? What grievances did they articulate? In what ways did they act on their dissatisfactions? What traditions of protest and resistance did they leave us above and beyond the women's rights movement?"[10] The result was a much broader picture of an emerging feminist consciousness in American culture — in social reform movements, benevolent organizations, foreign missions, in the domestic sphere — almost anywhere women met together to form the bonds of sisterhood.[11]

7. Linda K. Kerber, "Separate Spheres, Female Worlds, Woman's Place: The Rhetoric of Women's History," *Journal of American History* 75 (June 1988): 14.

8. See Joan Scott, "Women's History," in *Gender and the Politics of History* (New York: Columbia University Press, 1988), 15-27.

9. "Preface" to *Clio's Consciousness Raised: New Perspectives on the History of Women*, ed. Mary Hartman and Lois W. Banner (New York: Harper and Row, 1974), vii.

10. Ellen DuBois in "Politics and Culture in Women's History: A Symposium," 29.

11. Examples abound; see, for example, Blanche Hersch, *The Slavery of Sex: Feminist Abolitionists in America* (Urbana: University of Illinois Press, 1978); Keith Melder, *Beginnings of Sisterhood: The American Woman's Rights Movement, 1800-1850* (New York: Schocken Books, 1977); Ruth Bordin, *Woman and Temperance: The Quest for Power and Liberty, 1873-1900* (Philadelphia: Temple University Press, 1981); R. Pierce Beaver, *American Protestant Women in World Mission: A History of the First Feminist Movement in North America*, reprint ed. (Grand Rapids: Eerdmans, 1980);

The Politics of Women's Experience

By the 1980s, women's history was moving away from an egalitarian model to one that emphasized the power and pervasiveness of a "woman's culture," a world without men, or, to cite the name of a famous essay, a "female world of love and ritual."[12] This shift among feminist academics mirrored a larger change in the meaning of feminism in the early 1980s, from an across-the-board commitment to sexual equality to "essentialism," an emphasis on the psychological, biological, and spiritual differences between the sexes.[13] Essentialists argued that certain universal aspects of women's experience — childbearing, nurturing, dealing with masculine oppression — gave all women at all times and places a special understanding of each other's thoughts and feelings. "Elaborations on and extensions of female community multiplied rapidly," writes Nancy Hewitt, in a recent review essay. "Women on wagon trains heading west, worshippers in evangelical revivals and in Quaker meeting houses, prostitutes on the Comstock Lode, mill workers in Lowell boarding houses, and immigrants on the streets of Lawrence and the stoops of Providence loved and nurtured one another, exchanged recipes, gossip, and herbal remedies, swapped food and clothing, shared childrearing and domestic chores, covered for each other at work, protected one another from abusive fathers, husbands, lovers, and bosses, and supported each other in birth and death." Women's solidarity and resistance arose everywhere, leaping across social boundaries of class, color, and geographic location.[14]

Daniel Scott Smith, "Family Limitation, Sexual Control, and Domestic Feminism in Victorian America," in *Clio's Consciousness Raised*, 119-36.

12. Carroll Smith-Rosenberg, "The Female World of Love and Ritual: Relations Between Women in Nineteenth-Century America," *Signs* 1 (Autumn 1975): 1-29.

13. Psychological studies of women played an important role in the new formulation. See, e.g., Carol Gilligan, *In a Different Voice* (Cambridge: Harvard University Press, 1982); Mary Belenky et al., *Women's Ways of Knowing* (New York: Basic Books, 1986); Jean Baker Miller, *Toward a New Psychology of Women* (Boston: Beacon Press, 1976; 1986). For a specific, and famous, example of the equality vs. difference problem see Ruth Milkman, "Women's History and the Sears Case," *Feminist Studies* 12 (1986): 394-95.

14. Nancy Hewitt, "Beyond the Search for Sisterhood: American Women's History in the 1980s," in *Unequal Sisters: A Multi-Cultural Reader in U.S. Women's History*, 2nd ed., ed. Vicki Ruiz and Ellen Carol DuBois (New York: Routledge, 1994), 2-3.

The focus on women's experience was also useful in other ways. Honing in on women's individual lives allowed historians to overcome the relative lack of published literary sources about women. They could use materials like diaries and photographs that promised not objectivity but self-revelation; it didn't matter if a diarist was inaccurate, mistaken, or even dully repetitious in addressing historical events, for her words were valuable in themselves as a more deeply truthful record of the past.

But the frequently triumphalist subtext of this narrative didn't always make for "good" history in the traditional sense of the term, as Hewitt's subtle parody suggests. It was often hard-pressed to account for women who didn't get along with other women or (inexplicably) preferred the company of the opposite sex. Moreover, it also begged the logical question of whether or not men could ever write women's history (or women about men). Implicit in many reconstructions of women's experience was a strong feminist narrative that tended to exclude those experiences that didn't fit the paradigm of liberation. Critics soon began to notice an often suspicious similarity between the so-called experiences of women in the past and those of the middle-class, white, secular feminist historians who wrote about them.[15]

The critiques pointed toward the strength and the inherent weakness of a feminist methodology grounded on women's experience, particularly its radical subjectivism. Australian feminist Dale Spender explains that "at the core of feminist ideas is the crucial insight that there is no one truth, no one authority, no one objective method which leads to the production of pure knowledge" — one of the core assumptions of patriarchal thinking. Feminist knowledge "is based on the premise that the experience of all human beings is valid and must not be excluded from our understandings."[16] If each experience is so entirely different from the next, critics wondered, then how can anyone, especially a

15. See, e.g., Mary McClintock Fulkerson, *Changing the Subject: Women's Discourses and Feminist Theology* (Minneapolis: Fortress Press, 1994); Elizabeth Fox-Genovese, *Feminism Without Illusions: A Critique of Individualism* (Chapel Hill: University of North Carolina Press, 1991); Evelyn Brooks Higginbotham, "African-American Women's History and the Metalanguage of Race," *Signs: Journal of Women in Culture and Society* 17 (Winter 1992): 251-74; Christine Stansell, *City of Women: Sex and Class in New York, 1789-1860* (New York: Knopf, 1986); and Lori Ginzberg, *Women and the Work of Benevolence: Morality, Politics, and Class in the Nineteenth-Century United States* (New Haven: Yale University Press, 1990).

16. Dale Spender quoted in Reinharz, *Feminist Methods in Social Research*, 7.

historian whose subjects cannot speak for themselves, presume to draw meaningful conclusions about someone else's experiences?

In response to their critics, feminist historians argued that they were not after textbook style accuracy. They did not hope to achieve some perfectly recreated "truth" about the past, nor an historical realism based not on "facts." Their task was far more ambitious: to construct a new historical record based on connections derived from common feminine experience. Their assumption that all women by virtue of their sex share certain fundamental experiences allowed them a unique window into the past. Their power as narrators was necessarily limited, since no one can know more about a person's experience than the person herself, but they still claimed the ability to retrieve and restate historical data that would be meaningful for readers in the present.[17] Louise Newman explains that "Authority, which used to lodge in the historian as an objective narrator of the past, now lodges in experience, which has an ontological status of its own. Although history, the accounts of experience, may no longer be objective, the underlying experiences still are."[18]

Other critics, however, took issue with "herstory" for lacking any genuine political edge: again, it let men off too easily. To Ellen DuBois, the "women's culture" model was static and isolated, too particular; without any men in the picture "the concept of women's oppression begins to seem irrelevant," leaving an opening for a "sneaky kind of antifeminism" to emerge. By focusing exclusively on women, herstory could not fully explain why men oppressed them, or how their subjugation varied over time and place. DuBois' critique of women's culture echoed a gathering response to the "so what" quality of much of the new social history, stockpiling information without a clear narrative to give it meaning and context, "academic in the worst sense of the word."[19]

But herstory was, of course, pursuing a political agenda. It was

17. Recent years have also witnessed renewed interest among feminist historians in biography and autobiography. See, e.g., Sara Alpern et al., *The Challenge of Feminist Biography* (Urbana: University of Illinois Press, 1992); Julia Swindells, "Liberating the Subject: Autobiography and 'Women's History': A Reading of the Diaries of Hannah Cullwick," in *Interpreting Women's Lives: Feminist Theory and Personal Narrative* (Bloomington: Indiana University Press, 1989), 24-38.

18. Louise M. Newman, "Critical Theory and the History of Women: What's at Stake in Deconstructing Women's History," *Journal of Women's History* 2 (Winter 1991): 61.

19. DuBois in "Politics and Culture in Women's History," 33-34.

slowly beginning to dismantle the time-honored grand narratives of American history. During the 1980s, a huge gulf was forming between the cozy female world of love and ritual and the male-dominated historical narrative of politics and war. In this scholarly context, it is not surprising that some women's historians began to find men's history fundamentally irrelevant to their own work, and they raised troubling new questions about the story line. Did women have a Renaissance?[20] An American Revolution?[21] Did they experience religious conversion in the same way that men did?[22] Did it make any sense at all to demarcate human history in terms of political elections and wars if half the world's people did not participate in such events, by law or custom? Although women's historians had often criticized the narrative strategy of their male colleagues as a shallow attempt to "add women and stir," in part the awkwardness was of their own creation.

Gender and Postmodernism

One way to make men relevant once again was to widen the focus from women's history toward a history of gender — one of the implied goals of women's history from its beginning. Back in 1975 Natalie Zemon Davis had suggested that women's historians should "be interested in the history of both women and men" and "that we should not be working only on the subjected sex any more than a historian of class can focus entirely on peasants."[23] Gender studies built off of the classic distinction in American feminist thought between "sex" (biologically based) and "gender" (socially constructed), and took women's studies to its logical next level. It also promised to do for men what women's historians had already done, to a large degree, for women: describing and analyzing the

20. Joan Kelly-Gadol, "Did Women Have a Renaissance?" in *Becoming Visible: Women in European History*, ed. Renate Bridenthal and Claudia Koontz (Boston: Houghton Mifflin, 1977), 137-64.

21. Mary Beth Norton, *Liberty's Daughters: The Revolutionary Experience of American Women, 1750-1800* (Boston: Little, Brown Co., 1980).

22. Carolyn Walker Bynum, "Women's Stories, Women's Symbols: A Critique of Victor Turner's Theory of Liminality," in *Fragmentation and Redemption: Essays on Gender and the Human Body in Medieval Religion* (New York: Zone Books, 1991), 27-51.

23. Natalie Zemon Davis, "Women's History in Transition: The European Case," *Feminist Studies* 3 (1975-1976): 390.

different social meanings of gendered identities, for as Nancy Cott observes, "In contrast to women — who are too often seen only in terms of their sex — men have been the *un*marked sex."[24]

Gender studies also made women more relevant to the larger narrative. In American religious history, for example, the concept of religious "feminization" (i.e., the consistent predominance of women in religious institutions) forces historians to take account of women's presence, even when they are not participating directly in theological or institutional disputes.[25]

But much of the new scholarship on gender entailed far more than just a critique of old narratives; it also proved a "useful category of historical analysis" for postmodernist historians.[26] These scholars, exemplified by Joan Scott, used gender as a way to track the dualisms and power differentials that are the basis of all oppression in human society. Gendered language and imagery in texts don't just refer to masculine and feminine qualities of men and women, but offer insight into a dualism that transcends physical, sexual identity. All societies are based on disparities of power, Scott argues, and that underlying structure emerges in coded form in texts that make use of gendered words and images. This makes for a far more radical task for women's historians. Scott writes: "Feminist history then becomes not the recounting of great deeds performed by women but the exposure of the often silent and hidden operations of gender that are nonetheless present and defining forces in the organization of most societies. With this approach women's history critically confronts the politics of existing histories and inevitably begins the rewriting of history."[27]

Using gender as a means of social analysis gives it universal signif-

24. Nancy Cott, "On Men's History and Women's History," in *Meanings for Manhood: Constructions of Masculinity in Victorian America*, ed. Mark C. Carnes and Clyde Griffen (Chicago: University of Chicago Press, 1990), 206. A useful bibliographic essay is David Hackett, "Gender and Religion in American Culture, 1870-1930," *Religion and American Culture* 5 (Summer 1994): 127-57.

25. See Ann Douglas, *The Feminization of American Culture* (New York: Alfred A. Knopf, 1977); Ann Braude, "American Religious History *Is* Women's History," in *Retelling U.S. Religious History*, ed. Thomas Tweed (Berkeley: University of California Press, 1997), 87-107.

26. Scott, "Gender: A Useful Category of Historical Analysis," *American Historical Review* 91 (December 1986): 1053-75.

27. Scott, *Gender and the Politics of History*, 27.

icance. Gender is no longer a contingent subject matter, tacked onto a larger narrative as a separate chapter about "women's contribution," or worse still, relegated to discussions of the family, sexuality, and the so-called private sphere. Nor is it simply one leg in a triad with race or class, but resting at the bottom of all historical processes. Both race and class, Scott argues, are simply socially constructed metaphors for the more fundamental dualism of gender.

Postmodernist theory also draws from the earlier feminist critique of objectivity. Postmodernist feminists argue that objectivity is a masculine myth that lies at the bottom of all domination and control in human society, particularly all hierarchies of gender. Post-structuralist feminist theorists, as critic Elizabeth Fox-Genovese explains, have identified "the illusion that the human mind can identify and understand any independent reality" as "a specifically male pretension to intellectual domination." By this token, all of Western thought (and its love of dualisms in particular) is inherently "phallocentric."[28]

Postmodernist feminists in fact take feminist subjectivism even farther than many feminist historians would allow. Postmodernists argue that the very act of constructing a narrative about the past—even a feminist one—is an act of domination, since the narrator alone holds the power to decide what to include and what to leave out. History, Joan Scott writes, "creates its meanings through differentiation and in this way organizes knowledge about the world." Dominant historical narratives arise from "a politics that sets and enforces priorities, represses some subjects in the name of the greater importance of others, naturalizes certain categories, and disqualifies others. . . . In that way, history operates as a particular kind of cultural institution endorsing and announcing constructions of gender."[29]

Responding to Postmodernism

Not surprisingly perhaps, many women's historians view postmodernist feminist theory as a two-edged sword. Certainly postmodernism offers both challenges and opportunities for scholars like myself who write about women and religion. The older mode of women's history, with its

28. Fox-Genovese, *Feminism Without Illusions,* 146.
29. Scott, *Gender and the Politics of History,* 9.

implicit privileging of women whose experiences most closely resembled those of white, secular feminist historians, provided few rationales for studying women in conservative religious subcultures (except perhaps as a sad cautionary tale). Now, because historians do not have access to any predetermined narrative — feminist or otherwise — which might signal which past experiences are more significant than others, any group is a potential candidate for sustained historical analysis.

Scott's argument that gendered language provides important clues about social structures is also well-taken. Historians who study women in religious institutions, for example, need to look carefully at what is said and how, what gendered metaphors and images are called into play, and even more carefully at what is not said, at the spaces between the lines. Is masculinity always equated with godliness? What institutions or movements are designated feminine and why? Historians must not be too quick to assume that if things look fairly egalitarian from the outside, that this is the final truth of the matter, but listen for suppressed or excluded voices.

But, in terms of the two tasks of women's history outlined at the beginning of this essay — to create a more nuanced, accurate account of the past and to speak with "mythic power" — postmodernist approaches are deeply problematic. For one thing, postmodernism denies historians genuine access to women's experiences. What a historian may think is a valid reconstruction of a person's life in the past is really her own face in the mirror, completely obliterating the long-gone image of her subject. The very idea of constructing "herstory" is at best a naive sham, at worst a high-handed attempt to exploit people in the past unable to speak for themselves.

Postmodernist historians do not necessarily find it frustrating to be thus locked in the present and denied all true access to the past. As Newman writes, "for Scott *history is the representation that constructs experiences*," not a chronological account of historical events. "Historians write new histories not to relate existing experiences previously unknown but to give new meanings to experiences never before understood in such a way."[30] Stated this way, the goal is a humble one: postmodernists have given up any attempt to impose order on the past, or to act as literary ventriloquists for the people who lived there. History is essentially a commentary on the present, and nothing more.

Some feminist historians have criticized postmodernist theory as

30. Newman, "What's at Stake in Deconstructing Women's History," 62.

socially reactionary. Not only does it allow scholars to avoid responsibility for historical accuracy — if history is really only my own reflection in the mirror, who can argue that it's wrong? — it also removes intellectual discourse from larger issues of justice, oppression, and liberation — if there is no "story line," then there can be no heroes, villains, or meaningful attempts toward humanitarian progress. The landscape is completely flat, with no roads and no vanishing point at the horizon.

Some scholars see an even more threatening agenda behind the new neutrality of postmodernism. "The opening of higher education to nearly all who seek it, the rewriting of American history from a variety of cultural perspectives, and the dethroning of science as the source and model for all that is true are interrelated phenomena," one recent group of feminist critics has observed. It was as if "higher education was open to us — women, minorities, working people — at the same time that we lost the philosophical foundation that had underpinned the confidence of educated people."[31] Is it a coincidence, others have asked, that scholars have proclaimed the "death of the subject" just as women are poised to enter the historical mainstream as both authors and subjects?[32]

Christian historians may want to be alert to responsible feminist critics of postmodernism, particularly as they attempt to find the proper voice for writing and talking about history. As one recent book has argued, if history is, in the end, only about historians, then there is little incentive to treat one's subjects, who don't offer much beyond their own self-referential view of the world, with appropriate deference and care. "Relativism, possibly tinged with cynicism or arrogance," the authors write, "would characterize the historian's aesthetic stance toward such people, becoming the alternative to and replacement for respect. In the face of their myopia or futile discursive strategies, the ironic voice would overshadow the historian's wonder, presenting the passion to linger among human beings struggling to find truths as a quest for their 'truth-effects.'"[33]

31. Joyce Appleby, Lynn Hunt, and Margaret Jacob, *Telling the Truth About History* (New York: W. W. Norton, 1994), 2-3.
32. See also Scott's exchange with Gertrude Himmelfarb at the American Historical Association: Himmelfarb, "Some Reflections on the New History," *American Historical Review* 94 (June 1989): 661-70; Scott, "History in Crisis? The Other Side of the Story," idem, 680-92.
33. Appleby et al., *Telling the Truth About History*, 228.

The great strength of women's history, and one which speaks directly to the idea of a "Christian history," has been its interpretive power. Feminist historians have had a passion for their subjects, born out of a conviction that scholarship should ultimately contribute toward justice. Scholarly objectivity and ivory-tower attitudes, they argue, have no place in a world filled with pain and oppression, nor can it ever hope to engage the imagination of people living in the present. Preachiness, of course, is a constant temptation in this kind of historical approach; however, much of the new feminist scholarship on women has been deeply relevant, illuminating, and, in many cases, even fun to read.

But, as the field of women's history also illustrates, what some readers may find engaging, others will find easy to ignore. The burden of gender historians like Joan Scott is, in one sense, to find a way of resisting the "ghettoization" of women's history and to bring it back into meaningful dialogue with the history of labor movements, religion, war, business, art, race, and social class, to name only a few significant aspects of human experience. Unless women's historians themselves begin to forge those connections, to make clear the historical agency of women in the past, then their subjects will continue to dot the historical record as merely interesting footnotes. A narrow triumphalism that discounts the complexity and ambiguity of a larger social context can lead in the end to a genteel isolation. Christian scholars who are fundamentally uninterested in mill workers, army sergeants, society matrons, politicians, or policemen — any aspect of human experience — cannot expect a wide audience.

This kind of respect for the past also requires historians to recognize its deep ugliness. The insight of Christian historiography which perhaps most closely touches a feminist one is the utter consistency of social injustice, and the brokenness of people on both ends of the historical spectrum, *especially* around matters of gender. "The point," as Elizabeth Fox-Genovese writes, "is not to deny women's suppression, much less their anger at it, but to suggest ways of focusing the knowledge and the anger so as to save us from the twin evils of complacent acceptance of things-as-they-are and an imaginative turning of our world into a mess of broken crockery."[34]

A truly feminist, Christian history makes room for both of those powerful passions, wonder and anger. It assumes a deep respect for

34. Fox-Genovese, *Feminism Without Illusions*, 230.

women—and men—as subjects who create history in meaningful, sometimes awe-inspiring, ways. But respect should not verge over too quickly into celebration; one of the first human sins recorded in the Bible was Eve and Adam turning against each other, and the consequence was a world filled with similar enmity and recrimination. The sentimental uplifting of heroines from bygone days, or naive accounts of feminine virtue and masculine vice all fall far short of the stark reality, and the hope, of the Christian story, and the accompanying challenge to tell the "truth" about human history.

The Potential of Missiology for the Crises of History

MARK A. NOLL

The world, considered as "the regions beyond," has historically opened up to Christian believers in North America through the efforts of missionaries. Missionary efforts have traditionally stimulated hagiography of different sorts and provided an exalted standard for measuring seriousness of purpose. These older functions of missions may continue to be important for North American religious communities. Yet a different aspect of missionary service also deserves full attention from believers who are concerned about history, historical writing, and the increasingly contentious arguments about the nature (or possibility) of historical knowledge. A growing quantity of first-order historical writing, as documented for example in the pages of the *International Bulletin of Missionary Research,* along with an increasing weight of provocative reflection, often published in books from Orbis Press, on broad themes arising from the cross-cultural experiences of missionary-scholars highlights ever more clearly the potential importance of mission perspectives for more general purposes. As they build upon foundational work from the middle decades of the century by pioneers like Kenneth Scott Latourette, R. Pierce Beaver, and Stephen Neill,[1] contemporary

---

1. As examples, Latourette, *A History of the Expansion of Christianity,* 7 vols. (New York: Harper, 1937-1945); Beaver, *Ecumenical Beginnings in Protestant World Mission* (New York: Nelson, 1962); Neill, *A History of Christian Missions* (England: Penguin, 1964).

missiologists are providing a wealth of critical writing worthy of wide notice. Whether path-breaking syntheses about the shape of Christianity as it has come to exist around the world (e.g., David Barrett, Samuel Moffett, Adrian Hastings),[2] provocative arguments about the importance of cross-cultural missionary experience for understanding contemporary issues like the roles of women in the churches (e.g., Dana Robert, Ruth Compton Brouwer),[3] or luminous theological-historical reflection on the broader interpretation of Christianity as a world religion (e.g., Lesslie Newbigin, Andrew Walls, Lamin Sanneh),[4] it is increasingly clear that the history of missions has a wide potential for history more generally. This potential can be seen by considering briefly the current state of church historical study and then at somewhat greater length the stage at which general writing by Christian historians now exists and the current crisis of meaning in the historical profession more generally.[5]

Church History

Missiology is now of heightened importance for church history because the next great challenge for writing the history of Christianity is to attempt a genuinely global history. For at least two centuries the history

2. As examples, Barrett, *World Christian Encyclopedia* (New York: Oxford University Press, 1982); Moffett, *A History of Christianity in Asia* (San Francisco: Harper-San Francisco, 1992); Hastings, *The Church in Africa, 1450-1950* (New York: Oxford University Press, 1994).

3. As examples, Robert, *American Women in Mission* (Macon, GA: Mercer University Press, 1996); Brouwer, *New Women for God: Canadian Presbyterian Women and Indian Missions, 1876-1914* (Toronto: University of Toronto Press, 1990).

4. As examples, Newbigin, *Foolishness to the Greeks: The Gospel and Western Culture* (Grand Rapids: Eerdmans, 1986); Walls, *The Missionary Movement in Christian History: Studies in the Transmission of Faith* (Maryknoll, NY: Orbis, 1996); Sanneh, *Translating the Message: The Missionary Impact on Culture* (Maryknoll, NY: Orbis, 1989).

5. This essay is revised from "The Challenge of Contemporary Church History, the Dilemmas of Modern History, and Missiology to the Rescue," *Missiology* 24 (Jan. 1996): 47-64. That essay in turn revises and updates a few paragraphs from "Contemporary Historical Writing: Practice and Presuppositions," *Christianity and History Newsletter* [UCCF] (Feb. 1988): 15-32; and "Traditional Christianity and the Possibility of Historical Knowledge," in *Religious Advocacy and American History*, ed. Bruce Kuklick and D. G. Hart (Grand Rapids: Eerdmans, 1997), 28-53.

of Christianity, in fact as in contrast to historiography, has no longer been the same as Christianity in simply the Mediterranean, European, and North American worlds. In keeping with our temperamental conservatism, however, Western historians have been slow to catch on. But now at the end of the twentieth century excuses have run out. To put the matter concretely, the *World Christian Encyclopedia* of David Barrett and associates, the essays and bibliographies of the *International Bulletin of Missionary Research,* and Barrett's annual survey of the state of Christianity around the world in the *International Bulletin* demonstrate, even to the most blinkered Western historian, that Christian history now simply is *world* history.[6] We are at the end of a century where perspectives have been dominated by interpreters of Western and American Christianity — for example, Harnack, Lortz, Pelikan, Ahlstrom, Dolan, and Marty. The agenda for the next century, if history is going to keep up with historical reality, is now being set by another set of writers — Walls, Sanneh, Moffett, Hastings, an ever-broadening variety of Western missiologists, and an emerging cadre of Christians from outside Europe and North America. While the world history of Christianity will not exclude European and North American perspectives, it will relativize them. No one will have more insight into how that relativizing should proceed, and also how to weigh developments from around the globe, than the historians who in pursuit of missionary activity have already learned to balance the perspectives of various cultures and to explore the shape of Christian contextualization in a variety of widely scattered regions.

History as Theology and History as Science

When the issue is not so much what will be written, but how that writing is carried out, missiological perspectives may have even more to offer. In particular, missiologists offer to the Christian community an excellent way of keeping alive the all-important discussion between history considered as a function of Christian truth understood only by believers and history considered as a general social science open to all humanity. To show why missiology might be so important for this particular exercise it will be useful to risk caricature by attempting a retrospective sketch.

6. David B. Barrett, "Annual Statistical Table on Global Mission: 1997," *International Bulletin of Missionary Research* 26 (Jan. 1997): 24-25.

Serious academic history writing by Christians has come forth in a steady stream for over half a century; it has become a veritable deluge during the last two decades. Notable in this effort were pioneers at mid-century and earlier like Herbert Butterfield, Charles Norris Cochrane, Christopher Dawson, E. Harris Harbison, and Kenneth Scott Latourette. More recently the tide has been swelled with Lutherans like Martin Marty and Lewis Spitz; British believers — Anglican, Dissenter, and Roman Catholic — like Patrick Collinson, David Hempton, Margaret Spufford, Eamon Duffey, and David Bebbington; North American Catholics like Philip Gleason and James Turner; liberal Protestants like William Hutchison and E. Brooks Holifield; evangelical Protestants like Timothy Smith, George Marsden, Robert Frykenberg, Robert Swierenga, Dale Van Kley, and Allen Guelzo; and from different denominations many historians of the patristic and medieval periods.

The presence of such writers in the contemporary academic situation represents a striking reversal. In America, a thorough secularism in the mold of John Dewey's pragmatism had come to dominate the university world by the 1920s.[7] The same was true for Britain where by the 1930s various leftist theories had assumed the upper hand in the universities.[8] The shift in fortunes for academic historians who are also Christians benefited from many factors, but at least two conditions in recent Western culture as a whole can be singled out, along with two having more to do with religious developments themselves. First, at the end of the twentieth century we have witnessed the manifest failure of Marxism, Freudianism, and Social Darwinism, the principal "grand theories" in earlier decades of this century, to provide satisfactory comprehensive explanations for human history.

Second, successive stages in the collapse of liberal progressivism have allowed more space for alternative ways of explaining the past. The once proud certainty that the West by sheer exertion could lead the world from superstitious darkness into the light of self-sufficient day has

---

7. See Henry Warner Bowden, *Church History in the Age of Science: Historiographical Patterns in the United States, 1876-1918* (Chapel Hill: University of North Carolina Press, 1971), esp. 3-30, 225-38; and George M. Marsden, *The Soul of the American University* (New York: Oxford University Press, 1994).

8. A sprightly if tendentious account of British developments is Maurice Cowling, *Religion and Public Doctrine in Modern England,* 2 vols. to date (Cambridge: Cambridge University Press, 1980-).

been bludgeoned by a series of terrible blows — the First World War; economic collapse in the 1930s; the mass extermination of Armenians, Slavs, Ukrainians, Cambodians, and especially European Jews; the clouds over Hiroshima and Nagasaki; the recoil against the West among colonized peoples; abject wretchedness in both developing nations and the bosom of the West; the caprices of the global economy; Vietnam; and the painful uncertainties of a post-Communist Eastern Europe — as only a partial list. One by-product of the collapse of liberal optimism has been greater willingness to countenance the thought that God may again be relevant for the future.

From the side of the church, a powerful band of public voices has reasserted the gravity as well as the coherence of the Christian faith. First in the 1930s and 1940s was a strong group of neo-orthodox theologians. Even more important for recent decades has been the weighty appeal of voices emerging from under the rubble — especially Alexander Solzhenitsyn and Pope John Paul II. Such ones have revived the idea that God talk might not be completely foolish after all.

The second religious circumstance bears on what might be called "Christian history"; it is the place where missiology becomes important. In a climate that has become less antagonistic, or at least less monolithically antagonistic, to Christian perspective, Christian historians made a strategic adjustment that opened a door to their participation in the university world. This adjustment was to abandon — at least while working within university precincts — the tradition of providential historiography stretching back to Constantine's Eusebius. The adjustment was for Christian historians to consider history writing in the sphere of creation rather than in the sphere of grace, as a manifestation of general rather than special revelation. Put differently, Christian historians took their place in the modern academy by treating history not so much as a subdivision of theology but as an empirical science. This choice meant that they have constructed their historical accounts primarily from facts ascertained through documentary or material evidence and explained in terms of natural human relationships.

Usually without defining their theoretical commitments explicitly, these historians have hewn to a middle course.[9] They have eschewed

9. Exceptions where explanations occur include Herbert Butterfield, *Christianity and History* (New York: Charles Scribner's Sons, 1949); *Herbert Butterfield: Writings on Christianity and History*, ed. C. T. McIntire (New York: Oxford University

providential history. Most Christian historians in the academy have gone about their work under the assumption that a scholar working with the data of historical research cannot know God's mind for past events in the way that the inspired writers of Scripture did, and they assume that the primary purpose of historical writing is not apologetics or evangelism. On the other side, however, they have also eschewed reductionism. That is, even as academic Christian historians gave up the extremes of providential history, they have also opposed the modern tendency to treat religion as a product of deeper, more fundamental realities.

It is to such academic Christian historians that missiologists are able to offer special assistance. In particular, missiologists are in a propitious position to remind academic Christian historians how shrewdly it is necessary to negotiate between history as theology and history as science.

The prime focus of missiology is on those situations where, in the words of the preface to an outstanding new collection of missionary biographies, believers attempt "to effect passage [for others] over the boundary between faith in Jesus Christ and its absence."[10] Such situations are also attended by the widest possible cultural consequences, some recognized at the time, others unanticipated by either missionaries or those to whom the message is brought. These situations, moreover, are often marked by intense spiritual conflict, both with respect to individuals and the future of societies.

Such missionary situations, in other words, need to be described with simultaneous attention to the meaning of Christianity and to the record of actual human experiences. Missiologists writing about such matters are usually keenly aware of spiritual realities, and so are in a position as Christians to check the tendency in modern historiography to write as if God did not matter. On the other side, however, missiologists are also usually alert to the profound cultural dynamics at work in any cross-cultural religious proclamation. As such, they realize that in order to write the history of such encounters it is necessary to pay

---

Press, 1979); and George M. Marsden, "Afterword: History and Fundamentalism," in *Fundamentalism and American Culture* (New York: Oxford University Press, 1980), 229-30.

    10. "Preface to the Series," in *Mission Legacies: Biographical Studies of Leaders of the Modern Missionary Movement*, ed. G. H. Anderson et al. (Maryknoll, NY: Orbis, 1994), xii.

the most exacting attention to actual human actions, linguistic practices, ideological frameworks, political superstructures, and social consequences. The functional atheism of the academy often makes it difficult for missiologists to keep realities of the faith in focus. The functional gnosticism of sending churches often makes it difficult to keep the realities of lived human experience in view. Yet missiologists, as they attend to the actual dynamics of what they study, keep both atheism and gnosticism at bay.

It will remain as difficult for missiologists as for other Christian historians actually to show how the worlds of faith and of historical science can be brought together with integrity. Yet because of the nature of what they study — situations where unseen spiritual dynamics and visible cultural consequences are bound so inextricably together — missiologists are in a favored position to help the rest of us. Christian historians at work on standard historical, or even church historical, topics have made a good beginning at differentiating between history as a function of empirical inquiry and history as a function of theological deductions. We have even begun the task of providing reasons for why the treatment of history as a function of empirical inquiry can be a valid Christian vocation.[11] What we have not done so well is to show how the realms of history-as-science and history-as-theology may coexist or mutually support each other. Perhaps that inability arises from reactions against the excessive providentialism of earlier Christian history. However proper it may be to reform excesses, it is not a healthy situation for Christian historians to overreact. If balance — between the realms of faith and sight, between the dogmatic overstatements of the past and the confused possibilities of the present — can be found, it will probably be missiologists who find it. And they will be able to lead the way because of the sensitivities they have developed as historians of faith, historians of culture, and historians of the interactions between faith and culture.

---

11. See the hints scattered throughout the essays found in George Marsden and Frank Roberts, eds., *A Christian View of History?* (Grand Rapids: Eerdmans, 1975); C. T. McIntire and Ronald Wells, eds., *History and Historical Understanding* (Grand Rapids: Eerdmans, 1984); and Philip Gleason, *Keeping the Faith: American Catholicism Past and Present* (Notre Dame: Notre Dame University Press, 1987).

The Meaning of History in the Modern World

For a number of ideological, national, professional, social, and economic factors, historical study in the modern West is in a relatively troubled condition. Within the decade, distinguished historians have even spoken of an "epistemological crisis" concerning the status of knowledge about the past.[12] This sense of crisis is a response especially to radically unsettling theories concerning the use of language and the practice of intellectual life more generally that have swept through Western universities since the 1960s. The confusion with respect to historical knowledge may, however, be even more complicated, and also more severe, than the mere presence of radical new theories suggests. The fact is that the newer views have not simply replaced the old. Rather, radical new proposals now contest the terrain with remnants of older views. Especially for activities like history writing, older practices do not simply vanish when newer options appear. So the situation today is a field of combat where at least three antagonists struggle for ascendancy. These three may be called, to use our era's most plastic vocabulary, the premodern, the modern, and the postmodern — or, with slightly more precision, the ideological, the scientific, and the deconstructive. Again risking caricature, it will be necessary to say a little about each view in order to suggest why missiology might once again be able to lead other Christian historians in pacifying historiographical combat while also enabling more fruitful Christian employment of the wisdom of the world.

Premodern or Ideological

The first stance or attitude is the assumption that historical writing exists in order to illustrate the truth of propositions known to be true before study of the past begins. This stance may be called ideological or pre-

12. For the phrase, "epistemological crisis," see Peter Novick, *That Noble Dream: The "Objectivity Question" and the American Historical Profession* (New York: Cambridge University Press, 1988), 573; and Joyce Appleby, "One Good Turn Deserves Another: Moving Beyond the Linguistic," *American Historical Review* 94 (Dec. 1989): 1326, 1328. For a helpful recent survey which ends by defending the values of the Enlightenment, see Georg G. Iggers, *Historiography in the Twentieth Century: From Scientific Objectivity to the Postmodern Challenge* (Hanover, NH: Wesleyan University Press, 1997).

modern. Beyond question it has always been the most widely practiced kind of history. Herbert Butterfield called this way of encountering the past, "Whig History," which he defined as the telling of "a story which is meant to reveal who is in the right."[13] This stance approaches history as if it existed to illustrate how similar all of the past is to the present and how clearly the past reveals the inevitable emergence of those present conditions favored by the historian. We often think of Marxism as the major proponent of such ideological approaches, but this general way of writing history has a very long pedigree. When Polybius in his *Histories* of the Roman republic from the mid-second century B.C. described that state as the rise of an ideal political system, or when Livy did the same in the age of Augustus to glorify the empire, they were practicing a form of ideological history.[14] The most influential early church historians, Eusebius and Orosius, were also primarily ideologues in this sense, since they wrote in order to show how God had ordained the confluence of Jewish-Christian and Roman histories for the universal spread of the church.[15] This premodern conception of history prevailed among Christians in the Middle Ages. It has been a stock-in-trade of competing Christian denominations — Catholics vs. Protestants, Protestants vs. one another — to the present day.[16] It is probably the most widely practiced form of Christian history, for it specializes in exploiting historical data to show why my group is right and the opponents of my group are wrong.

In other venues, premodern history is one of the most potent allies of nationalistic blood lust. Under the influence of various romantic movements, ideological history flourished in the nineteenth century as an effort to discover the distinctive *Geiste* of the individual European *Völker,* or tribes. Its evil fruit is visible in post-communist Europe as well. This approach has, however, always also been important to the self-conception of American historians. Puritans tracing the rise of God's Kingdom in the howling American wilderness, nineteenth-century his-

13. Herbert Butterfield, *The Whig Interpretation of History* (1931; New York: W. W. Norton, 1965), 130.

14. Ernst Breisach, *Historiography: Ancient, Medieval, and Modern* (Chicago: University of Chicago Press, 1983), 45-50, 63-69.

15. Ibid., 77-78; Charles Norris Cochrane, *Christianity and Classical Culture* (New York: Oxford University Press, 1944).

16. See especially A. G. Dickens and John Tonkin, *The Reformation in Historical Thought* (Cambridge, MA: Harvard University Press, 1985), 7-89.

torians like George Bancroft describing the rise of a free and democratic society, early professional historians like Henry Adams (who proclaimed that "Democracy is the only subject for history"),[17] modern interpreters of America as the cradle of liberating capitalism or the source of materialistic racism — all share an ideological view of the past. In recent years, a particularly active form of ideological history in the United States has drawn together national, Christian, and political elements. It is the view that history shows how the American way of life enjoys the special providential care of God.[18]

Another way of referring to this approach is to call it tribal history, which historian Grant Wacker describes in the following terms: "This is scholarship that is fashioned with private, factional, parochial, or ethnic — in a word, non-public — criteria for what counts for good evidence, reliable warrants, and sound conclusions. Tribal history rarely suffers from factual inaccuracy in the strict sense of the term. More often the problem proves the opposite: an inordinate attention to details, yet all linked by explanatory frameworks that only insiders find credible."[19]

Premodern or ideological history has few defenders in the academy, but intellectuals are probably no less prone to practicing this form of history than the not so intellectual. The key to a premodern stance is its instinctive, non-reflective partisanship. Premodern history may engender prodigious research, but it is research with a purpose, and a purpose firmly fixed before the research even begins.

Modern or Scientific

The second position holds that genuine knowledge of the past must be derived through verifiable procedures modeled directly on a strictly empirical conception of the physical sciences. This position no longer exercises the dominance it once enjoyed, but nonetheless retains con-

---

17. Quoted in Cushing Strout, *The Pragmatic Revolt in American History* (1958; Ithaca, NY: Cornell University Press, 1966), 15.

18. This view, with examples, is examined in Mark A. Noll, George M. Marsden, and Nathan O. Hatch, *The Search for Christian America*, expanded ed. (Colorado Springs, CO: Helmers & Howard, 1989).

19. Grant Wacker, "Understanding the Past, Using the Past: Reflections on Two Approaches to History," in *Religious Advocacy and American History*, 169.

siderable influence among both academics and in the public at large. It had some vogue in England as early as the mid-nineteenth century, especially in the work of H. T. Buckle.[20] It added a component, in a particularly European fashion, to the work of French historians of the *Annales*. It has flourished intermittently in America since the 1870s. The flavor of this approach is suggested by the statement of the nineteenth-century Lincoln biographer Albert J. Beveridge that "facts when justly arranged interpret themselves" or from the literary historian Moses Coit Tyler's belief that he and his colleagues could "write the whole absolute truth of history."[21] George Burton Adams summed up this general opinion in his presidential address before the American Historical Association in 1908. The job of historians, he affirmed, was "to ascertain as nearly as possible and to record exactly what happened." Questions about the "philosophy of history," he sneered, are wisely left to "poets, philosophers and theologians." Historians knew, Adams went on, that "at the very beginning of all conquest of the unknown lies the fact, established and classified to the fullest extent possible." Others may yield to "the allurements of speculation," but "the field of the historian is, and must long remain, the discovery and recording of what actually happened."[22]

Philosophers and historians of science, not to speak of most practicing historians, have long since abandoned the extremes of this position, but still it lingers on, often among historians most closely identified with sociology, the American academic discipline where the greatest naiveté remains concerning the use of scientific method. Scientific history also feeds off a popular perception of history among the public at large. Thanks to pedestrian teaching, the impression can still prevail that history simply is a faceless regiment of meaningless potentates arranged across an iron grid of random dates. In both the academy and among the populace, where this type of historical modernism survives, knowledge of the past is assumed to mean the discovery of the pristine fact, nothing more and nothing less.

20. Breisach, *Historiography*, 274-75.
21. Beveridge, *Abraham Lincoln* (1928), as quoted in W. Stull Holt, "The Idea of Scientific History in America," *Journal of the History of Ideas* 1 (1940): 358. Tyler is quoted in Bowden, *Church History in the Age of Science*, 19.
22. George Burton Adams, "History and the Philosophy of History," *American Historical Review* 14 (1909): 223, 226.

Postmodern or Deconstructive

Most recently a range of sophisticated academic positions have challenged the scientific approach to history. Some of these challenges make a point of praising premodern approaches as a way of attacking scientific views for *their* naiveté. The sources for this challenge are many. The seriousness of the challenge has left modern historical study troubled.[23]

Modern critics of scientific notions of history have stressed the extent to which historical writing is and always has been political. To be sure, the development of "professional history" in the universities over the last two centuries obscured the political character of historical writing for some time. Early leaders of academic history in Europe and in the United States prided themselves on a detachment and an objectivity that they felt defined their advance over earlier, amateur, and much more obviously partisan historians of previous generations.[24] Recent appeals to self-reflection, however, have made it increasingly clear that history-writing has always served political purposes, not just in what historians write but also in how they conceive the nature of their tasks. This conclusion is the point of compelling formal studies, of which Peter Novick's *That Noble Dream: The "Objectivity Question" and the American Historical Profession* is the most impressive.[25] In retrospect, it is evident that the first great professional historians in nineteenth-century Europe stimulated the rising sense of nationalism among the European peoples. Just as clear in our own day is the way that political considerations (again, in the broad sense of the term) shape historical writing. This generalization was most obviously true for works written by officially sponsored historians of communist countries and by dissidents within those countries. But it is just as true for Western chroniclers of the Cold War, where Leftist historians followed the evidence and assigned substantial responsibility for the Cold War to the United States, and Rightist historians followed the evidence and assigned substantial responsibility for the Cold

23. For a clear summary, and vigorous rebuttal, of postmodern trends affecting writing about the past, see Keith Windschuttle, *The Killing of History* (New York: Free Press, 1997).

24. Breisach, *Historiography*, 272-90; D. W. Bebbington, *Patterns in History: A Christian View*, rev. ed. (Grand Rapids: Baker, 1990), 68-91.

25. For an excellent discussion of Novick's stimulating volume, see James T. Kloppenberg, "Objectivity and Historicism: A Century of American Historical Writing," *American Historical Review* 94 (Oct. 1989): 1011-30.

War to the Soviet Union. It is illustrated by historians of the Reconstruction period in American history, where an individual historian's degree of sympathy with the modern civil rights movement invariably has correlated with that historian's interpretative conclusions about the efforts of radical Reconstructionists. It is true for historians of homosexuality, where gay liberationists find widespread acceptance of homosexual practice in the past and defenders of traditional values find persistent opposition to homosexual practice in the past. Political intent is also manifestly apparent in the writing of church historians. An immense distance, for example, separates the tone of Roman Catholic histories of the Reformation written after the Second Vatican Council, which urged Catholics to new charity when evaluating other groups of Christians, and those histories of the Reformation written by Catholics before these injunctions took hold. The same is true for at least some Protestant accounts of the Catholic past. Recently, in short, even historians with their noses deeply buried in the archives have come to sense that more is at work in reporting their findings than simply letting the facts fall where they may.

A second modern condition that pushes history in a postmodern direction is a proliferation in almost all academic disciplines of voices questioning the once widely-shared ideal of detached, rational, scientific inquiry. The reasons for questioning that ideal are various and are now well-known. The ideal is described as the tool of patriarchialist, capitalist, and racist oppressors; it is denounced as dehumanizing; it is depicted as intellectually incoherent. But in each case, the effect is to call into doubt the ability of researchers to move smoothly from a collection of facts to the presentation of universally valid truth. Such voices, with their flat rejection of objective, value-neutral research, have become increasingly important among historians because of the trend that has been strengthening throughout the twentieth century for opening up historical work to the concepts, materials, and strategies of the various social sciences and humanities. Simon Schama's *Dead Certainties* (1991) is a prime example that such postmodern views can ground impressive historical writing, as well as simply theories about history.

A third influence rousing historians from dogmatic slumbers is even more unnerving. It is the conviction proposed most influentially by Thomas Kuhn in his 1962 essay, *The Structure of Scientific Revolutions,* that even natural science — the intellectual standard since Newton for hard, real, genuine knowledge — may itself be less fixed, less intellectually pristine, less value-neutral than all of Western civilization once assumed. Such a suggestion is significant for historians because the goal of most professional historians over the last century had been to justify their existence by demonstrating that they too were scientific, that they were shedding the burdens of value-laden, subjective, and partisan history. But Kuhn's shocker, though disconcerting enough, was only an opening salvo. His focus was on the internal operations of science, and his intent was to mount a backhanded defense of "normal science" on a pragmatic foundation more in line with the lived realities of scientific experience instead of the self-gratifying myths of scientific heroism. Other, more radical historians of science went far beyond Kuhn. They argued that scientific knowledge was relative not only to intellectual shifts internal to the guild of professional scientists. It was also relative to the very same social, political, racial, sexual, and economic conventions of culture that seem to have shaped so decisively the social sciences and the humanities. These historians of the external relations of science have made their most impressive cases studying the age of Newton and the rise of Darwinism in Britain, as well as the American commitment to conceptions of common-sense, Baconian empiricism in the early United States. The recent biography of Charles Darwin by Adrian Desmond and James Moore (1991), as well as Steven Shapin's study of modern science in the age of Robert Boyle's England, *A Social History of Truth* (1994), are brilliant examples of history written under such convictions.[26] In these instances, along with many others, it has not been difficult to show that what scientists and awed non-scientists held to be the sanitized results of pristinely objective inquiry were in fact products, at least in large part, of religious or social preconceptions, competition for status, eagerness for warrants to justify influence, and still other factors having nothing directly to do with the study of nature as such. With the anchor of scientific objectivity drifting, if not lost altogether, aspirations to write history scientifically were cast adrift on a very choppy sea.

A recent book by three distinguished historians, Joyce Appleby, Lynn Hunt, and Margaret Jacob, *Telling the Truth About History,* provides a readable summary of these new challenges. According to the authors: "In the decades since World War II the old intellectual absolutisms have

---

26. For a recent, readable distillation of such approaches to the scientific past, see Steven Shapin, *The Scientific Revolution* (Chicago: University of Chicago Press, 1996).

been dethroned: science, scientific history, and history in the service of nationalism. In their place — almost as an interim report — the postwar generation has constructed sociologies of knowledge, records of diverse peoples, and histories based upon group or gender identities. . . . The postwar generation has questioned fixed categories previously endorsed as rational by all thoughtful men, and has denaturalized social behavior once presumed to be encoded in the very structure of humanness. As members of that generation, we routinely, even angrily, ask: Whose history? Whose science? Whose interests are served by those ideas and those stories? The challenge is out to all claims to universality. . . ."[27]

*   *   *

The task facing Christian historians is to know what to do on the contemporary battlefield. Premodern history plugs along tenaciously, with wide effect in the world (especially in churches of the sort that send and receive missionaries) and with some influence in the academy. Modern history is battered, but survives as a practical stance for many working historians and as an intellectual refuge for those who cannot abandon the high ideal of truth that created the modern university. Postmodern history flourishes as theory, and sometimes generates impressive practice, but how long can it fend off the deadly embrace of nihilism?

On this battlefield, the dilemma posed to believing historians is also an opportunity, for Christianity itself both recommends and condemns certain aspects of each stance. To defend such a thesis would take a full monograph, but at least hints can be offered here about how Christian faith is both at home, and not at home, with each of the three major historiographical trajectories.

With the premoderns, believers may affirm that it is appropriate to think of history as the vindication of the Right and True, but in this case the Right and True as defined by the progress of the gospel and the worldwide spread of Christianity. In addition, the premodern use of intuition as a guide to the meaning of the past is strikingly similar to the central place that a kind of intuition — more properly called "faith" — occupies at the core of every believer's life, no matter how adept in reason or research that believer may be.

27. Joyce Appleby, Lynn Hunt, and Margaret Jacob, *Telling the Truth About History* (New York: Norton, 1994), 3.

Yet looked at from another angle, premodern approaches to history fall dangerously short of Christian standards. They appear to open up the human experience of bygone generations, but in fact often shut off the past and silence the voice of the dead. The major sin of ideological history is to prevent people from looking at the past as a way of finding out about the past. It encourages an idolatrous sense of one's own powers and a dangerously dismissive attitude toward the ways in which divine providence has actually sustained human existence. Ideological history, whether Marxist or Presbyterian, democratic capitalist or Maoist, has been a bad currency driving out the good with unusual effect during the twentieth century.

It is the same way with modern or scientific historiography. Christians may commend it for taking empirical procedures with great seriousness in the same way that they can commend the stress on induction among early modern scientists. In both cases Christians may be pleased with the scientist's and historian's confidence in the contingency of events — that is, the belief that knowledge depends more upon an ability to perceive the event in its own development than upon deductive explanations brought to the event. Early modern scientists and positivist historians both overstated significantly the degree to which they were free from pre-understandings. Yet they also displayed a laudable confidence in the worlds outside themselves that God made, sustains, and opens to humans through mental abilities that also come from his gracious hand.

But if there is a positive side to scientific history, there is also a negative side. The perversion of modern history lies not in its empiricism, but in its short-sightedness about the process that culminates in written history. The agents of history — those who act and witness actions, those who make and transmit records, those who attempt to reconstruct past actions on the basis of those records — are people with worldviews, biases, blindspots, and convictions. Moreover, their most important actions — responsible moral choice with consequences — are the very ones most resistant to the kind of replication and control required for a strictly empirical science. Scientific history implicitly recognizes the God-ordained shape of the past, but also easily falls prey to an idolatrous assessment of the historian's own powers.

Again, the postmodern stance deserves, from a Christian angle, both commendation and condemnation. Individuals do in fact write history from the standpoint of their own circumstances, and in order to promote the interests of their own class, nation, or denomination. From a Christian perspective, there is even strong justification for expecting history to be impaired by the historian's point of view. The Christian concepts of the Fall and of human finiteness account for perceptual blinders that are as limiting for historical knowledge as for the knowledge of God. Put positively, the fact that God assigned humans the stewardship of the earth implies divine sanction for the particular adaptation to different landscapes, climates, and cultures that such a stewardship requires. In addition, the Incarnation and the outworking of redemption in the particular culture of first-century Judaism suggests something — if only a dim shape within a mystery — about the dignity of human actions and perspective rooted in very specific historical circumstances. So, for a postmodernist to claim that historical knowledge is inevitably particular, limited, and perspectival can be to make a kind of Christian claim.

At the same time, Christians hold that a realm of reality beyond the immediate sensory perception of this generation is the fundamental reality that makes possible the perception of all other realities. They believe, furthermore, that this more basic reality was manifest with unique force in events and circumstances of history. And they affirm that this reality is supernatural as well as natural, that it stems originally from God. It is hard to imagine a sharper antithesis than between such Christian views and postmodern denials of the past.

The contemporary situation may offer a golden opportunity for believers concerned about history. I do not myself know anyone from the community of faith who has seized fully that opportunity, but it seems to be there for the taking. That opportunity is created both by modern intellectual confusion and by the specific forms of contemporary thought that, in striving against each other, create the confusion. The opportunity is to practice a history that accepts with discrimination, but also eagerly, the historiographical wisdom of the world. That opportunity is to show how the beauty, power, and coherence of the Christian faith make it possible to learn from the modern world without falling prey to intellectual confusion or anti-Christian conclusions.

Who in the tribe of Christian historians is in the best position to work simultaneously with aspects of the premodern, the modern, and the postmodern? The answer certainly must be missiologists. Missiologists resonate with the premodern in their sympathy with sending churches and receiving cultures, where constructs from the academy — whether modern or postmodern — make no sense at all. Missiologists themselves usually believe that something like a direct, nonrational (if not antirational) knowledge of God — whether expressed in terms of the Holy Spirit, the sacraments, or in other ways — is not only possible, but is in fact the heart of life itself. Missiologists who share these aspects of the premodern worldview are surely in a position to write about it when they find it in others.

Missiologists are also modern because they can see how standards of objectivity have made it possible for Catholic researchers and Protestant researchers to benefit from each other's insights, and together to benefit from the research insights of many who are not Christian in any sense. Missiologists who recognize such gifts as the contributions of modern or scientific historical study are surely in a position to write as moderns themselves.

Missiologists, because they study other cultures and study them with cross-cultural sensitivity, are also primed to benefit from the insights of postmodernity. Their intense focus on the diverse incarnations of the gospel in cultures very different from each other reinforces postmodern awareness of the relativity of knowledge. Missiologists who find valid insights in postmodern history are surely in a position to write with heightened savvy about what they see.

But in the end, missiologists will not be defined primarily as premoderns, moderns, or postmoderns. They will continue to be defined above all else as Christians. That ultimate identification will preserve them from the blood lust of ideology, the desiccation of scientific pretense, and the silence of deconstructive solipsism.

It is, I realize, a mind-defying task that I want to assign to missiologists. But mission historians are already leading other historians geographically beyond our tight preoccupations with Europe and North America, and mission historians have already begun to show how the history of Christianity can encompass the most diverse expressions of particular cultures. It would seem that mission historians might also show the way in historical method. That hope, of course, does not rest ultimately in the missiologists, but in the fact that they study so intensely, and study from so many cultural angles, allegiance to the Way, the Truth, and the Life.

Whose Story, Which Story?
Memory and Identity among Baptists in the South

BILL J. LEONARD

The Southern Baptist Convention is the largest Protestant denomination in the United States, claiming more than fifteen million members in almost forty thousand churches. While its strength remains primarily in the South and Southwest, its influence and constituency are spread throughout the nation. Founded in 1845 as a result of the controversy over slavery, the SBC created a powerful programmatic identity for its people, a spiritual and regional legacy closely connected to Southern cultural and social consciousness. The convention linked local churches, regional associations, and state conventions with a national connectional system of boards and agencies which facilitated programs in education, missions, publication, historical studies, annuity, and other benevolent activities. Although plagued by continued controversy, the SBC remained reasonably intact throughout most of the twentieth century, united around evangelistic and missionary zeal, certain basic Baptist principles, Southern cultural contexts, and a wide variety of common programs. To be a "Southern" Baptist was to be distinguished, not only from Baptists in the North (call them Yankees), but also from those Baptists in the South who were not affiliated with the Southern Baptist Convention. These included Independent/Fundamentalist, Primitive, Old Regular, and Free Will Baptists, among others. Through a Cooperative Program, the denomination's collective funding plan, churches contributed to the state and national ministries of the convention, funding theological education, sending missionaries, addressing ethical issues, evangelizing the unconverted, and instructing the faithful.

Early denominational histories and biographies of convention leaders were often given to an unabashed hagiography, detailing the lives of the Southern Baptist saints as paragons of devotion and self-sacrifice at home and abroad. In a statement which I used as the title for a book on recent SBC controversies, Alabama preacher/statesman Levi Elder Barton, commented on the significance of the SBC, not simply in the present age, but in the Kingdom of God. In June 1948, he noted: "I am more tremendously convinced than ever that the last hope, the fairest hope, the only hope for evangelizing this world on New Testament principles is the Southern Baptist people represented in that Convention. I mean no unkindness to anybody on earth, but if you call that bigotry then make the most of it."[1] The SBC "story" in its traditional populist expression was thus a providential history which traced the work of God through chosen vehicles serving God as part of this peculiar people. The SBC experience was shared by generations of members from Richmond, Virginia, to El Paso, Texas. I introduced my earlier work on the SBC with the following description of certain norms which were passed on to generations of youth reared in the denomination and its churches.

Growing up Southern Baptist once seemed relatively easy. Elaborate denominational programs created a surprising uniformity among an otherwise diverse and highly individualistic constituency. . . . Sundays meant church, all-day church. Off you went to Sunday school armed with the three great symbols of Southern Baptist faith: a King James Version, "genuine cowhide," zippered edition of the Bible; a Sunday school quarterly outlining the prescribed lesson; and an offering envelope containing the weekly tithe. The Sunday school envelope also offered an opportunity for detailing personal spirituality based on the denomination's "six point record system," which included points for attendance, being on time, having a prepared lesson, bringing a Bible, giving an offering, and attending preaching.[2] Such uniformity and common experience could not last forever, however. By the late twentieth

1. *Alabama Christian Advocate,* June 29, 1948; and Bill J Leonard, *God's Last and Only Hope: The Fragmentation of the Southern Baptist Convention* (Grand Rapids: William B. Eerdmans, 1990), vi.
2. Leonard, *God's Last and Only Hope,* 1-2.

century, Southern Baptists were experiencing institutional transitions created by changing dynamics of American (and Southern) cultural and religious life. Theological and political conflicts also took their toll on denominational solidarity.

In 1979, a controversy over biblical inerrancy and denominational control divided the SBC into factions often labeled fundamentalists and moderates. Fundamentalists, convinced that segments of the convention had departed from orthodoxy (particularly in the colleges, seminaries, and denominational staff), pressed the doctrine of biblical inerrancy as the essential doctrinal principle of the denomination. Through a ten-year process (1979-1990) of electing a series of convention presidents who appointed only inerrantists to SBC trustee boards, fundamentalists succeeded in achieving a "course correction," by gaining control of the national denominational infrastructure. Moderates opposed fundamentalist methods, if not their theology, and resisted what they saw as a "hostile takeover" of denominational agencies, funds, and identity. Their attempts to elect convention leaders who were sympathetic to their cause were largely unsuccessful.

As their losses deepened in the late 1980s, moderates formed new organizations for publication, mission action, theological education, ethics, and other endeavors. Many congregations developed de facto dual alignments, retaining membership in the SBC while also identifying with such new organizations as the Alliance of Baptists and the Cooperative Baptist Fellowship. Fundamentalists soon set about reorganizing the convention, downsizing, reconfiguring, or eliminating numerous denominational agencies and commissions. For example, the Southern Baptist Historical Commission, charged with promoting the denomination's heritage, was disbanded and its work transferred to a council of the six seminary presidents. The related Southern Baptist Historical Society now maintains a tenuous, though autonomous, existence at Oklahoma Baptist University in Shawnee, Oklahoma.

Some fundamentalist churches, while asserting their loyalty to the newly re-formed convention, were quite willing to utilize non-SBC organizations, publications, and educational materials, shopping around for resources inside and outside the denominational system. Some even chose to minimize the name Baptist and identity in their public appeals, attempting to reach a new constituency of non-Christians and non-Baptists with the gospel. During the 1990s "messengers" to the convention's annual meeting frequently attracted national media attention by passing

126

resolutions opposing abortion, homosexuality, women pastors, and the Disney corporation.

At century's end, while fundamentalists retained control of the national denominational network, battles continued for control of state conventions and local congregations alike. Some state Baptist groups such as Texas and Virginia seemed clearly in the moderate camp, while Florida and South Carolina were dominated by fundamentalists. Other states saw control of state systems move back and forth between the two factions.

In Virginia, the SBC experienced its first clear-cut schism as a result of the controversy. Fundamentalists, frustrated in their efforts to secure a voice in state convention affairs, broke away in 1996 to establish their own state organization, Southern Baptist Conservatives of Virginia. The Southern Baptist Convention recognized the new body, thus establishing connections with both the new and the old state conventions.

The turmoil in the states also was evidenced by the decision of numerous Baptist colleges and universities to distance themselves from their parent bodies, the state Baptist conventions. Baylor University in Texas, Samford University in Alabama, Furman University in South Carolina, and Meredith College in North Carolina were among those schools which reorganized their trustee selection process in order to secure greater autonomy from the state Baptist bodies.

These developments had significant effect on the old denominational system, long a powerful mechanism for inculcating identity among the people called Southern Baptists. Through the denominational network, churches, institutions, and individuals found their "place" as Baptists in the South. This network created a sense of "Southern Baptistness" passed on to generations of practitioners in the churches. Controversy, factionalism, realignments in denominational loyalties along with the loss of programmatic uniformity, led many to ask not only what it means to be Baptist, but which Baptist story is the most appropriate one for which Baptist group? Whose story is it? How will Baptists pass on a discernable identity to new generations of young people reared outside the twin cocoons of Southern culture and Southern Baptist program? Which of the many Baptist stories will churches use to communicate their identity?

Baptist Origins: The Theories

Telling the Baptist story has never been easy. Historians have long noted the presence of various theories of origin in Baptist historiography. In his classic work, *The History of the Baptists*, Robert Torbet documented three such theories. The first he labeled the "Jerusalem-Jordan-John" hypothesis, that effort to trace Baptist churches in unbroken succession back to the New Testament community, and Jesus' baptism at the hands of John the Baptist. This successionism was an attempt to establish Baptists as the one true church, existing from the first century, not through apostolic succession, but through a succession of apostolic churches, dissenting, evangelical, and persecuted, which were Baptist in everything but name. Successionists pointed to the Montanists, the Waldenses, the Cathari, the Anabaptists, and others as part of the Baptist line. Although lacking historical veracity, this theory became a popular method by which some Baptists promoted their orthodoxy as the true New Testament church over against other Christian communions.[3]

A second theory of origins Torbet called the "Anabaptist Spiritual Kinship" theory, which sought to establish links between the seventeenth-century Baptists and the Radical Reformers of the sixteenth century. The idea of "kinship" reflects the disagreement among historians as to whether direct links between Baptists and Anabaptists can be established. Clearly, the two groups shared many of the same ideals — believers' church, believers' baptism, and congregational authority, among other things. British Baptists in the Netherlands began alongside the Anabaptists, though not directly out of their communities. Baptists contacted the Dutch Anabaptists, particularly Mennonites, regarding many subjects, particularly the question of believers' baptism.[4] Yet early Baptists also sought to distinguish themselves from the Radical Reformers. One seventeenth-century Baptist confession of faith was composed by a group of Baptist believers, who noted that they were "(falsely) called Anabaptist."[5]

3. Robert G. Torbet, *A History of the Baptists*, 3rd ed. (Valley Forge: Judson Press, 1963), 18-21.

4. Ibid., 21-29.

5. William Lumpkin, *Baptist Confessions of Faith*, rev. ed. (Valley Forge: Judson Press, 1969), 224. The Confession of 1660 begins: "A brief confession or declaration of faith set forth by many of us, who are (falsely) called Ana-Baptists. . . ."

A third idea of origins dominates Baptist historiography and is called the "Puritan Separatist" theory. This view suggests that Baptist groups—both Arminian and Calvinist—grew out of segments of English Puritanism, particularly the Separatist tradition. The General or Arminian Baptists who constitute history's first Baptist community in 1608 were a group of English Separatists in exile in Amsterdam. They broke with the Separatists over infant baptism and constituted a church on the basis of the believers' profession of faith and succeeding baptism. The Particular or Calvinist Baptists originated in London in the 1630s as part of a congregation of Puritan Independents known to historians as the Jacob-Lathrop-Jessey church. They instituted believers' baptism by immersion in 1641, affirming basic Baptist beliefs within the context of Reformed theology.[6]

Thus, considerable theological diversity characterized Baptist identity, with various groups claiming doctrinal ideals from Arminian to Calvinist. The earliest confessions of faith approved by Baptist churches and associations reflected theological divergence over issues of election, predestination, and free will, while affirming common ideas regarding a believers' church, a profession of faith followed by immersion, congregational polity, the priesthood of all believers, the ordination of ministers, religious freedom, and the liberty of conscience under God. Historically, many Baptist communions were seedbeds of dissent against those ecclesiastical and political establishments which sought to dominate the church and the culture.

In the United States, Baptists have often been an unruly lot, a case study in contradictions and polarities. Nowhere is this more evident than among Baptists in the American South. Dominated by the Southern Baptist Convention, the South is also home to a number of other Baptist groups including Primitive Baptists, Old Regular Baptists, and assorted other subdenominations located primarily in the Appalachian region, as well as large numbers of African-American Baptists, Independent Baptists, Free Will Baptists and other Baptist-related churches, associations, and denominations.

6. Torbet, *A History of the Baptists*, 29-37.

Southern Baptist Origins: Unexpected Diversity

Although the Southern Baptist Convention was not formed until 1845, historians identify numerous historical traditions or "stories" which informed Baptist identity in the South. They represent an unexpected diversity of theology and practice. First, the Regular Baptist tradition was evident in the founding of the first Baptist church in the South at Charleston, South Carolina. Led by William Screven (1629-1713), these Baptists came south from Kittery, Maine, in the 1690s. The Regular Baptists affirmed Reformed theology, preferred an educated ministry, and sang the Psalms as part of their orderly worship. Evangelical Calvinists, they preached as if all could be saved, believing that God would use such proclamation as a means of awakening the elect. Regular Baptists left their mark on churches in Charleston, Richmond, Augusta, Savannah, Atlanta, and other population centers.[7]

A second group, known as Separate Baptists, settled in North Carolina in 1755, led by Shubal Stearns (1706-1771) and Daniel Marshall (1706-1784), former congregationalists converted in the New England awakenings. Convinced that all believers should receive baptism by immersion, they became Baptists, moving to North Carolina and founding the Sandy Creek Baptist Church, from which over forty other churches would be established. Separate Baptists preached a gospel characterized by "enthusiastical" religion, dramatic conversion, spontaneous worship, and a mistrust of educated or paid clergy. Although they were Calvinists, their evangelistic concerns led them to a greater interest in free will and the general atonement. Separate Baptists participated in the revivals and awakenings which shaped frontier churches in the early nineteenth century.

A third source of Baptist identity in the South came from the so-called Gospel Landmark movement, an effort to trace Baptists all the way back to the Jordan as the one true church of Christ. Taking its name from Proverbs 22:28, "Remove not the ancient landmarks which thy fathers hath set," the movement arose over the question of whether ministers from Christian traditions which did not practice immersion (pedobaptists) should be permitted to preach or pray in Baptist pulpits.

---

7. Walter B. Shurden, "The Southern Baptist Synthesis: Is It Cracking?" in the 1980-81 Carver Barnes Lectures, published by Southeastern Baptist Theological Seminary, 1981. Shurden delineated these three traditions in this series of lectures.

Landmark leaders such as J. R. Graves (1820-1893) and J. M. Pendleton (1789-1858) rejected the idea, insisting that Baptist churches alone maintained the marks of the true church. Baptists alone could trace an unbroken succession to the New Testament church. Landmarkism was perhaps the most popular of the successionist views of Baptist origins. Again, while there is little historical basis for the Landmark claims, it became a popular formula for explaining Baptist beliefs, practices, and uniqueness.

Another source of Baptist identity can be traced to the founding of the Southern Baptist Convention in 1845. With a constituency influenced by multiple theological and liturgical traditions, i.e., Regular, Separatist, and Landmark, Southern Baptist denominational leaders were required to find those ideas and actions around which a diverse people could unite. This was particularly difficult given the Baptist mistrust of "hierarchical" organizations beyond the local church. In their efforts at achieving unity and cooperation, denominationalists created a connectional system by which convention boards and agencies were linked in common educational, missionary, publication, and other endeavors. Likewise, local congregations were encouraged to participate in the varied programs available through the denominational system. This network linking local, regional, and national efforts created a powerful source of identity for the participants. Through the denomination, churches and individuals were schooled in scripture, history, ethics, and a sense of "Southern Baptistness." Denominational resources, programs, and institutions aided churches in delineating and extending Baptist identity from one generation to another.[8]

The nature of Southern Baptist ministry is a case in point. Children were nurtured from the "cradle roll" to adulthood, through Sunday school, Baptist Young Peoples' Union (BYPU), and youth activities. Many "surrendered for full-time Christian service" in decisions often made public at summer youth camps and revival services. Many of these would-be ministers went to a Baptist college or university, then to one of the six denominationally funded seminaries. Those who did not attend college or seminary could also receive ordination and acceptance as ministers in churches which affirmed their call and spiritual gifts. For

8. John Franklin Loftis, "Factors in Southern Baptist Identity as Reflected by Ministerial Role Models, 1750-1925" (unpublished Ph.D. dissertation, Southern Baptist Theological Seminary, 1987), 232-50.

its ministers (at least the males), the denominational system functioned much as a large corporation, enlisting, training, and placing ministers in positions as pastors, staff members, missionaries, denominational administrators, or professors in Baptist-related schools.

Baptist piety also sent women to seminaries. Youth camps, Sunday schools, and revival services impressed upon Baptist youth the need to "do whatever God calls you to do." Indeed, Southern Baptist young people grew up singing such hymns as "Wherever He Leads, I'll Go," or "I Surrender All." When females took those admonitions to their logical conclusions and moved toward all facets of Christian ministry (include pastorates), some Southern Baptists protested. Divisions over the role of women in ministry paralleled, even contradicted, some of the pious generalizations about the boundaries of Christian service.

By the twentieth century, therefore, numerous influences shaped Southern Baptist subgroups, including fundamentalism (significantly), liberalism (minimally), the Social Gospel (minimally), women in ministry (significantly), and revivalism (significantly). Indeed, Southern revivalism was an important source for defining the nature of evangelism, conversionism, and spirituality for churches and individuals in the SBC. Southern Baptist identity has not been unaffected by the decline of the revivalist milieu among the churches. While an emphasis on evangelism continues, and concern for baptisms and church growth remain strong, the decreasing use of revival methodology has created questions as to what new models for doing evangelism might be developed.

Much Southern Baptist history was characterized by the extensive utilization of revivals as a resource for awakening churches and bringing sinners to conversion. Baptists were heirs of the camp meetings and "protracted" gatherings, services of renewal and evangelism utilized by many churches well into the twentieth century. For rural congregations, revival meetings were held seasonally, often in spring after planting and in fall after harvest. Preaching was usually carried out by a visiting evangelist/preacher during meetings which lasted two weeks or more. Often these were community events, drawing large crowds from many Christian traditions. Revivals were characterized by lively music, "personal testimonies" from the converted, colorful sermons by the evangelist, and the urging of sinners to repentance. Church members were encouraged to bring the unconverted to the services, sometimes through friendly competition in "pack the pew nights," in which prizes were given to those who brought the most people. Indeed, Southern Baptists created an extensive revivalist culture which shaped the methods and theology for accomplishing evangelism. While they were particularly significant in rural areas and small towns, revivals were also brought to the city with "crusades" held in urban stadiums and convention centers. Billy Graham was not the only Southern Baptist evangelist to fill stadiums across the South during the second half of the twentieth century. With time, and the distractions of modern life, however, many churches shortened revival meetings to a week, then to Sunday to Wednesday. The revival culture became less appealing to many urbanites inside and outside the churches. Revival methods, established in an earlier, more rural, less secular, era, were increasingly difficult to sustain. By the latter twentieth century, while some churches continued to conduct revivals, many had dropped them from the church calendar, substituting spiritual renewal services, or other occasions not characterized by revival formats. Yet the revivals had provided an important and tangible means of converting sinners. With the loss or decline of those specific methods, Southern Baptists confronted the dilemma of what to offer in its place.

One recent alternative to revivalism is found in the methodology and philosophy of the so-called megachurch, a phenomenon impacting large segments of American evangelicalism, including significant portions of the SBC. A megachurch may be defined as a congregation of several thousand members, led by a charismatic pastor/authority figure/CEO, providing specialized ministries targeted at particular constituencies, and organized around intentional marketing techniques. Many are self-defined as "seeker-oriented" churches aimed primarily at persons who are religiously non-affiliated. Their worship is often more contemporary, with praise-choruses projected on screens around the "worship centers," replacing traditional hymns. Services are informal in liturgy and dress, often including drama or skits. Many of these churches eschew or relinquish denominational "brand" names, in favor of the designation "community church," or "fellowship." They often have multi-staff ministries which stress small group experiences for Bible study, prayer, fellowship, recreation, and mutual encouragement.

Some Southern Baptist churches have appropriated these megachurch characteristics, often minimizing their Baptist connections. Others utilize elements of the megachurch methodology, developing "alternative" worship services, or seeker-oriented activities, while retaining traditional denominational programs. Some have dropped the Baptist name from their publicity, while retaining Baptist practices in baptism and the

133

Lord's Supper, and continuing their official affiliation with the Southern Baptist Convention. Praise worship has sometimes introduced charismatic elements into some of these churches, invigorating services but also dividing the congregation. While popular and highly successful, megachurches have yet to show that they can pass on a tradition or identity to a second generation of believer/consumers. Indeed, given the tendency of megachurches to maintain a looser, more generic form of Christianity, it remains to be seen what kind of identity might be passed on.

Given the fragmentation, realignment, or re-formation of the SBC denominational system, what might congregations and individuals do to extend Baptist identity toward the future generations? Numerous approaches are already evident. Some seek security of faith and practice in confessions of faith, specifically the Baptist Faith and Message, revised in 1963. Many view it as a guide, perhaps even a mandate, for maintaining doctrinal correctness in denominational agencies and churches, identifying who Baptists are by what they must believe. Some confessionalists even propose to use one specific theological tradition — Calvinism — to inform their reading of the denomination's confession of faith and other doctrinal statements.

Others insist the Baptist essence is found, not in "man-made" creeds, but in being a "free and faithful" people, bound to scripture, community, and individual conscience. Still others are concerned to understand the Baptist heritage in light of the broader mainline, evangelical, or even charismatic, movements in the church at large. Some, however, seem to act as if the old mechanisms are still intact, relying on the denominational system to inform identity. Certain segments of the denomination show greater interest in regional connections, understanding themselves as "Texas Baptists," or as members of a specific Baptist congregation which defines the nature of the tradition locally.

Still others wonder which of the innumerable subgroups once or yet related to the SBC can claim to be heir of the Baptist story. Fundamentalists insist that theirs is the true Baptist vision because they, like early Baptists, are committed to the infallible and inerrant Word of God. Moderates declare that they possess the identity passed on from "free and faithful" Baptists to a new generation of believers. Women wonder if they can ever get beyond the "woman's sphere" or the ecclesiastical "glass ceiling" to claim full identity among the people who nurtured them to faith and ministry. Many others question the continuing divisions between Baptists, black and white, in the American South.

In light of this diversity in Baptist self-definition, what strategies might Baptists use in recovering, renewing or restating their identity? First, local congregations must exercise greater intentionality in exploring and defining the nature of the Baptist heritage for themselves. In an earlier time, the denomination was the chief resource for identity, communicated through literature, programs, and the general ethos of the convention and the culture. Toward the future local congregations must be intentional about the need for identity and, given the diversity of Baptist stories and traditions, the specific traditions they seek to communicate, preserve, and promote.

Second, Baptists should not succumb to the fallacy of origins, that noble but naive belief that there exists a pristine, systematic, and unified source of Baptist identity in the beginning that need only be discovered and installed. In fact, there are multiple Baptist traditions — theological, regional, and institutional — from which churches may choose. There are many Baptist "stories" from which congregations and individuals may draw, some complementary, others contradictory. Discovering the story or stories which most inform what kind of Baptist one person or community of faith wishes to be is one of the great adventures for Baptist people toward the new century.

Third, Baptists might come to understand their classic "distinctives" as significant ideals which are ever held in tension, in a continuing and elusive quest for balance. For example, like their forbears, Baptist communions might seek to maintain a robust biblicism informed by an equally robust concern for "soul liberty," the freedom of individual and communal interpretation. Their concern for a church of believers might lead them to bring persons to conversion by means of both gentle nurture and dramatic religious experience. They could reexamine the meaning of believers' baptism and the Lord's Supper and the role of these sacraments (ordinances), not simply within the congregation, but within the entire church of Jesus Christ. Given the transitions, even breakdowns, in old denominational connections, Baptists in the South must reconsider the relationship between local autonomy and associational or ecumenical cooperation. Likewise, the concern for the priesthood of all believers should not lead to the idea that being a Baptist means that one can believe anything at all. Rather, the individual "priest" exists within and is informed by the community of "priests," the church.

Perhaps no question deserves more attention from twenty-first century Baptists than that of religious liberty. In a sense, the Baptist vision of religious liberty for believer, heretic, and atheist prevailed in America, evident in the Bill of Rights and the freedom of all to believe or not believe without sanction from the state. Recently, however, some Baptists have also become concerned about the growth of a secular religious establishment which they believe to be aggressively antagonistic toward religious faith in the public square. Such issues divide Baptists and other religious traditions in the U.S. and must be given close attention by Baptist communities of faith.

Fourth, Baptists would do well to continue to cultivate their role as religious dissenters from establishments political and religious. Clearly, Baptists themselves will not agree on when and where dissent is necessary, but they should struggle with it nonetheless. Whether fighting for religious liberty in Virginia or civil rights in Alabama, Baptists in the South (black and white) have upheld a proud tradition of dissent. Toward the future, they might pursue the essence of religious dissent and the wisdom to know when to exercise it.

Fifth, Baptists might remember that there are many "ways" to be a Baptist. There are many stories, some contradictory, which inform Baptist identity. In the future, Baptists are called upon to choose which story or stories best informs who they are and wish to be under God. They might also think long and hard before relinquishing the name Baptist in favor of some nebulous, generic religious ethos. Religion has specificity and offers a place to stand from which to relate to other movements and ideas in the religious marketplace.

Finally, on the way to the future, Baptists might remember and reexamine the ideas which gripped their unruly forbears. They might be summarized as follows: There are many "ways" to be Baptist and many Baptist "stories" to be claimed. Ideas are worth fighting over. Dissent is a worthy pursuit. The Bible is the written Word of God. Jesus is the living Word of God. Faith is both personal and communal. Baptism and the Supper are life-changing, grace-filled moments that mark the Christian journey. The people can be trusted. God alone is judge of conscience. Doctrines can and should be articulated by communities of faith. Controversy is inevitable. Religion at its best is never generic; it has specificity and peculiarity. Being a Baptist is messy, controversial, divisive, and energizing. That's just how it is, on the way to the Kingdom.

Selves and Others in Early New England: Refashioning American Puritan Studies

RICHARD POINTER

Who am I? Who are we? Who are you? Simple questions. Yet not-so-simple questions. Questions of definition. Questions of identity. Questions of bonds and boundaries. Questions about the self. Questions about the other.[1]

Ten years ago David D. Hall found the coherence of American Puritan studies in historians' and literary critics' shared "confidence in language, . . . new concern for spiritual experience, and . . . recognition of ambivalence." Examining developments in the field since his earlier historiographical assessment in 1970, Hall saw cultural studies supplanting intellectual and social history as the dominant focus and approach among Puritan scholars. Armed with new or renewed convictions about the close connections between language and action, specifically that people behave on the basis of how their language constructs "reality," historians were once again paying careful attention to Puritan texts, some familiar and some not. In particular, a wave of

1. Much of my thinking in this essay is indebted to the members of the seminar on "Puritanism and Its Discontents" sponsored by the Pew Charitable Trusts and hosted by Calvin College during the summer of 1997. A special word of thanks is due its leader, Laura Lunger Knoppers, for her insightful and gracious direction.

RICHARD POINTER

new works had appeared on Puritan spirituality. Among other things, they argued that for lay Puritans, as well as for their ministerial shepherds, the words of piety matched the experience of piety. Meanwhile, students of theological discourse were showing that New England's Puritans were neither exceptional nor static in their religious system. Instead, adaptation and ambiguity marked their seventeenth-century movement, helping it to survive and confounding modern attempts to define it simply.[2]

Today the definitional beat goes on, fueled by many of the theoretical influences Hall was beginning to notice in the mid-1980s. At one level, the last decade's attempts to figure out who the Puritans were seem anything but new. No movement (if it was such) has elicited so much scholarly effort in the twentieth century merely to define it. At another level, however, recent pursuit of what Hall called the "elusive Puritan" embodies enough new twists and turns (including the linguistic one) to warrant seeing it as something new indeed. In particular, much of the fresh work on Puritanism in the last few years concerns itself in one way or another with the character and construction of Puritan identity.[3] Herein may lie one source of coherence in current Puritan studies. How Puritans as a whole saw themselves is once again an open question.

2. David D. Hall, "On Common Ground: The Coherence of American Puritan Studies," *William and Mary Quarterly*, 3d Ser., 44 (1987): 193-229. Hall's earlier essay, "Understanding the Puritans," had appeared in *The State of American History*, ed. Herbert J. Bass (Chicago: Quadrangle Books, 1970), 330-49.

3. My focus on Puritan identity precludes discussion of many other vital areas of recent Puritan scholarship including the character of the Great Migration (see David Cressy, *Coming Over: Migration and Communication between England and New England in the Seventeenth Century* [New York: Cambridge University Press, 1987], Virginia DeJohn Anderson, *New England's Generation* [Cambridge: Cambridge University Press, 1991], and Cedric B. Cowing, *The Saving Remnant: Religion and the Settling of New England* [Urbana, Ill.: University of Illinois Press, 1995]); Puritan colonization outside of New England (see Karen Ordahl Kupperman, *Providence Island, 1630-1641: The Other Puritan Colony* [Cambridge: Cambridge University Press, 1993]); the character of New England towns (see John Frederick Martin, *Profits in the Wilderness: Entrepreneurship and the Founding of New England Towns in the Seventeenth Century* [Chapel Hill: University of North Carolina Press, 1991]); and the supernatural cosmology of early New Englanders (see David D. Hall, *Worlds of Wonder, Days of Judgment: Popular Religious Belief in Early New England* [New York: Alfred A. Knopf, 1989], and Richard Godbeer, *The Devil's Dominion: Magic and Religion in Early New England* [New York: Cambridge University Press, 1992]).

138

However that query is answered, some scholars, inspired by literary critic Stephen Greenblatt and others, are more interested in how individual Puritans represented themselves. In Greenblatt's terms, in what ways did they fashion a self?[4] Closely related is a growing interest in how Puritans related to those they saw or defined as different, as "other." Scholars are asking how did Puritan encounters with the other shape who they thought they were? And how did this change over time? Queries about selves and others in early New England run through many current discussions of Puritanism, sometimes dominating, sometimes augmenting, but collectively pushing toward ever more nuanced understandings of this "people of the Book" and their place in early America. Examining some of this literature will help illumine not only what we think Puritans thought of themselves and their neighbors but where Puritan studies seem headed overall.

Any discussion of what the Puritans who came to Massachusetts Bay thought they were about begins with Perry Miller's formulation of the Puritan errand. Drawing heavily upon Governor John Winthrop's lay sermon delivered aboard the *Arbella* en route to New England, Miller in the 1950s portrayed these English Protestants as seeing themselves engaged in a two-dimensional errand. On the one hand, they went to care for their own religious welfare, to concern themselves with their own business. On the other hand, they intended to create nothing less than a "City upon a Hill" that could serve as a model of a godly society for all of Europe, but especially England, to follow.[5] Despite Miller's slight evidence and careful choice of words regarding the latter errand, his view of Puritans as a people persuaded that God had chosen them to fulfill a special mission remains preeminent among efforts to define their collective aim and image. Numerous scholars have not only taken Miller's idea as axiomatic but extended it to argue that the Puritans understood their assignment in millennial terms; they thought God had

---

4. Stephen Greenblatt, *Renaissance Self-Fashioning: From More to Shakespeare* (Chicago: University of Chicago Press, 1980).

5. Perry Miller's classic account is in "Errand into the Wilderness," in *Errand into the Wilderness* (Cambridge, Mass.: Belknap Press of Harvard University Press, 1956), 1-15. For Miller's fuller perspective on American Puritans see *The New England Mind: The Seventeenth Century,* 2d ed. (Cambridge, Mass.: Harvard University Press, 1954) and *The New England Mind: From Colony to Province* (Cambridge, Mass.: Harvard University Press, 1953).

picked them to lead the way for the ushering in of his kingdom.[6] Particularly influential in this regard have been the writings of literary historian Sacvan Bercovitch. Though differing with Miller on many points, Bercovitch's two major books of the 1970s echoed the emphasis on the Puritan sense of chosenness and prophetic destiny. In his view, the Puritan myth became America's national myth, the Puritan self nothing less than the American self.[7]

Miller and Bercovitch's Puritans hoped to be, and in their minds became, models for later generations, in America if nowhere else. But what if these transplanted English Protestants were less concerned with being imitated and more concerned with being imitators? What if they imagined Massachusetts less as a "City upon a Hill" and more as a place of refuge and exile? What if they devoted less energy to being the vanguard of the coming millennium and more energy to being the restorers of a biblical past? For T. Dwight Bozeman, such questions arise from a careful review of Puritan language and form the heart of his strikingly revisionist account of Puritanism. *To Live Ancient Lives* stands out as the boldest reinterpretation of Puritan aims and collective identity to appear in the last decade. While admitting that Puritans occasionally spoke of themselves on an errand in Miller's second sense, he insists that much more often (and hitherto overlooked by historians) they talked about their quest to recover "primitive" Christianity. This primitivist impulse, along with Puritan pietism and moralism, began in England as they sought to rid their church of human "inventions." When hopes dimmed there for restoring gospel simplicity, Puritans departed like Old Testament exiles seeking a place of refuge. In New England, they were freer to create civil and ecclesiastical forms patterned on biblical models. Whatever reforms in English ways they initiated were considered returns to ancient practice, not innovations. Puritans looked backward not forward. The biblical past held far more importance to them than any future, including the eschatological one (at least prior to 1640).[8]

6. This tendency is discussed in Theodore Dwight Bozeman, "The Puritans' 'Errand into the Wilderness' Reconsidered," *New England Quarterly* 59 (1986): 234-35.
7. Sacvan Bercovitch, *The Puritan Origins of the American Self* (New Haven: Yale University Press, 1975); Sacvan Bercovitch, *The American Jeremiad* (Madison: University of Wisconsin Press, 1978).
8. Theodore Dwight Bozeman, *To Live Ancient Lives: The Primitivist Dimension in Puritanism* (Chapel Hill: University of North Carolina Press, 1988), 4-32, 42-56, 73-80, 193-94, 217-29.

Bozeman's arguments temper claims that Puritans self-consciously moved toward "modern" ways. If in the end aspects of Puritanism aided and abetted modernization, those consequences, he says, were unintentional. He would rather scholars notice the Puritan contribution to the strong restorationist bent within later American Protestantism and American thought. As for "assertions of a national mission to mankind," they would come to shape much American action in the centuries ahead, "but to represent the Great Migration as the first installment upon such claims is to misunderstand the origins of New England."[9]

If Bozeman challenges Miller's "errand," Janice Knight questions Miller's "orthodoxy." In her book, *Orthodoxies in Massachusetts,* she argues that *The New England Mind* portrayed American Puritans as homogeneous and univocal. Since then, scholars have either presumed or insisted (e.g., Sacvan Bercovitch) there was a single Puritan orthodoxy embodied in the thought of men like Thomas Hooker, Thomas Shepard, and John Winthrop. But in New England's early years, according to Knight, an alternative perspective existed "within the mainstream of Puritan religious culture." John Cotton, John Davenport, and Henry Vane brought to the colonies a piety and a theology learned at the Cambridge colleges that differed significantly from that of other Puritan leaders. In brief, Cotton and the others were more Augustinian, more mystical, more millennialist, more affective, more Sibbesian, less preparationist, less anxiety-ridden, less Amesian. Because they lost "a series of contests over political and social dominance in the first American decades," these Cambridge Brethren have been ever since subsumed into a mythical Puritan consensus that supposedly existed from the start. Instead, they need to be understood as powerful evidence of real diversity at the center (not just on the sectarian fringes) of Puritanism.[10]

By finding little difference between English and American pro-

<hr/>

9. Bozeman, *To Live Ancient Lives,* 344-55; Bozeman, "'Errand into the Wilderness' Reconsidered," 251. Andrew Delbanco, *The Puritan Ordeal* (Cambridge, Mass.: Harvard University Press, 1989), is similarly concerned with misrepresentations of the Great Migration. His reinterpretation of the Puritan errand emphasizes the Puritans as prototypical immigrants to America. Also see Andrew Delbanco, "The Puritan Errand Re-Viewed," *Journal of American Studies* 18 (1984): 343-60.

10. Janice Knight, *Orthodoxies in Massachusetts: Rereading American Puritanism* (Cambridge, Mass.: Harvard University Press, 1994), 1-12, 34-37. Knight emphasizes the differences between and influence of English Puritan theologians Richard Sibbes and William Ames.

ponents of either strand of Puritan thought, Knight casts doubt on claims for American exceptionalism. By insisting on the important links between English and American Puritans, she makes clear the necessity of seeing them through a transatlantic perspective. By revealing variety at the very heart of Puritanism, she presents a more fluid, more ambiguous movement. All three of those tendencies (and virtues?) continue lines of analysis most recently and most persuasively set out by Stephen Foster. Foster is that rare Puritan scholar equally conversant with the movement and its historiography on both sides of the Atlantic. He brings all of that expertise to bear in *The Long Argument*, arguably the most important book on Puritanism published in the last decade. Foster's contribution lies principally in conceptualizing Puritanism as a *movement* rather than as an intellectual construct (Perry Miller's "mind"). He tackles the age-old problem of definition with fresh vigor and resolves it by emphasizing Puritanism's adaptability and ambivalence. No single set of ideas or tactics can be listed to capture the totality of the movement. Even the godly's self-identification vacillated. Who they were or what they stood for evolved as they confronted and adjusted to changing historical circumstances. For example, the attitudes and preferences of Puritan migrants differed dramatically depending on when they left England in the 1630s. Those who departed in the second half of the decade were more radical in their church politics than earlier immigrants due to their deteriorating situation under Archbishop Laud in England. Once in America, they pushed New England Puritanism in a more sectarian direction, as reflected in the stricter religious policies adopted by the founders of the Connecticut and New Haven colonies. Thus, events in England played a crucial role in "sharply altering the character of the Puritan faith as it was in the process of translation to New England."[11]

Foster carries on the story of how Puritans adapted to the changing realities of the colonies in the second half of the seventeenth century and even offers an intriguing final chapter that locates Puritanism's denouement in the First Great Awakening.[12] Throughout the book, he adeptly builds upon or complements other recent scholarship on English and American Puritans. On the English side, he openly acknowledges

11. Stephen Foster, *The Long Argument: English Puritanism and the Shaping of New England, 1570-1700* (Chapel Hill: University of North Carolina Press, 1991), x-xii, 3-32, 138-174.

12. Foster, *The Long Argument*, 175-314.

his large debt to Patrick Collinson, whose voluminous writings on Elizabethan and Jacobean Puritanism are a critical part of a broader re-evaluation of Puritan (and English) history that cannot be recounted here. Suffice it to say that Collinson similarly interprets Puritanism as a movement that evolved with the times.[13] On the American side, Foster cuts more of his own path but heads in a direction (i.e., "Puritanism's American history as adaptive process") towards which many other historians have pointed.[14] *The Long Argument*'s particular achievement is putting the whole thing together so we see the Puritan way from beginning to end. Overall, Foster gives us both a compelling broad view (a truly transatlantic interpretation) and a fascinating long view (sixteenth through eighteenth centuries) of Puritanism's historical development.

Cursory summaries can do little more than hint at the breadth and depth of the arguments made by Bozeman, Knight, and Foster in their recent books. But they may indicate a bit about which way the wind is presently blowing in Puritan studies. For instance, however much David Hall thought in 1987 that the reaction to Perry Miller had "begun to run its course," these works make clear that saying something new and substantial about Puritanism's collective identity still requires "taking on" some significant part of the Miller edifice.[15] That identity itself now begins to look more and more like *identities* as historians stress the multiple Puritanisms that existed both at any one time and across time. Meanwhile, place remains an important shaping influence on the movement's character but not in terms of some kind of American exceptionalism. At least not for these authors. Instead, emphasis is "placed" on

13. Ibid., xiii-xiv. Among Patrick Collinson's voluminous writings see especially *The Elizabethan Puritan Movement* (Berkeley: University of California Press, 1967) and *Godly People: Essays on English Protestantism and Puritanism* (London: Hambledon Press, 1983).

14. Charles Cohen makes this point in his review of Foster's book in the *William and Mary Quarterly*, 3d Ser., 49 (1992): 524-26. Cf. David D. Hall, *The Faithful Shepherd: A History of the New England Ministry in the Seventeenth Century* (Chapel Hill: University of North Carolina Press, 1972); Charles Cohen, *God's Caress: The Psychology of Puritan Religious Experience* (New York: Oxford University Press, 1986); Charles E. Hambrick-Stowe, *The Practice of Piety: Puritan Devotional Disciplines in Seventeenth-Century New England* (Chapel Hill: University of North Carolina Press, 1982); Harry S. Stout, *The New England Soul: Preaching and Religious Culture in Colonial New England* (New York: Oxford University Press, 1986).

15. Hall, "On Common Ground," 193. Hall recognized, however, that Miller's "structure of interpretation" remained a "focus of discussion" (194).

how England's unique set of religious circumstances in the late sixteenth century gave rise to Puritanism and how English events, ideas, and policies in the seventeenth century largely shaped the movement's history on this side of the Atlantic. For the moment, scholars seem more impressed by what was shared across the ocean than by what was held alone. Still, even this threesome of historians follow the well-worn path toward finding the roots of some important strain of later American thought or culture in American Puritanism.[16]

The quest to understand Puritans as a group is being matched by a growing effort to explore and explain Puritan personal identity. The last few decades have witnessed an explosion of interest across a variety of disciplines in the nature of the self. Insights from psychology, anthropology, literary analysis, and material culture are now regularly informing historians' discussions about selfhood.[17] An important sign that scholars of colonial America have moved in this direction is a new collection of essays entitled *Through a Glass Darkly: Reflections on Personal Identity in Early America*. Philip Greven's contribution may serve as an appropriate starting point for considering recent work on the Puritan self. In it he revisits his book of twenty years ago, *The Protestant Temperament*, which anticipated much of the current interest in the self.[18] Greven reasserts his claim that in colonial America a person's religious beliefs largely corresponded to the character of her upbringing. In the Puritans' case, child-rearing practices that emphasized breaking the child's will and suppressing the self produced adults theologically preoccupied with predestination, divine sovereignty, and free grace. Psychologically, those same adults were beset with "feelings of anxiety, fear, anger, depression, obsessiveness, and paranoia that were directed against the body and the self and against other

16. Foster is the least inclined towards this tendency but even his final chapter offers some hints. Foster, *Long Argument*, 286-314; Bozeman, *To Live Ancient Lives*, 344-55; Knight, *Orthodoxies*, 198-213. Also see Delbanco, *Puritan Ordeal*, 224-43, for a similar tendency.

17. For a listing of much of this theoretical literature, see the bibliographic note at the end of Mechal Sobel, "The Revolution in Selves: Black and White Inner Aliens," in *Through a Glass Darkly: Reflections on Personal Identity in Early America*, ed. Ronald Hoffman, Mechal Sobel, and Fredrika J. Teute (Chapel Hill: University of North Carolina Press, 1997), 200-205.

18. Philip Greven, *The Protestant Temperament: Patterns of Child-Rearing, Religious Experience, and the Self in Early America* (New York: Alfred A. Knopf, 1977).

people."[19] Greven responds to his critics by citing a string of works that have appeared since 1977, all of which he argues support his grim picture of Puritan and later evangelical child-raising techniques.[20] So grim in Greven's view were the childhoods of typical Puritans to warrant calling them abused and to "say that their sense of selfhood was misshaped by the sufferings of their early life experiences."[21]

Greven's portrait of Puritan selves as deeply disturbed carries forward, albeit in a somewhat exaggerated form, an older emphasis on the Puritan saint as forever riddled with anxiety about his spiritual condition. As Hall's 1987 article detailed, however, new analyses of Puritan spirituality published in the late 1970s and early 1980s had reached different conclusions. A variety of books, but especially those by Charles Hambrick-Stowe and Charles Cohen, spoke about how Puritans regularly and repeatedly resolved their anxiety through devotional practices and an understanding of religious experience that centered on God's love. Conversion narratives or "confessions" offered by applicants for membership in Thomas Shepard's church in Cambridge, Massachusetts, for example, provided strong evidence that Puritan piety focused more on seeing conversion as a lifelong process of "growth in grace" than as a momentary crisis experience bound to arouse "profound anxiety" and an "overwrought conscience."[22]

---

19. Philip Greven, "The Self Shaped and Misshaped: *The Protestant Temperament* Reconsidered," in *Through a Glass Darkly*, 348-54.

20. Ibid., 350-58. Greven is responding particularly to the criticisms levelled in Cohen, *God's Caress*, 18. Greven cites in his own favor Lawrence Stone, *The Family, Sex, and Marriage in England, 1500-1800* (New York: Harper & Row, 1977); David Leverenz, *Language of Puritan Feeling: An Exploration in Literature, Psychology, and Social History* (New Brunswick, N.J.: Rutgers University Press, 1980); John Owen King III, *The Iron of Melancholy: Structures of Spiritual Conversion in America from the Puritan Conscience to Victorian Neurosis* (Middletown, Conn.: Wesleyan University Press, 1983); Julius H. Rubin, *Religious Melancholy and Protestant Experience in America* (New York: Oxford University Press, 1994); and John Stachniewski, *The Persecutory Imagination: English Puritanism and the Literature of Religious Despair* (Oxford: Oxford University Press, 1991).

21. Greven, "Self Shaped and Misshaped," 360.

22. Hall, "On Common Ground," 215-22. Besides Cohen *(God's Caress)* and Hambrick-Stowe *(Practice of Piety)*, other important recent works on Puritan spirituality that make use of the Cambridge texts are listed in Michael McGiffert, ed., *God's Plot: Puritan Spirituality in Thomas Shepard's Cambridge*, rev. ed. (Amherst, Mass.: University of Massachusetts Press, 1994), 227-30.

Michael McGiffert has extended this line of argument in a revised and expanded edition of *God's Plot*. It now contains not only Shepard's autobiography and selections from his journal but thirty-three lay confessions from his congregation. McGiffert thinks the ritual of public confession served constructive ends for both Puritan individuals and communities. Laity were afforded a rare (especially for women) opportunity to present themselves before their spiritual leader and peers. Through their words they could define themselves, fashion themselves, and "no matter how negative their self-judgments, the subtext . . . [was] a positive sense of self." This was their moment in the limelight and although nerve-wracking, it was a chance to tell their story, to affirm their importance in the eyes of God and themselves. It was also the moment in which they were affirmed and embraced by the congregation and became one of the "enfolded saints." They in turn would in future days listen to the stories of other potential members and reenact a ritual that allowed the community to "reaffirm its essential identity, validity, and stability . . . [and] remind itself of its reason to be."[23]

McGiffert's discussion of the Cambridge confessors argues that however much Puritans emphasized sublimation of the self, they did not destroy or misshape it. Instead, the "collective persona of the Puritan saint" constructed by their individual stories was marked by a healthy dose of assurance, confidence, and happiness. Doubts they had aplenty but they were reassured that such were to be expected along the journey of faith. McGiffert's analysis also points up how investigation of individual acts of Puritan self-definition can yield important insights into broader social and cultural patterns in early New England. In this case, he finds that the rite of confession bound church communities together and paved the way outside of church for the formation of particular political and social networks within the village as a whole.[24]

Conversion narratives were certainly not the only "texts of self" that Puritans produced in the seventeenth century.[25] Jeffrey A. Hammond's *Sinful Self, Saintly Self* sheds new light on what the old verse of

23. Ibid., 144-45.
24. Ibid., 145-48.
25. I borrow this phrase from Greg Dening, "Texts of Self," in *Through a Glass Darkly*, 157-62. Dening defines "texts of self" as "the expressions of experience, the masks" in which "the self is materialized," whether "in song, dance, sculptured stone, [or] words on paper. Being texts, they are available to be read" (159).

Michael Wigglesworth, Anne Bradstreet, and Edward Taylor reveals about Puritan personal identity. His reading of Wigglesworth is particularly noteworthy. Rather than seeing the minister's poetry (and the minister himself) as symptomatic of schizophrenia or an unstable identity, Hammond argues that instead it made plain to readers their sinful selves and their need to begin a process of "self-emptying" that would move them toward saintly selves. Wigglesworth's words also provided comfort and the right dose of reassurance for those along the way. Pilgrim souls were to travel an unending road in this life as they struggled to put off the old fallen self and put on the new. Within such an understanding, Puritan personal identity was viewed "more as a process than a fixed entity."[26]

Captivity narratives represent a third genre in which the Puritan self found expression. Mary Rowlandson's 1682 account of her capture by and sojourn among Narragansett Indians remains the archetypal text. Among recent interpretations, Margaret H. Davis's article in *Early American Literature* is particularly enlightening.[27] Perhaps above all else, it illustrates the strong influence of Stephen Greenblatt and the New Historicism upon current studies of selfhood in colonial America. Greenblatt believes that the self is defined on the one hand in relation to some overarching authority and on the other in relation to some threatening other that the authority has labeled as alien.[28] In Rowlandson's case, Davis locates that authority in "the entire patriarchal hierarchy [of Puritanism] including God, the Bible, males in general, and her own husband in particular." The place of the other is filled by her native captors. In the *Narrative*, Rowlandson constructs herself as a model Puritan housewife "conforming to the only role she knows and the only role approved for Puritan females." Such an identity makes her story and her otherwise subversive act of writing (women's writing was widely disapproved in

26. Jeffrey A. Hammond, *Sinful Self, Saintly Self: The Puritan Experience of Poetry* (Athens, Ga.: University of Georgia Press, 1993), 22-27, 48-56.

27. Margaret H. Davis, "Mary White Rowlandson's Self-Fashioning as Puritan Goodwife," *Early American Literature* 27 (1992): 49-60. Alden Vaughan and Edward W. Clark, eds., *Puritans among the Indians: Accounts of Captivity and Redemption, 1676-1724* (Cambridge, Mass.: Belknap Press of Harvard University Press, 1981), 1-28, provide an excellent introduction to captivity narratives.

28. Greenblatt, *Renaissance Self-Fashioning*, 8-9. The New Historicism blossomed as one of the leading literary critical methods among scholars of early American literature in the 1980s.

the seventeenth century) acceptable in the eyes of Puritan authorities. Yet within the text are hints of other subversive elements that neither those authorities nor Rowlandson herself fully recognized. In particular, her encounter with Indians pushed her on occasion towards a very different identity, a "selfhood of independent will and self-assertion." In the end, Rowlandson chose to suppress "the claim to individualized selfhood" and "reinforce the identity of submissive goodwife to God and man that she value[d]."[29]

Whether Davis's extreme characterization of Puritan patriarchy or discovery that Rowlandson's text has a more assertive self lying below the surface can withstand scholarly scrutiny (after all, did any Puritan want to claim individualized selfhood?) may be less important for the moment than recognizing what it shows about recent work on Puritan personal identity. Alongside the research of Greven, McGiffert, Hammond, and others, Davis's brings into view the threefold general concerns of current studies of not only the Puritan self but any selves in early America. First, scholars want to know who or what someone thought he was; that is, what was the content of this person's self-definition? Second, they are interested in how someone defined herself; that is, in what ways or through what means did this person give definition to herself? And third, they wonder about the relationship between the individual self and the larger world; that is, what might those self-definitions and ways of defining oneself (ends and means) reveal about the broader society and culture of which one was a part? The works discussed here also make plain that no consensus exists at present on the character or health of the Puritan self. More studies of individual Puritan efforts at self-definition could change that. Conversely, they could make generalizations about a Puritan "collective persona" or "metaself" more suspect not less.[30] Like Puritan group identity, Puritan personal identity may have

29. Davis, "Rowlandson's Self-Fashioning," 51-53, 56-59.

30. Other recent studies of Puritan selves may be sampled in Mary Cappello, "The Authority of Self-Definition in Thomas Shepard's *Autobiography* and *Journal*," *Early American Literature* 24 (1989): 35-51; Margo Todd, "Puritan Self-fashioning: The Diary of Samuel Ward," *Journal of British Studies* 31 (1992): 236-63, Ivy Schweitzer, *The Work of Self-Representation: Lyric Poetry in Colonial New England* (Chapel Hill: University of North Carolina Press, 1991), and Kathleen M. Swaim, "'Come and Hear': Women's Puritan Evidences," in *American Women's Autobiography: Fea(s)ts of Memory*, ed. Margo Culley (Madison, Wisc.: University of Wisconsin Press, 1992).

been plural, diverse, and changing. There were limits, of course, to who a Puritan could be, boundaries set by the larger community. As Davis puts it, Rowlandson projected "a self demanded by her theological milieu."[31] Herein lies one of the ironies, however, of studying the self. Forasmuch as historians want to reconstruct individual experiences of self-definition for the sake of understanding what they can tell us about a larger society, they seem bound to make sense out of those individual experiences on the basis of what they already believe to have been true about that larger society. Hence, Davis's presumptions about Puritan patriarchy *inform* rather than *derive* from her reading of Rowlandson. And as a result, they naturally color the kind of personal identity that Davis thinks was possible for someone like Mary. Differences among scholars on Puritan personal identity, then, would seem to have as much to do with their conflicting and preexisting assessments of Puritanism as a whole as with divergent evidence in Puritan texts of self. How to surmount this text-context conundrum deserves ongoing attention.

Deciding who Puritans thought they were or fashioned themselves to be seems more and more connected to Puritan interaction with those they considered "other." At least that is the message conveyed in both the dominant theoretical literature on the self and many recent works on early New England. As noted above, Greenblatt's emphasis on the role of a strange and hostile other in the construction of the self has become widely accepted. In Puritan studies, this is evident, for example, in Andrew Delbanco's recent assertion that Puritan migrants, having been freed from their enemies in England, "created new enemies" in America to retain their sense of themselves as an "outgroup." Their new opponents included Indians, Antinomians, Quakers, and witches.[32]

While important books have appeared on Puritan relations with these and other groups, my concern here will be with Puritan encounters with Native Americans.[33] Growing interest in that subject has been part

31. Davis, "Rowlandson's Self-Fashioning," 58.
32. Delbanco, *Puritan Ordeal*, 13-14.
33. On Antinomians and other sectarians, see Philip Gura, *A Glimpse of Zion: Puritan Radicalism in New England, 1620-1660* (Middletown, Conn.: Wesleyan University Press, 1984), and Amy Schrager Lang, *Prophetic Woman: Anne Hutchinson and the Problem of Dissent in the Literature of New England* (Berkeley: University of California Press, 1987). On Quakers, see Jonathan Chu, *Neighbors, Friends, or Madmen: The Puritan Adjustment to Quakerism in Seventeenth-Century Massachusetts Bay*

of a larger renaissance of scholarship on the period of first contacts between Europeans and indigenous peoples, and on the place of Indians within early American history as a whole.[34] These historiographical trends emerged independent of and somewhat prior to the more recent fascination of colonial historians with the self. Now these strands of inquiry overlap more and more as students of Native American history look closely, for instance, at changes in Indian personal identity and scholars of colonial selves reexamine how European newcomers were shaped by their encounter with native neighbors.[35]

Discussions of Puritan-Indian relations in the last thirty years have been dominated by the sharply opposing views presented in Alden Vaughan's *New England Frontier* and Francis Jennings's *The Invasion of America*.[36] Writing in the mid 1960s, Vaughan found Puritan sources reliable and Puritan dealings with Indians "remarkably humane, considerate, and just."[37] Later editions of his book have somewhat backed off that claim in response to critics and taken a dimmer view of Puritan

---

(Westport, Conn.: Greenwood Press, 1985), and Carla Gardina Pestana, *Quakers and Baptists in Colonial Massachusetts* (New York: Cambridge University Press, 1991). On witchcraft, see Carol Karlsen, *The Devil in the Shape of a Woman: Witchcraft in Colonial New England* (New York: Norton, 1987), Godbeer, *Devil's Dominion*, Bernard Rosenthal, *Salem Story: Reading the Witch Trials of 1692* (Cambridge: Cambridge University Press, 1993), Peter Charles Hoffer, *The Devil's Disciples: Makers of the Salem Witchcraft Trials* (Baltimore: Johns Hopkins University Press, 1996), and Elaine G. Breslaw, *Tituba, Reluctant Witch of Salem: Devilish Indians and Puritan Fantasies*, The American Social Experience Series, Volume 35 (New York: New York University Press, 1996).

34. This scholarship is far too voluminous to cite. An excellent synthesis of much of it may be found in Colin Calloway, *New Worlds for All: Indians, Europeans, and the Remaking of Early America* (Baltimore: Johns Hopkins University Press, 1997).

35. Cf. Robert James Naeher, "Dialogue in the Wilderness: John Eliot and Indian Exploration of Puritanism as a Source of Meaning, Comfort, and Ethnic Survival," *New England Quarterly* 62 (1989): 346-68, and Rosalie Murphy Baum, "John Williams's Captivity Narrative: A Consideration of Normative Ethnicity," in *A Mixed Race: Ethnicity in Early America*, ed. Frank Shuffleton (New York: Oxford University Press, 1993), 56-76.

36. Hall, "On Common Ground," did not address the historiography on Puritan-Indian relations. An early assessment of the Vaughan-Jennings debate may be found in David C. Stineback, "The Status of Puritan-Indian Scholarship," *New England Quarterly* 51 (1978): 80-90.

37. Alden Vaughan, *New England Frontier: Puritans and Indians, 1620-1675* (Boston: Little, Brown, 1965), vii.

actions.[38] But Vaughan's view is still not nearly so dim as Jennings's. His 1975 work offered a stinging and at times polemical, revisionist account of Puritan-Indian relations, emphasizing the greed, duplicity, and ethnocentrism of the Europeans and the horrific consequences for the Native Americans. Jennings distrusted Puritan sources, seeing economic ambition lying behind even Puritan missionary efforts.[39]

Two years before Jennings, an equally provocative and controversial book by Richard Slotkin *(Regeneration Through Violence)* had argued that the Puritans initiated a long American pattern of violent subjugation of the wilderness and its inhabitants. Drawing heavily upon Puritan war narratives, Slotkin explored the Puritan psyche and concluded they had projected their own worst qualities and fears upon the Indians of southern New England. The act of destroying Pequots, Narragansetts, and other Indian groups became a means of regenerating their own Puritan selves.[40]

Interest in Puritan-Indian relations blossomed further in the early 1980s. Works by Neal Salisbury, William Cronon, and James Axtell employed more interdisciplinary methods (each used an "ethnohistorical" approach) and reached more complex conclusions. Though more tempered than Jennings, Salisbury nevertheless offered a severe critique of Puritan policies and ideology. He argued that the expropriation of Indian lands and conquest of New England flowed from the mutually reinforcing economic and religious motives of the English settlers and forced the Indians of the area to pass through a "sequence of radical transformations" that eventually resulted in their "descent to the position of a sub-proletariat."[41] Cronon examined New England's ecological history and found a similar pattern of change and destruction. As Indians were drawn into the orbit of European trade and a globally expanding capitalist economy, as well as exposed to devastating diseases, their traditional need-based economic and ecological ethics and their resource use pat-

38. Alden Vaughan, *New England Frontier: Puritans and Indians, 1620-1675,* 3d ed. (Norman, Okla.: University of Oklahoma Press, 1995).

39. Francis P. Jennings, *The Invasion of America: Indians, Colonialism, and the Cant of Conquest* (Chapel Hill: University of North Carolina Press, 1975). Jennings had already stated his position on Puritan missions in "Goals and Functions of Puritan Missions to the Indians," *Ethnohistory* 18 (1971): 197-212.

40. Richard Slotkin, *Regeneration Through Violence: The Mythology of the American Frontier* (Middletown, Conn.: Wesleyan University Press, 1973), chs. 1-6.

41. Neal Salisbury, *Manitou and Providence: Indians, Europeans, and the Making of New England, 1500-1643* (New York: Oxford University Press, 1982).

terns were dramatically transformed, debilitating both native cultures and the environment. Then, as colonial settlement advanced, English forest-clearing and farming techniques added to the area's ecological woes through deforestation, overgrazing, soil exhaustion, and resource depletion.[42] Axtell focused his attention upon the religious dimensions of the Puritan-Indian encounter. Building on a small flurry of works by himself and others from the previous ten years, Axtell's balanced treatments and measured judgments showed the maturing of the field of early American ethnohistory: Puritan missionary efforts were largely doomed by their insistence on civilizing as well as Christianizing natives; Indian conversions to Christianity were bona fide; surprising numbers of Europeans culturally converted to Native American ways; and Christian Indians were authentically Christian and Indian.[43]

No works of the last decade match the topical breadth or interpretive clout of Salisbury, Cronon, or Axtell. Still, scholarship on Puritan-Indian relations is alive and well as historians reexamine narrower pieces of the pie equipped with new resolve to understand what happened from both sides and with new knowledge about southern New England's native peoples and cultures. The latter comes from the burgeoning research of archaeologists, linguists, and ethnologists on the region's Indians before and after European contact.[44] Anthropological studies like Kathleen Bragdon's *Native People of Southern New England, 1500-1650*, enable historians to be less exclusively dependent on European sources and to interpret more sensitively the Indians in those sources.[45] A fine example is Charles

42. William Cronon, *Changes in the Land: Indians, Colonists, and the Ecology of New England* (New York: Hill and Wang, 1983).

43. James Axtell, *The Invasion Within: The Contest of Cultures in Colonial North America* (New York: Oxford University Press, 1985), chaps. 7-9. Cf. James Axtell, "Were Indian Conversions Bona Fide?" in James Axtell, *After Columbus: Essays in the Ethnohistory of Colonial North America* (New York: Oxford University Press, 1988), 100-121, and James P. Ronda, "Generations of Faith: The Christian Indians of Martha's Vineyard," *William and Mary Quarterly*, 3d Ser., 38 (1981): 369-94.

44. Much of this scholarship is noted and incorporated in Neal Salisbury, "The Indians' Old World: Native Americans and the Coming of the Europeans," *William and Mary Quarterly*, 3d Ser., 53 (1996): 435-58. Also see Bruce G. Trigger, "American Archaeology as Native History: A Review Essay," *William and Mary Quarterly*, 3d Ser., 40 (1983): 413-52.

45. Kathleen J. Bragdon, *Native People of Southern New England, 1500-1650* (Norman, Okla.: University of Oklahoma Press, 1996). Another important recent work is Robert S. Grumet, *Historic Contact: Indian People and Colonists in Today's Northeastern*

Cohen's recent essay on Indian confessions for admission into John Eliot's Roxbury church in the 1650s. According to Cohen, the conversion narratives of Massachusett saints reveal an appropriation of Christianity mediated "not only by Puritan standards and expectations, but by the converts' socio-psychological backgrounds." The natives' Eastern woodland culture conditioned how they apprehended Christianity and adapted it to their own preconceptions. If on the whole few Massachusett crossed the religious divide, it was in part because "their own cultural legacies threw stumbling blocks on the way to [Puritan] faith."[46]

Other dimensions of Puritan-Indian relations similarly benefit from a more sophisticated understanding of native ways. In *The Pequot War,* Alfred Cave reinterprets the 1636-37 conflict in the light of a revised view of the Pequots' political, economic, and military place among southern New England Indians. He refutes longstanding claims that the Pequots posed a serious threat to the Puritans and their Indian allies.[47] Virginia DeJohn Anderson sheds new light on the coming of New England's later war, King Philip's (1675-76). She argues that conflicts between Indians and colonists over a growing livestock population, conflicts rooted in part in different cultural attitudes about domestic animals, contributed to "innumerable occasions for friction, tested the limits of cooperation — and led, in the end, to war."[48] Michael Puglisi's *Puritans Besieged* examines the troublesome consequences of that war for Englishmen and natives alike.[49] The acculturation of "Praying Indians" is the focus of studies by Dane Morrison and Harold Van Lonkhuyzen. Although telling somewhat different stories, both attempt to explain changes in native identity based on more knowledge about various

---

United States in the Sixteenth Through Eighteenth Centuries, Contributions to Public Archeology (Norman, Okla.: University of Oklahoma Press, 1996).

46. Charles L. Cohen, "Conversion Among Puritans and Amerindians: A Theological and Cultural Perspective," in *Puritanism: Transatlantic Perspectives on a Seventeenth-Century Anglo-American Faith,* ed. Francis J. Bremer (Boston: Massachusetts Historical Society, 1993), 233-56.

47. Alfred Cave, *The Pequot War* (Amherst, Mass.: University of Massachusetts Press, 1996).

48. Virginia DeJohn Anderson, "King Philip's Herds: Indians, Colonists, and the Problem of Livestock in Early New England," *William and Mary Quarterly,* 3d Scr., 51 (1994): 601-24.

49. Michael Puglisi, *Puritans Besieged: The Legacies of King Philip's War in the Massachusetts Bay Colony* (Lanham, Md.: University Press of America, 1991).

aspects of Massachusett culture including uses of space, rituals, material culture, religious authorities, and economic organization.[50]

These few examples hint at the range of recent work on Puritan-Indian relations.[51] Scattered throughout are suggestions concerning how the encounter with the Indian other shaped the Puritan self.[52] Influenced by Slotkin, the emerging story, in brief, goes something like this. Puritan migrants came to the New World determined not to have their identity changed by their new surroundings. They "worried that conquering the American wilderness and coming into contact with American Indians would alter . . . [their] English culture and their sense of themselves as English people." As they interacted with Native Americans, Puritans "defined themselves in opposition to Indians." What Indians were, they were not. What was deemed Indian savagism thus clarified for Puritans what it meant to be civilized. Meanwhile, Indian defeats, depopulation, and displacement clarified for Puritans what it meant to be divinely

50. Dane Morrison, *A Praying People: Massachusett Acculturation and the Failure of the Puritan Mission, 1600-1690* (New York: Peter Lang, 1995); Harold W. Van Lonkhuyzen, "A Reappraisal of the Praying Indians: Acculturation, Conversion, and Identity at Natick, Massachusetts, 1646-1730," *New England Quarterly* 63 (1990): 396-428.

51. Other topics recently reexamined include Indians and Puritan law (see Yasuhide Kawashima, *Puritan Justice and the Indian: White Man's Law in Massachusetts, 1630-1763* [Middletown, Conn.: Wesleyan University Press, 1986]), and the career of John Eliot (see Richard Cogley, "John Eliot in Recent Scholarship," *American Indian Culture and Research Journal* 14 (1990): 77-92.

52. My summary here of the scholarship on how contact with Indians shaped the Puritan self is based on the works cited in notes 48 through 51, and Roy Harvey Pearce, "'The Ruines of Mankind': The Indian and the Puritan Mind," *Journal of the History of Ideas* 13 (1952): 200-217; Slotkin, *Regeneration Through Violence*, 54-56, 77-93, 97-115; G. E. Thomas, "Puritans, Indians, and the Concept of Race," *New England Quarterly* 48 (1975): 3-27; Charles Segal and David Stineback, eds., *Puritans, Indians, & Manifest Destiny* (New York: Putnam, 1977); Richard Slotkin and James K. Folsom, *So Dreadfull A Judgment: Puritan Responses to King Philip's War, 1676-1677* (Middletown, Conn.: Wesleyan University Press, 1978), 35-37, 61-75, 265-66; James Axtell, *The European and the Indian: Essays in the Ethnology of Colonial North America* (New York: Oxford University Press, 1981), 302-9; William S. Simmons, "Cultural Bias in the New England Puritans' Perceptions of Indians," *William and Mary Quarterly*, 3d Ser., 38 (1981): 56-72; Dennis L. Cerrotti, "The Negative Myth of the Other: Puritan and Indian Relations in Colonial New England" (D. Min. diss., Andover Newton Theological School, 1995); Calloway, *New Worlds for All*.

chosen. Still, second and third generation Puritans had occasions for self-doubt when God used natives (of all people) as the instruments of divine judgment upon them. And plenty of fears could still be aroused among late seventeenth-century Puritans about being "Indianized." Indian captives were naturally in the most precarious position; their redemption was crucial for reaffirming the superiority of Puritan ways and symbolizing the larger redemption of Puritanism from the snares of the alien environment and its demonic inhabitants. In the end, most Puritans "did not become Indians, but they did become something other than what they, or their ancestors, had been."[53]

Finding that contact with Indians (and other "others") made differences in who Puritans thought they were and how they behaved should not surprise us. Nor would it have surprised many Puritans. After all, as one historian has put it, "their very efforts not to change indicated that they sensed the pressures to change."[54] What may surprise us is that it has taken so long for historians to change enough to see those differences.

American Puritan studies may no longer have the prominence within the discipline it once held when Perry Miller was in his prime or even when a younger generation of social historians shifted attention to New England towns and communities.[55] Yet the work of the last decade indicates that furnished with new theoretical frameworks, a more interdisciplinary and transatlantic approach, and a willingness to reexamine texts closely, historians and other scholars are still capable of producing rich new studies of those perhaps overstudied folks known as Puritans. Much of the best of that work, it seems to me, concerns matters of the self and matters of otherness. As noted above, in moving in that direction, Puritan studies both reflect and contribute to broader scholarly fascinations, which are themselves reflections of a culture caught up with questions of identity and difference.

53. The quotes in this paragraph are taken from Calloway, *New Worlds for All,* 7, 196-97. More radical claims for a certain type of Puritan "Indianization" are put forward in John Canup, *Out of the Wilderness: The Emergence of an American Identity in Colonial New England* (Middletown, Conn.: Wesleyan University Press, 1990).

54. Calloway, *New Worlds for All,* 196.

55. Charles L. Cohen, "The Post-Puritan Paradigm of Early American Religious History," *William and Mary Quarterly,* 3d Ser., 54 (1997): 695-722.

Those questions seem especially ripe for and demanding of Christian scholarly attention, whether asked by seventeenth-century Englishmen or contemporary Americans. For that reason I find much to applaud in recent assessments of Puritanism. For example, by investigating more fully how Puritans considered and interacted with those outside their circle, historians provide a picture of early New England that comes closer to doing justice to all participants in the story. Moreover, by recognizing the nature of the injustices and the reasons for the tragedies that often characterized those relations, we get strong reminders of humanity's fallen condition. But it was not all darkness. Alongside the conflict and death stood native resourcefulness and Puritan adaptability, friendships made and kept, souls touched and changed. By occasionally highlighting these redemptive elements in colonial New England's history, recent accounts have moved collectively nearer to achieving some kind of balance in descriptions of Puritan encounters with the other.

Scholarly concern about otherness is itself a welcome development. Insight in this case into why Puritans usually found it so difficult to affirm the other as another self created in God's image and therefore worthy of respect rather than vilification, is telling for what it reveals not only about Puritans but also about a longer-lasting legacy of religious, racial, and ethnic antipathy. On the other hand, the theoretical models informing current discussions of otherness (and, for that matter, the self) include assumptions that seem problematic. At the very least, they deserve careful Christian consideration. What, for instance, should be made of the prevailing presumption, derived from anthropologist Clifford Geertz, that "there is no such thing as a human nature independent of culture"? Is the self merely the invention or construction of a particular set of social or cultural constraints, the by-product of "control mechanisms . . . for the governing of behavior"?[56] Was who a Puritan could be (or who I am) so severely limited by these control mechanisms (culture) as to make any claims for or sense of self-determination fictive? And were Puritans so bound to identify some kind of other as alien for the sake of knowing and protecting themselves, that they had no choice but

---

56. As quoted in Greenblatt, *Renaissance Self-Fashioning,* 3; Clifford Geertz, "'From the Native's Point of View': On the Nature of Anthropological Understanding," in *Culture Theory: Essays on Mind, Self, and Emotion,* ed. Richard A. Shweder and Robert A. Levine (Cambridge: Cambridge University Press, 1984), 123-36.

to castigate Indians as savages, Antinomians as heretics, marginal women as witches, and Quakers as madmen?

The suspicions about human freedom implicit in the regnant Geertzian model are matched by growing suspicions about any kind of overarching Puritan metanarrative. Clearly, many historians remain convinced that it is possible and legitimate to speak of *Puritanism.* Even among them, however, there is strong emphasis on the evolving and plural character of the movement. Meanwhile, other scholars seem increasingly persuaded that while there may have been Puritan selves, there was no Puritan self. Some would even prefer to give up use of the term altogether, believing that it confuses more than it clarifies. Would greater use of the label Puritans applied to themselves, "the godly," ease any of the definitional difficulties related to these English Protestants? More important, would loss of any sense of "Puritan" beyond what applies to a particular individual be just that, a loss? Does focus on Puritan personal identity inherently push us toward too individualistic a view of what was fundamentally a communal enterprise? Should Christian scholars be suspicious of suspicions that there are no metanarratives in history, Puritan or otherwise?

Hope for resolving such thorny issues is offered in the very works under examination here. Greater awareness of, and openness to, the insights of scholars from a wide array of disciplines promises to supply historians with a steady stream of alternative ways of understanding how selves are defined. Some of them may prove to be more complementary to Christian conceptions of the self. Meanwhile, increased recognition of the need to see American Puritans in transatlantic perspective has generally inclined scholarship toward more holistic and less individualistic (and less exceptionalist) interpretations, thereby counterbalancing some of the trends noted above. The confidence in language highlighted by David Hall ten years ago has persisted, suggesting that close scrutiny of texts may still yield new insights. So, too, has the interest in Puritan spirituality. The willingness to take seriously and on their own terms the religious experiences and expressions of all Puritans — clergy and laity, men and women, English and Native American — is as bright a sign as any that understanding of who Puritans thought they were and what they were about will move forward.

On the other hand, since historians seem as convinced as Aristotle that "it is nobler to write tragedy than comedy," it is probably important not to conclude on too hopeful a note about the future of Puritan studies.[57] Perhaps it is sufficient to say that we, too, see through a glass darkly, whether looking at Puritans or ourselves. For as Puritan minister John Cotton put it in 1637, "our native corruptions and selves we still carry about with us."[58]

57. I have borrowed this thought and line from Foster, *The Long Argument*, 311.
58. John Cotton to John Dodd, 19 December 1637, in Everett Emerson, ed., *Letters from New England: The Massachusetts Bay Colony, 1629-1638* (Amherst, Mass.: University of Massachusetts Press, 1976), 217.

The Little White Church:
Historiographical Revisions
about Religion in Rural America

ROBERT P. SWIERENGA

In Garrison Keillor's Lake Wobegon, the Lutheran church and Our Lady of Perpetual Responsibility Catholic church grace the center of the community, overshadowing the other venerable institutions in town — the Chatterbox Cafe, Ralph's Grocery, Sidetrack Tap, and school-house.[1] The proverbial little white church and little red schoolhouse defined rural America. Spires marked the horizon in church villages, and schools with their bell towers dotted country lanes. The preacher and the schoolmaster worked hand in hand. The church instructed adults in their religious obligations, and the school indoctrinated the children.

Schools far outnumbered churches in the countryside, but churches had more staying power.[2] Schools stand abandoned while many churches still thrive, despite the conclusion of the Country Life Commission in 1908 that rural churches were an anachronism that "deserve extinction."[3]

1. Garrison Keillor, *Lake Wobegon Days* (New York: Viking, 1985).
2. Wayne E. Fuller, *The Old Country School: The Story of Rural Education in the Middle West* (Chicago: University of Chicago Press, 1982).
3. Benson Y. Landis, *Rural Church Life in the Middle West as Illustrated by Clay*

This chapter is adapted from my 1997 presidential address to the Agricultural History Society, which was published in *Agricultural History* 71 (Fall 1997), and is used here with permission. I am indebted to Janel Curry-Roper, Brian Beltman, and Jay Green for helping me sharpen the focus of this essay.

Rural churches outlasted the Grange, Old Settler's societies, the Odd Fellow's, Ladies' Aid societies, and other voluntary clubs of all kinds. Indeed, the importance of the rural church has grown over time, rather than diminished in its influence.

The tolling of the church bell each Sunday morning set the pattern of the week for most believers and nonbelievers alike—six days labor and one day rest. Only in the critical days of planting and harvesting did some farmers take to the fields on Sunday. In a world where leisure was a luxury, Sunday activities provided a welcome break from the week's work. Reserved as a day of rest and relaxation, a "foretaste of Heaven," as believers phrased it, the Christian Sabbath provided time for worship, family visits, community picnics, and music. "No one need talk to me of 'Puritan' Sundays—long and tedious treaded," wrote Katherine Elspeth Oliver. "We 'kept' Sunday. It was full of delightfully 'different' things . . .—the long drive to 'town,' church and Sunday school and a picnic lunch eaten in the wagon on the way home." North Dakotan Russell Duncan recalled in his youth not wanting "to miss church even though many times we had to walk the two and a half miles to our church."[4] Countless rural folk offer similar testimonies to the vital place of the church in their lives.[5]

County, Iowa and Jennings County, Indiana with Comparative Data from Studies of Thirty-five Middle Western Counties (New York, 1922), 53; James H. Madison, "Reformers and the Rural Church, 1900-1950," Journal of American History 73 (Dec. 1986): 645-68; Merwin Swanson, "The 'Country Life Movement' and the American Churches," Church History 46 (Sept. 1977): 358-73.

4. Joanna L. Stratton, Pioneer Women: Voices from the Kansas Frontier (New York: Simon and Schuster, 1981), 183; Russell Duncan, I Remember, second ed. (privately printed, 1978), 116, 119.

5. Dave Wood, ed., Wisconsin Prairie Diary, 1869-1879 (Whitehall, WI, 1978), cited in June Marie Pederson, Between Memory and Reality: Family and Community in Rural Wisconsin, 1870-1970 (Madison: University of Wisconsin Press, 1992), 117; Diary of Benjamin F. Gue in Rural New York and Pioneer Iowa, 1847-1856, ed. Earle D. Ross (Ames: Iowa State University Press, 1962), 12-13, 34-35; Mary Neth, Preserving the Family Farm: Women, Community, and the Foundations of Agribusiness in the Midwest, 1900-1940 (Baltimore: Johns Hopkins University Press, 1995), 53-54, 68-69; Brian W. Beltman, Dutch Farmer in the Missouri Valley: Life and Letters of Ulbe Eringa, 1866-1950 (Urbana: University of Illinois Press, 1996), 78-79, 198-99; Harvey M. Sletten, Growing Up on Bald Hill Creek (Ames: Iowa State University Press, 1977), 11-17; Alfred C. Nielsen, Life in an American Denmark (New York: Arno Press, 1979), 25-32, 85-89; Clarence A. Andrews, Growing Up in Iowa: Reminiscences of Fourteen Iowa Authors (Ames: Iowa State University Press, 1978).

The church was more than a religious meeting place; it was a cultural nest, integrating families, social classes, and nationality groups. It gave members a cultural identity and status and socialized them into the community.[6] "As forces of order," said John Mack Faragher, "churches reinforced the basic cultural assumptions, guiding tender consciences and influencing personal behavior at home and at work."[7] The reach of rural churches was remarkable. They provided charity and aid in times of sickness and disaster, educated children, offered recreation and leisure activities, facilitated marriages, consoled the grieving and buried the dead in the adjacent cemetery, and sought to legislate morality through political action. Rural life truly was church-centered.[8]

In the immigrant communities that dotted the Midwest, churches actually built communities by attracting newcomers, drawing them together in a protective cocoon, and providing a feeling of security, a "community of feeling."[9] Churches were the "strongest institution" in town; they "acted as centers of family and community rituals and sociability," and were vitally important in the retention of European cultural identity. Not to be a part of it meant to cut oneself off from family and community.[10] In the German Lutheran community of Block, Kansas, for example, Carol Coburn found that the church and school "functioned as the hub around which the entire community lived and worked"; the church trained "young and old in how to think and how to live." Ronald Jager recalled that "families, churches, and denominations were the rel-

6. Louis Bultena, "Rural Churches and Community Integration," *Rural Sociology* 9 (Sept. 1944): 257-64; Sonya Salamon, *Prairie Patrimony: Family, Farming, & Community in the Midwest* (Chapel Hill: University of North Carolina Press, 1992), 47; Barbara Jane Dilly, "A Comparative Study of Religious Resistance to Erosion of the Soil and the Soul Among Three Farming Communities in Northeast Iowa" (Ph.D. diss., University of California, Irvine, 1994), 187.

7. John Mack Faragher, *Sugar Creek: Life on the Illinois Prairie* (New Haven: Yale University Press, 1986), 168.

8. Michael Winter, "The Sociology of Religion and Rural Sociology: A Review Article," *Sociologia Ruralis* 31 (1991): 205-6.

9. Faragher, *Sugar Creek,* 170.

10. Pederson, *Between Memory and Reality,* 125, 129-38; George M. Stephenson, *The Religious Aspects of Swedish Immigration: A Study in Immigrant Churches* (Minneapolis: 1932), 407-8; Deborah Fink, *Open Country, Iowa: Rural Women, Traditions, and Change* (Albany: State University of New York Press, 1986), 92; Robert C. Ostergren, "The Immigrant Church as a Symbol of Community and Place on the Landscape of the American Upper Midwest," *Great Plains Quarterly* 1 (Fall 1981): 224-38.

evant units of social accounting" in his Dutch immigrant community of six hundred families in Michigan's cutover lands.[11]

That rural folk and modern scholars alike repeatedly speak of the centering influence of the rural church suggests that churches likely had an impact on farming behavior as well as on the farm family. In the 1950s Lee Benson showed that voting, at least in the nineteenth century, was an expression of the deepest values and beliefs of the electorate concerning what constituted the good society. With this insight about the meaning of voting, the ethnocultural historians swept the field of political history with their behavioral studies of religiously-based voting patterns.[12]

If religion explained voting patterns, it may also explain farming behavior. One can substitute for the question "what is voting?" the question "what is farming?" Farming is a business enterprise, of course, but it is also a way of life, a "calling," an expression of ultimate commitments. As the farm family carries on its daily tasks, the members put flesh on their deepest beliefs and values. Farming, in this sense, is an act of faith, and to farm is to practice one's religion as much as is gathering for Sunday worship. Decisions about cropping, fertilization, animal husbandry, and land inheritance, all reflect, consciously or unconsciously, the beliefs or "worldview" farmers hold dear.[13]

Although political historians now accept religion as a key variable in voting studies, agricultural historians, rural geographers, and rural sociologists have largely ignored it. This is remarkable because the Weberian school of social science taught that religion is a primary force shaping behavior which drives all institutional change. A perusal of the pages of *Agricultural History*, which aims to embrace all aspects of rural life, reveals a general neglect of religion. In the annual indexes from volume one in 1927 to the present, I found only one entry under "church" and none under "religion." Agricultural historians have overlooked the

11. Carol K. Coburn, *Life at Four Corners: Religion, Gender, and Education in a German-Lutheran Community, 1868-1945* (Lawrence: University Press of Kansas, 1992), 152-53; Ronald Jager, *Eighty Acres: Elegy for a Family Farm* (Boston: Beacon Press, 1990).

12. Robert P. Swierenga, "Ethnoreligious Political Behavior in the Mid-Nineteenth Century: Voting, Values, and Cultures," in Mark A. Noll, ed., *Religion and American Politics: From the Colonial Period to the 1980s* (New York: Oxford University Press, 1990), 146-71.

13. Wuthnow defined worldview as "all the *beliefs* that an individual holds about the nature of reality," in "Two Traditions in the Study of Religion," *Journal for the Scientific Study of Religion* 20 (March 1981): 24.

steeples in favor of the grain elevators. Michael Winter, director of the Centre for Rural Studies at the Royal Agricultural College in Gloucestershire, rightfully concluded in a 1991 review article that "those whose interests are rural, or rather agricultural, rarely consider religion to have anything important to contribute to their understanding."[14]

Agricultural historians and geographers have made nativity rather than religion the dependent variable. The progression of research studies since the 1960s by Allan Bogue, Terry Jordan, Robert Ostergren, and more recently Sonya Salamon, among others, compared cropping and livestock patterns of native-born and immigrant farmers. Early studies generally concluded that farmers, whether immigrant or native-born, readily adapted to the environment and only minor or very subtle differences set groups apart. More recent work has focused on cultural islands and the results, not surprisingly, have highlighted the contrasts between entrepreneurial Yankees and communal European peasants. Yankees ran large grain farms as a business and were mobile geographically and economically; peasants practiced diversified agriculture on smaller holdings and emphasized continuity. Keeping the farm in the family and preserving the community were more important than short-term profit maximization. Europeans valued local control, cooperation, sustainability, and communal life; Yankees were capitalists who commodified resources and prized self-interest.[15]

These studies are seminal because they provide the first solid data on ethnocultural patterns in farming. But the research has several limitations. Most studies used nationality cohorts without accounting for local and regional differences in Europe, where lifestyles and even languages varied within a small geographic area. The pioneering work also slighted the importance of religious group differences, because the federal censuses never reported religion or denominational affiliation. Thousands of church-centered, ethnic colonies in rural America were culture islands that preserved native languages and traditions for several

14. Winter, "Sociology of Religion and Rural Sociology," 202.
15. For Bogue, Jordan, and Ostergren, see Robert P. Swierenga, "Ethnicity and American Agriculture," *Ohio History* 89 (Summer 1980): 323-44; Salamon, *Prairie Patrimony,* 15-23, 93, 253-55; Gary Foster, Richard Hummel, and Robert Whittenburger, "Ethnic Echoes Through 100 Years of Midwestern Agriculture," *Rural Sociology* 52 (Fall 1987): 365-78; Jan L. Flora and John M. Stitz, "Ethnicity, Persistence, and Capitalization of Agriculture in the Great Plains during the Settlement Period: Wheat Production and Risk Avoidance," *Rural Sociology* 50 (Fall 1985): 341-60.

generations. These cohesive enclaves differed greatly from settlements composed of a mixture of mainline "church" groups, even if all were Protestant.[16]

Agricultural historians must find ways to include religious beliefs as a basis for explaining the contrasts among some of these cultural islands, and between them and the so-called mainstream. Religious values may have shaped farm behavior and the construction of rurality. Salamon hinted at that line of research by acknowledging that religion undergirded ethnic culture and that culture matters in the "making of economic and social trends." Yet her anthropological orientation and socioeconomic assumptions limited her vision. She left the door ajar but unopened.[17]

Historical geographers have opened that door and discovered that religious values affect behavior on the farm more than does ethnicity or other socioeconomic variables. James Lemon, John Rice, and Aidan McQuillan broke the ethnic mold in the 1970s and first introduced religion as a variable. Lemon showed that the sectarian "plain folk" of southeastern Pennsylvania — the Mennonites, Friends, "Dunkers," and Moravians — resided in tighter clusters, farmed more intensively, owned the most valuable land, and were less transient than their neighbors of other denominational roots — Lutherans, Reformed, Anglican, and Presbyterians. In this relatively homogeneous agricultural region, significant differences in farming behavior derived from religious rather than ethnic origins.[18]

In a study of Kandiyohi County, Minnesota, Rice found that Norwegian, Swedish, Irish, and native-born farmers were similar in their cropping patterns, livestock holdings, persistence rates, and economic status. But one community of conservative Swedish Lutherans, transplanted en masse from the village of Gagnef in Dalarna province, stood out as unique. They were the most stable and economically prosperous, and advanced from the poorest of the Swedish settlements to the wealthiest. Thus, the experience of the church-centered Gagnef group differed

16. Terry Jordan, "A Religious Geography of Hill Country Germans of Texas," 109-28, esp. 116, in Frederick C. Luebke, *Ethnicity on the Great Plains* (Lincoln: University of Nebraska Press, 1980).

17. Salamon, *Prairie Patrimony*, 255, 257, 57-90.

18. James T. Lemon, *The Best Poor Man's Country: A Geographical Study of Early Southeastern Pennsylvania* (Baltimore: Johns Hopkins University Press, 1976).

markedly from the neighboring immigrant settlements, even those of other Scandinavians.[19]

McQuillan specifically considered the role of religious values in the cultural adaption process among Swedish Lutheran, German Mennonite, and French-Canadian Catholic immigrant farmers in the more arid region of central Kansas. The Swedes' "deep pietistic faith helped them to persevere in Kansas. . . . The rough labor that was required to convert prairie sod into bountiful farmland could be turned to spiritual advantage if it was accepted as a means of self-discipline to check one's emotions." Swedish pastors rode tight herd on the moral behavior of parishioners, reining in drunkenness, unchastity, cursing, and card playing, and insisting that Sunday was a day for worship not pleasure. Despite their piety, the individualistic Swedes acculturated most rapidly.[20]

The equally pious but communal Mennonites maintained their identity the longest. Among them "religious values permeated every aspect of their daily life, emphasizing the importance of frugal consumption, hard work, perseverance, and a cheerful acceptance of stinging environmental setbacks as the will of God." Thus, they withstood drought, fires, and grasshoppers better than others because of their strong faith-based community. They also obtained the best farmland, farmed it intensively, built the largest territorial base, and were the greatest innovators in farming. McQuillan concluded that the communal group, the Mennonites, coped more successfully with the physiographic challenges of prairie agriculture than did the individualistic Swedes and French-Canadians.[21]

Historians Royden Loewen and June Pederson built on the foundation of the geographers to relate religious values to rurality. In a fine-grained analysis of Mennonite communities in Manitoba and Nebraska, Royden, a descendent of the Manitoba clan, compared three generations over eighty years. Their conservative lifestyle, he found, was rooted in religious tenets carried over from ancestral Anabaptist practices of nonresistance, simplicity, separation from the world, and strict church discipline. The church congregation, Loewen explained, "ordered the public sphere . . . [and] encouraged a deep piety, articulated life's mean-

19. John Rice, "The Role of Culture and Community in Frontier Prairie Farming," *Journal of Historical Geography* 3 (1977): 155-75.

20. D. Aidan McQuillan, *Prevailing Over Time: Ethnic Adjustment on the Kansas Prairies, 1875-1925* (Lincoln: University of Nebraska Press, 1990), 51, 59.

21. Ibid., 64, 39, 41-42, 69-70, 193-99.

ing, defined community, undergirded social hierarchies, and specified the social boundaries." While Mennonites did not withdraw from the world, religious beliefs tempered their involvement in the marketplace and, reciprocally, the market shaped their ideology.[22]

The Norwegian Lutherans of Trempealeau County, noted Pederson, brought from the homeland a work ethic that went well beyond the traditional peasant view of "a man's got to work." Their tough strain of Lutheranism, which had been refined in the spiritual "awakenings" in Norway, made work "a sacred calling—a means of worshiping God," which for at least three generations governed their understanding of farming. Work "defined life's purpose, measured character, and was the essence of one's identity."[23]

This research shows that for some culture islands, community-wide ideological patterns keyed to religious values affected farming practices, capitalization and commercialization of farm enterprises, risk-reduction strategies, and land inheritance customs. Particular communities shared common lifestyles, ranging from communitarian, like the Mennonites and Mormons at one extreme, to individualistic, like the Yankees and German Reformed at the other extreme.[24]

The common ideology or worldview, what farmers think and believe, is derived in turn from their shared religious traditions. Clark Roof and Robert Wuthnow have argued that such worldviews, forged by interactions among family and friends, are usually taken for granted within communities, which makes them all the more powerful, because they do not require frequent articulation.[25]

Given the strength of the shared beliefs, it is likely that they affected agricultural behavior. The more individualistic the orientation, the more capitalistic and commercial the agriculture. Conversely, the more communitarian the worldview, the more likely a farming community will

22. Royden K. Loewen, *Family, Church, and Market: A Mennonite Community in the Old and New World* (Urbana: University of Illinois Press, 1993), 4.

23. Pederson, *Between Memory and Reality*, 143, 147.

24. Michael E. Sobel broadened the Weberian concept of lifestyle to include "a set of expressive, observable behaviors reflecting values and attitudes." This is the way I use the term. See Emily H. Schroeder, Frederick C. Fliegel, and J. C. van Es, "Measurement of Lifestyle Dimensions of Farming for Small-Scale Farmers," *Rural Sociology* 50 (Fall 1985): 309.

25. Clark Roof, *Community and Commitment* (New York, 1978), cited in Wuthnow, "Two Traditions in the Study of Religion," 28.

practice sustainable agriculture. In societies grounded in cooperative action, according to the "community of goods" principle, individuals are constrained by the formal rules of the community but also by the informal discipline of social control. In communal colonies, particularly, religious beliefs permeate every aspect of daily life, from work routines and uses of farm machinery to modes of travel. Farming is valued above all other work because of the creation mandate to Adam to till the ground and keep it. Even the inward facing of buildings, laager style, in Hutterite communities is patterned after the order and harmony that God imparted to the universe.[26]

Most of the ethnic historians and geographers to some degree have recognized the religious basis of the various farming communities they studied, and they repeatedly noted the piety of communal groups. But was it social values or religious beliefs, or both, that explained the behavioral differences? If religion and its cultural trappings, and not ethnicity per se, determined farming behavior among these various groups, then scholars face the task of explaining the mechanism of that behavior. Thus far, none have developed a comprehensive theoretical framework to explain the behaviors they observed.

Field research by geographers and sociologists is beginning to explore the religious dimension of agriculture and land use. An early example is Anne Van den Ban's 1960 article in *Rural Sociology*, based on data drawn from a cluster-sample of the Wisconsin Farm and Home Development Study. Van den Ban compared readiness to adopt new farm practices in a Dutch Reformed township (Alto in Fond du Lac County) and a Norwegian and German Lutheran township (Deerfield in Dane County), and found that the Reformed were slower to innovate than the Lutherans. After ruling out individual socioeconomic characteristics such as education, farm size, or net worth, the author considered direct religious influences that might be at work.[27]

26. Dorothy Schweider, "Agrarian Stability in Utopian Societies: A Comparison of Economic Practices of Old Order Amish and Hutterites," in *Patterns and Perspectives in Iowa History*, ed. Dorothy Schweider (Ames: Iowa State University Press, 1973), 431-53, esp. 436 and 441; John W. Bennett, *Northern Plainsmen: Adaptive Strategy and Agrarian Life* (Chicago: Aldine Publishing, 1969), 246-75; Victor Stoltzfus, "Amish Agricultural: Adaptive Strategies for Economic Survival of Community Life," *Rural Sociology* 38 (Summer 1973): 196-206.

27. Anne Willem Van den Ban, "Locality Group Differences in the Adoption of New Farm Practices," *Rural Sociology* 25 (Sept. 1960): 308-20.

Both Calvinists and Lutherans believe that God created and sustains the earth and assigned Adam and his descendants as caretakers of it, but Calvinist preachers emphasized more that God would hold farmers accountable to him on the Judgment Day for their stewardship. Thus, Calvinists view their farming as a religious task while Lutheran farmers "see no clear connection between their religion and their way of farming."[28] This very limited case study raised religious beliefs to the forefront, but the author backed away from a serious study of Calvinist and Lutheran theologies that might explain the contrasting farm behaviors.

Rural sociologist Ingolf Vogeler similarly found in a study of Wisconsin farmland transfers in the years 1950 to 1975 that ethnicity and religion were highly correlated, especially in intra-family transfers, and religion was a stronger variable than ethnicity. In Trempealeau County, where Polish Catholics dominated, three-quarters of the land transfers passed within the family, as did nearly one-half of the farms in the Norwegian Lutheran-dominated county of Pierce. That Catholics sold farms to their "own kind" more than did Lutherans is a tantalizing finding, but Vogeler made no attempt to explore possible theological explanations for the contrasting behaviors.[29]

A more ambitious attempt to include religion as a variable in analyzing sustainable farming practices is that of Barbara Dilly in her 1994 dissertation at the University of California, Irvine, but she too failed to work out the theological underpinnings of the behavior. Dilly's mentor, Joseph Jorgensen, director of the Program in Comparative Culture and a student of American Indian religion, had argued in 1984 that religion determines land use because "land is cultural." Following Jorgensen's lead, Dilly examined the role of religious doctrines and values in farming behavior, choosing as her subjects the Old Order Amish, Mennonite Brethren, and Evangelical Lutheran communities in northeast Iowa near Prairie City. These German Protestant subcultures practice diversified grain/livestock farming using methods that nurture the soil, treat animals humanely, minimize waste, and produce wholesome foods.[30]

28. Van den Ban, "Locality Group Differences," 312, 315.

29. Ingolf Vogeler, "Ethnicity, Religion, and Farm Land Transfers in Western Wisconsin," *Ecumene* 7 (1975): 6-13, esp. 11.

30. Dilly, "Religious Resistance"; Joseph G. Jorgensen, "Land is Cultural, so is a Commodity: The Locus of Differences among Indians, Cowboys, Sod-busters, and Environmentalists," *Journal of Ethnic Studies* 12 (May 1984): 1-21.

The explanation for this responsible behavior, Dilly claims, is that these farmers hold to a "sacred ecology of the soil and the soul . . . [that] incorporates soil, plant, and animal life" in a symbiotic relationship between the land and the community. Religious ideology is the lens, she states, that informs their conceptions of technology, economics, politics, and education. They are motivated by a "Christian ideology of steward-ship that places a spiritual value on land, labor, and capital." In their various ways each ties economic security to the "productive capacity of the soil, . . . and seeks profit in terms of individual peace of mind, [and] intimate affinal and kinship relations."[31]

To test her theory that "religion is a dynamic force . . . in agricul-tural sustainability," Dilly interviewed seventy-five families on fifty-one farms and assembled current data on the scale of their farm operations, acreages owned and rented, crops, tillage methods, livestock operations, and wage labor patterns. She analyzed the data by correlating the vari-ables of ethnicity, age, education, and livestock mixes.[32]

Despite their common Christianity, the German-American groups in Dilly's study differ in the rate of adoption of new techniques. The Old Order Amish, as extreme separatists, resist technological changes that erode their way of life, while the Mennonite Brethren, who assimi-lated quickly, embraced scientific advances even as they try to resist its corrosive effects on family and church life. The very ethnic Evangelical Lutherans, as "stubborn old Germans," reluctantly adopt technology and seek to insulate themselves from rapid social change. Other differences show up in land ownership and inheritance practices. Amish families hold land in joint tenancy, Brethren prefer family corporations, and Lutherans create formal father and son holdings. Amish parents help all their children get on the land, but the Brethren and Lutherans designate one child to keep the farm intact in the next generation.[33]

In farming and livestock practices, the Amish retain a traditional multiple-crop rotation and have fewer hogs, dairy, and feeder cattle. Brethren generally rotate between corn and soybeans, are more willing to contour plow and retain pasture that Lutherans plow under. Brethren raise large numbers of cattle, hogs, and dairy. Lutherans follow a tight corn and soybean rotation with livestock specialization, but do no dairy-

31. Dilly, "Religious Resistance," 1-5.
32. Ibid., 25, 222-30.
33. Ibid., 4-5, 25-26, 134-35, 156, 171.

ing. Only Brethren use hired help; but Lutherans and Brethren exchange work within family and among immediate neighbors while the Amish exchange within the whole church community. Amish and Lutherans are most averse to risk.[34]

These findings raise many intriguing questions: why do Lutheran farmers cultivate to the fencerows and Brethren retain pasture land? Or why are Brethren more willing to take risks than Amish or Lutherans? The broader question is why these groups, which are defined by a common religion and nationality, and who live in the same area, behave so differently on the land? From the outset Dilly insists that religion is a better predictor of farm behavior than ethnic background, and she specifically rejects Salamon's opposing view that ethnicity explains more than religion.

Dilly's thesis is based on the Augustinian idea of the two kingdoms, the kingdom of God and the kingdom of man, which have existed side by side since the dawn of human history in perpetual tension. Some Christians are very aware of this antithesis and try to live within the kingdom of the godly, while others plant their feet in both realms and attempt to synthesize them. Dilly aligns the three communal groups in her study along a continuum from dualists to synthesists. The Amish as radical dualists value separation from the world and its materialism; they "connect all that they do" to their religious ethos. The Brethren, at the other extreme, synthesize the two kingdoms. This allows them, and to a lesser extent the Lutherans — who maintain a tension between synthesis and dualism — to live comfortably in both worlds by minimizing the antithesis between believers and nonbelievers. Logically, therefore, the Amish place the highest value on community solidarity and preservation of traditions, followed by Brethren and Lutherans. Conversely, the Brethren are most open to technological modernization, Lutherans are less so, and the Amish lag far behind.[35]

The role of religion in Dilly's two-kingdom construct is that of a brake rather than a steering wheel.[36] The theology of dualism slams the brakes on progress, while the "worn-out" brakes of synthesis allow one quite easily to slide into modernity. Her dualism-synthesis scale may

---

34. Ibid., 139-66.
35. Ibid., 156, 25-26, 177-84; Salamon, *Prairie Patrimony*, 32-33.
36. Dilly, "Religious Resistance," 187, borrows the brake metaphor from Guy Swanson, *Religion and Regime* (Ann Arbor: University of Michigan Press, 1967).

explain Amish behavior, but it is not as helpful for understanding Lutherans and Brethren, let alone Calvinists or other Protestant groups. The main problem with Dilly's study is that in her interviews she collected data on farm practices but not on religious values; she then inferred how religious beliefs of the group as a whole might have impacted on their farm behavior. Even though the religious teachings of these groups are well documented, Dilly may have assumed too much.

Another innovative study of the intersection of religion and agriculture is that of Janel Curry-Roper, a rural geographer at Calvin College, who has measured directly the place of religious values in farming behavior.[37] Curry-Roper theorizes that "distinct worldviews exist that are grounded in common, theologically identifiable religious belief systems and [are] associated, in turn, with specific cultural traditions." Such discernable differences ought to be evident on the land, she assumed, just as William Cronin, in his study of early New England, found relationships between communal orientation, property rights, and perceptions of the environment. Curry-Roper constructed a community scale that ranked groups according to their conceptualization of society from individualistic to communal, based on answers to the questions: "How do I think of myself? Do I think of myself as an autonomous, independent person, or do I see myself principally as part of a network of human relationships?"[38]

The scale had five points: on one end, (1) individualistic and utilitarian, and (2) individualistic and non-utilitarian; at the other end, (4) communal and non-utilitarian, and (5) communal and utilitarian. In the middle (3) stood groups that were neither individualistic nor communal. Curry-Roper hypothesized that where each community lies on the scale is a predictor of other value decisions concerning the relation-

37. Janel Curry-Roper, "Trust and the Social Construction of Reality," unpublished paper, 1997; "Worldview and Agriculture: A Study of Two Reformed Communities in Iowa," in *Signs of Vitality in Reformed Communities,* ed. Donald Luidens, Corwin Smidt, and Heijme Stoffels (Lanham, MD: University Press of America, forthcoming); and "Community-Level Worldviews and the Sustainability of Agriculture," in *Agricultural Restructuring and Sustainability: A Geographical Perspective,* ed. Brian Ilbery, Quentin Chiotti, and Timothy Rickard (Wallingford, UK: CAB International, 1997), 102-15.

38. Curry-Roper, "Trust and the Social Construction of Reality," 14-15; William Cronin, *Changes in the Land: Indians, Colonists, and the Ecology of New England* (New York: Hill and Wang, 1983).

ship between people and the natural environment; the priority of individual, communal, or environmental "rights" in farming practices; and even the fundamental question of whether farming is, in essence, a business or a way of life. Conventional agriculture involves specialization, technology, world markets, and competition. Alternative agriculture emphasizes diversification, domestic markets, a skeptical use of science and technology, and cooperation among farmers and with their consumers.[39]

Curry-Roper carried out field research across Iowa in seven farming communities among eight small, homogeneous social groups, ranging in character from individualistic to communal, including Mennonite, Reformed, Lutheran, German and Irish Catholic, Swedish Lutheran, Dutch Reformed, Anglo and Norwegian Quaker, and Anglo Reorganized Church of Latter Day Saints.[40] Sampling four German communities with differing religious perspectives allowed her to control for ethnicity.

Curry-Roper developed a questionnaire and held group discussions to determine the residents' attitudes about religion, farming, land use, government, and other sociocultural issues. Like Dilly, she took into account the historical traditions and theological orientations of each village, which derived from their unique ethnic and religious character. Rather than attempt to measure church attendance or religiosity, she asked respondents their opinions about problems facing society and solutions, believing that the opinions reflect community views more than individual views. She also asked how religious beliefs affect their lives in general and their farm practices in particular, and especially how farmers perceive their relationship to nature.[41]

39. Curry-Roper, "Trust and the Social Construction of Reality," 13-15, 20-33.

40. Ibid., 16-17.

41. Ibid., 16-20, following Milton Yinger, "A Structural Examination of Religion," *Journal for the Scientific Study of Religion* 8 (Spring 1969): 88-99. Yinger said that the most crucial question is "How is a person religious?" rather than "How religious is he?" Curry-Roper interviewed ninety farmers and their spouses representing fifty-eight families drawn from the churches. She used content analysis to assess the transcripts of the group discussions, based on themes as the unit of measurement, and she statistically analyzed the questionnaires of some thirty respondents. Finally, she conducted personal interviews with thirty-two individuals and couples (four from each group) to determine basic religious commitments. The comments were grouped into various categories and compared by gender, age, and education, none of which were significant.

The villages diverge in their thinking about land use, animal husbandry, and farm inheritance. The German Reformed group most clearly typified the individualistic-utilitarian type (1): they stressed personal property rights and capitalistic agricultural goals even at the expense of some environmental degradation. English and Norwegian Quakers, and Irish and German Catholics, were also individualistic but non-utilitarian (2). Quakers de-emphasized property rights and accepted the social redistribution of wealth in the interests of greater social harmony. Catholics likewise accepted limitations on property rights in the interests of Christian stewardship. Both groups valued associational efforts but were not communal.[42]

Three groups on the communal end of the scale were German Mennonites, Dutch Reformed, and Anglo Reorganized Church of Latter-Day Saints; all expressed sustainable farming attitudes. But the Mennonites, in contrast to the Calvinists and Saints, held a utilitarian view of nature (5); preservation of the earth has little place in their theology, whereas Calvinists and Saints emphasized stewardship of resources and the duty to bring all activities of life under biblical norms (4).

The Lutheran Augustana Synod Swedes and Missouri Synod Germans did not fit into either the individualistic or communal positions (3). Among the Germans the men were communal and the women individualistic. Both Lutheran groups accepted the teaching of stewardship, but considered nature primarily to be for human use. They both viewed farming as a business; the Germans being more capitalistic than the Swedes. Curry-Roper again suggests that the cause may lie in Lutheran theology, which emphasized the personal and individual element of faith. This blend of religious piety and worldly activity stemmed from Martin Luther's teaching that "work itself, rather than 'the fruits of labor,' will set you free."[43]

Most interesting is the contrast between German and Dutch Reformed farmers, who share the same Calvinist theology but have different ethnic histories. Curry-Roper compared the Ost Frisian Germans

---

42. This and the next two paragraphs rely on Curry-Roper, "Trust and the Social Construction of Reality," 20-33.

43. The Lutheran work ethic, recalled Howard Kohn, former senior editor of *Rolling Stone*, was the essence of his father's life as the proverbial "last farmer" in the Missouri Synod community of Beaver in Michigan's Saginaw Valley, *The Last Farmer: An American Memoir* (New York: Summit Books, 1988), 102-3.

of Wellsburg in north-central Iowa (Grundy County) to the Dutch of Hull in northwest Iowa (Sioux County). The Germans she found to be extremely individualistic while the Dutch are more communal. Germans draw social boundaries around each farm unit and rarely cooperate beyond familial lines. The average farm size in 1980 was third from the top in Iowa (305 acres) and increasing, while their population decline was the highest. "Their individualistic, farm-unit-oriented worldview has not encouraged the type of social embeddedness that . . . is necessary to counter the pressures in these directions," Curry-Roper concluded.[44]

The Dutch placed communal needs above individual benefits, even though they are as strongly committed to property rights as the Germans. From the outset they wanted a homogenous ethnoreligious enclave and they built the institutional structure of churches, Christian day schools, and Christian agricultural societies to support it. This communalism reflects the centuries-old Dutch character of working together against the elements (water) and common enemies (Spain, France, Germany, England). The Dutch learned early the lesson "Een voor allen, allen een." Not surprisingly, Dutch farm sizes in Hull did not rise much in the crisis of the 1980s; they are the smallest in the state (185 acres) and their population decline in the 1980s was the lowest.[45]

The late Stanley Wiersma of Calvin College, who grew up in Sioux County — the largest Dutch Protestant farm settlement in America, tried to capture the Dutch sense of "ought" in a prose poem about planting corn, entitled "Calvinist Farming."[46] In a somewhat tongue-in-cheek

44. Curry-Roper, "Worldview and Agriculture," 25.

45. Ibid., 16-27; Hans van der Horst, *The Low Sky: Understanding the Dutch* (The Hague: Scriptum Books, Scheidam/Nuffic, 1996).

46. Sietze Buning [pseud. of Stanley Wiersma], *Purpaleanie and Other Permutations* (Orange City, IA: Middleburg Press, 1978), 61-63. See also Sietze Buning's prose poem, "An Open Letter," in *Style and Class* (Orange City, IA: Middleburg Press, 1982), which contrasts the values of religion and agricultural science with the theme, "Dordt vs. Ames." Dordt was the historic Dutch Reformed synodical creed of 1618-19 and a synonym for the Reformed soil of Sioux County; Ames, of course, was the Iowa State Agricultural University. "Dad's first commandment was: 'Watch out for Ames,' and the last commandment too," Wiersma writes (55-59, quote 55). Kohn's Missouri Synod Lutheran father sounds the same theme: "He and his farm, I said, were paradoxes. He had refused to apply the wonders of the land-grant laboratories, and yet his crops were somehow immune, or so it seemed, to bugs and fungi and other pests" (*Last Farmer*, 207-8).

style, Wiersma described the apprehension of these immigrant farmers about the newfangled practice of contour plowing. By fitting the curvilinear pattern precisely to the topography according to scientific principles, contouring produced the highest possible yields, while simultaneously being conservationist in the sense of minimizing agricultural runoff and soil erosion. But contour plowing required the heavy use of chemicals to control weeds and, more important, it seemed to defy order on the land.

Listen to Wiersma's story:

> Our Calvinist fathers wore neckties with their bib-overalls and straw hats, a touch of glory with their humility. They rode their horse-drawn corn planters like chariots, planting the corn in straight rows, each hill of three stalks three feet from each hill around it, up and over the rises. . . . Each field was a checkerboard even to the diagonals. No Calvinist followed the land's contours.
>
> Contour farmers in surrounding counties improvised their rows against the slope of the land. There was no right way. Before our fathers planted a field, they knew where each hill of corn would be. Be ye perfect, God said, and the trouble with contour farmers was that, no matter how hard they worked at getting a perfect contour, they could never know for sure it was perfect — and they didn't even care. At best they were Arminian, or Lutheran, or Catholic, or at worst secular. . . .
>
> We youngsters pointed out that the tops of our rises were turning clay-brown, that bushels of black dirt washed into creeks and ditches every time it rained, and that in the non-Calvinistic counties the tops of the rises were black. We were told we were arguing by results, not by principles. Why, God could replenish the black dirt overnight. The tops of the rises were God's business.
>
> Our business was to farm on Biblical principles. Like, let everything be done decently and in good order; that is keep weeds down, plant every square inch, do not waste crops, and be tidy. Contour farmers were unkingly because they were untidy. They could not be prophetic, could not explain from the Bible how to farm. Being neither kings nor prophets, they could not be proper priests; their humility lacks definition. They prayed for crops privately. Our whole county prayed for crops the second Wednesday of every March.

Here Wiersma abruptly changed the direction of the story.

175

God's cosmic planter has thirty years' worth of people since then, all checked and on the diagonal if we could see as God sees. All third-generation Calvinists now plant corn on the contour. They have heard the word from the State College of Agriculture. . . . [Now] there's no easy way to tell the difference between Calvinists and non-Calvinists. . . . When different ideas of God produced different methods of farming, God mattered more.

Wiersma obviously longed for the old distinctives after modern methods came into vogue. But he put his finger on an important point — "Our business was to farm on Biblical principles."

Other Calvinist writers recognize the salience of religion in shaping the behavior of their farming people. James Schaap, who grew up in a Dutch enclave in Sheboygan County, Wisconsin, and teaches in Sioux County, Iowa, recalls spending all day on hands and knees helping his father-in-law weed an eighty-five-acre soybean field. Then, at the evening meal the man prayed: "'Bless that all we do, we do to thy honor.'" Even weeding a bean field? asks Schaap incredulously. "It seemed to me that was stretching Calvinism a bit too far. . . . How on earth was I to believe that this milkweed stain on my hands was somehow related to the kingdom? . . . Maybe when my father-in-law looks up and down the cleaned rows of soybeans," Schaap opines, "he sees the beauty of God's creation well managed — subdued, in fact. . . . He has accomplished his calling as well as he can. . . . Maybe that's what he means. I'm not sure I know exactly, because I'm not a farmer."[47]

Skeptics might rightfully demand more evidence for the religious basis of farming behavior than limited field interviews and writers' anecdotes. If "theology rode the tractor seat," it must be shown by solid evidence from farm records.[48] Dilly compared data on cropping, livestock, and land use in religious communities, but she failed to ask questions about beliefs and so could not link worldview directly with farming practices. Curry-Roper raised the right questions about moral attitudes

47. James C. Schaap, "Bean-Walking," in *Thirty-five and Counting* (Sioux Center, IA: Dordt College Press, 1985), 85-86. See also Schaap, *Sign of a Promise and Other Stories* (Sioux Center, IA: Dordt College Press, 1979), 61-80; and Schaap, *CRC Family Portrait: Sketches of Ordinary Christians in a 125-Year Old Church* (Grand Rapids: CRC Publications, 1982), 147-50.

48. Karen Schnyders De Vries, "Theology from the Tractor Seat" [interview with Janel Curry-Roper], *Calvin Spark* (alumni magazine) 42 (Winter 1996): 18-20.

and farming, but her small number of interviewees (less than one hundred among eight groups) was too few to make a statistically valid data base to compare cropping and livestock patterns. And the studies of isolated ethnoreligious groups must be expanded to include the larger numbers of Baptists, Methodists, Disciples of Christ, Episcopalians, Pentecostals, and other farm populations.

If one concedes the primacy of theological beliefs in farming, the task remains to develop an explanatory theory that is widely applicable. Curry-Roper's individualist-communal continuum needs to be scaled two-dimensionally with the religious orientations of farmers. In another context, she suggested that church teachings on the doctrine of eschatology or the "last things," that is, the future of human history and the natural world, lead to a general orientation toward life and work that could influence behavior.[49] Those who believe they are partners with Christ in ushering in his earthly kingdom should take better care of the land than those who believe Satan controls the earth and Christ will utterly destroy both him and the earth with fire in the near future. Put another way, Calvinists preferred to sing the hymn "This is my father's world," rather than the spiritual, "This world is not my home, I'm just a'passing through."

Whether the creation mandate, two-kingdom dualism, millennial eschatology, or any other religious typology can help us understand farming decisions is still an open question, but it deserves more serious study. Ethnic studies since the 1960s have strongly suggested that religion mattered on the farm as in the voting booth. Agricultural specialists would do well to include the long-neglected religious variable in their research. Religious worldviews must enter the scholarly discourse with at least the interpretive priority now given to race, class, and gender.

49. Janel M. Curry-Roper, "Contemporary Christian Eschatologies and Their Relationship to Environmental Stewardship," *Professional Geographer* 42, no. 2 (1990): 157-69. Loewen, *Family, Church, and Market,* 185, similarly found that the Anabaptist premillennial view was a threat to the Mennonites' traditional teachings, because it lessened their commitment to a community-oriented, socially responsible stewardship of the land and to true discipleship, and instead focused attention on personal peace in a futuristic "Kingdom of God."

Decoding Conflicted History:
Religion and the Historiography
on Northern Ireland

RONALD A. WELLS

The last third of the twentieth century has offered many surprises, most notably the disintegration of the Soviet Union and the fall of apartheid in South Africa. But the two ethno-religious communities in Northern Ireland seemed to remain at fundamental odds with each other, although the peace process in the province offers some hope. Those communities are known by different names: on the one side it is Catholic, nationalist, and republican; on the other it is Protestant, unionist, and loyalist. While the names in each set are not exactly interchangeable there is, however, an affinity between them that the respective participants understand and act upon. The state of Northern Ireland, created as a stopgap measure by Britain following the establishment of responsible government for most of Ireland under a Dublin-based parliament, existed for a half-century (1922-1972) with its own parliament at Stormont. In 1972, because of Stormont's apparent inability to govern the province, the British government in London intervened, prorogued the provincial parliament, and asserted direct rule from Westminster. If Stormont failed it did so because it lacked that ingredient essential for all successful governments, a sociopolitical consensus.[1] The historian does not take a position on the unionist desire to see Northern Ireland work or on the republican desire to see it fail. One merely notes that the

1. Richard Rose, *Governing Without Consensus* (London: Faber, 1971).

events from at least 1969 onwards have illustrated the bitterly contested nature of the state's legitimacy.

A commonplace expression when referring to Northern Ireland has it that "the inevitable never happens while the unexpected always does." By "inevitable" it is meant that Ireland as a whole is "natural" for the nation-state. John Donne to the contrary notwithstanding, an island can be a thing unto itself, and in the view of many outside observers, it must be "inevitable" that the peoples inhabiting an island realize their essential commonality and, in the end, form a nation. By "unexpected," in the expression noted above, something always has emerged to prevent the seeming inevitability that all people on the Irish island will accept that their collective future depends on no one but themselves alone (e.g., the name of the republican, nationalist, and Catholic political movement, Sinn Fein, or, "ourselves alone"). The loyalist, unionist, and Protestant faction, of course, is the group that supplies the objections which, taken together, prevent the supposed inevitability from happening. They are therefore put on the defensive when asked to explain themselves to an incredulous world opinion when it observes the two factions engaging in a horrific civil war in the north of Ireland, historically known as the province of Ulster.

The loyalist, unionist, and Protestant group is a numerical majority in the state of Northern Ireland, and they have repeatedly exercised their constitutional rights in voting to remain a part of the United Kingdom. They believe that they already have a nation to which they belong, so to live in an all-Ireland republic would be an unacceptable change of nationality. As to why they abhor so deeply living with their fellow islanders the loyalists note that they would become a minority in a state at least guided (some would say dominated) by a church whose ideas and values they cannot accept.

Up until now in this chapter we have carefully referred to the two factions using political, attitudinal, and religious terms. While one would not wish merely, or simplistically, to reduce the subtle interconnection between the three terms, it is necessary to single out the religious component for explicit analysis because many of the participants themselves (especially Protestants) see it that way. It is, as noted above, the bedrock objection of Ulster Protestants to an all-Irish nation-state that Ireland is a "confessional state," informed by a church they disdain. Even as much as one sees the multi-dimensionality of the so-called "troubles," the religious dimension has — in the view offered here — been relatively discounted in scholarship over the past twenty-five years. The remainder of this chapter has two objectives: to restore the balance in the discourse about "the troubles" in respect of religion; and to look again at the 1920s to examine the founding of the state of Northern Ireland and to the role of evangelical, revivalist Protestantism in cementing a broad consensus among all social classes which would result in the unique solidarity that continues to say "no" to the putative inevitability of an "Irish" nation. We will look to the United States for comparative possibilities in linking Protestant evangelicalism and political conservatism.

The difficulty of interpreting Northern Ireland does not obtain because scholars have too little information with which to work. To the contrary, the province of Ulster has been one of the most-studied parts of the world over the past twenty-five years (one thinks of T. S. Eliot in wondering about the wisdom that eludes us in gaining information). While new discoveries of fresh data are always welcome, the questions that concern us here are: what frames of reference do we employ in our studies, i.e., how do we interpret Northern Ireland?[2] And, since we are herein asking about the connection between revivalist Protestantism and the state in Northern Ireland we need to inquire into the intersection of religion, society, and politics in a state that has not functioned well.

Most serious writers, in trying to decode the subtexts that cause disfunction in Ulster, have suggested that religion has had little more than a superficial role. While acknowledging that the participants in civil strife refer to themselves by religious names, nearly all historians and social scientists have insisted that the realities of conflict lie elsewhere. Duncan Morrow, a political sociologist in Ulster, argues that the answer to why academics cannot see religion's importance lies in the social construction of knowledge among British academics. Morrow reminds us that British academy is decidedly secular, therefore assuming a world in which religion either has disappeared or exists only among socially marginal peoples.

At its worst religion is equivalent to obscurantism and superstition. In this context religion, particularly in its organized form, is a strange

---

2. The best single book on this subject is the magisterial work of the late John Whyte, *Interpreting Northern Ireland* (Oxford: Clarendon, 1990), to which we shall refer again in the discussion to follow. I have discussed some of these issues in a similar way elsewhere: "Protestant Ideology and the Irish Conflict: Comparing Ulster Protestantism and American Evangelicalism," *Fides et Historia* 23 (Fall 1993): 3-17.

and difficult territory, easier to dismiss than to explore. The obsessive religiosity of the Irish is at best embarrassing and at worst dangerous.[3]

If social scientists believe religion to be epiphenomenal in Ulster, it may well turn not on the intrinsic merits of the case, but on their own failure of imagination about the persistence of religion in the modern world. Scholars whose presuppositions that religion — both as institutional form and as cultural affect — cannot be significant social phenomena often, therefore, accuse of "false consciousness" those participants in Ulster whose self-description insists that religion is vital in shaping their worldview and in guiding the actions that proceed therefrom. Having used the term "false consciousness" we must say a word about the contribution of Marxist scholars, especially those in sociology and political science.

In the middle-to-late 1960s, Marxist interpretations of all sorts were gaining a wide hearing in all areas of social analysis, no less so in interpreting the civil strife that began again in Ulster in 1969. James Connolly (1870-1916), of the revolutionary generation, had restated in Irish terms the basics of Marx's and Engels's ideology, i.e., that national independence and democratic socialism had to proceed hand in hand in Ireland. Indeed, even noting the knotty problem of Ulster Protestants, Connolly held the position still held by many nationalists, that when Ireland was united the true class interests of Ulster workers would become clear to them and they would, either out of conviction or necessity, align themselves with their class allies throughout Ireland. Of the many Marxist works to appear since 1968, Liam De Paor's *Divided Ulster* is one of the most often discussed.[4] He uses the colonial argument, both because it is dear to the heart of Marxist orthodoxy, and because, prior to 1921, it was probably a correct description of relations between Britain and Ireland. Further, by 1970, the time of De Paor's writing, to make the colonial argument stick in a postcolonial era was to seal the doom of British control in Ulster. Yet the argument's greatest weakness is that were the British government to withdraw its troops from Northern Ireland, it would not mean "Brits out," because a majority of the population in Ulster would nevertheless regard themselves as British. To

3. Duncan Morrow, *The Churches and Inter-Community Relationships* (Coleraine: Centre for the Study of Conflict, University of Ulster, 1991), 2.
4. Liam De Paor, *Divided Ulster* (Harmondsworth: Penguin, 1970).

summarize, the colonial argument — appropriate as it may have been for all of Ireland prior to 1921 — does not apply to contemporary northeast Ireland because the absence of putative colonial power would not change the ethnocultural realities in the area.

Michael Farrell's otherwise interesting, well-researched, and well-written work of 1976[5] is equally defective in its reasoning from a Marxist viewpoint. He founded his argument on the classic Marxist staple of the manipulation of the Ulster Protestant working class. While he, and other writers, were on to a valuable theme in articulating the economic and social differences between working-class and bourgeois Protestants, the argument breaks down if pressed to the conclusion that the Protestant proletariat would assert Irish consciousness if liberated from the double duplicity of Protestant identity and bourgeois manipulation. Even fellow-Marxists Paul Bew, Peter Gibbon, and Henry Patterson[6] allow for an objective reality in Protestant consciousness. Further, as to the question of the essential Marxist assumption that Ireland must be united and independent to be socialist, Gibbon and Patterson, in their own specialized studies, revised the Marxist model of interpretation even further, to allow for an objective reality in Protestant resistance to a unified, socialist Ireland.[7] Well does John Whyte remark that "during the 1970s, then, the unity of the Marxist school of thought on Northern Ireland disappeared,"[8] and with it, one might add, much of its interpretive power (though toward the end of this chapter, we will return, approvingly, to that staple product of Marxist analysis, i.e., cultural alienation). Economic and class conflict is undeniably present in all nations, and no less so in Ulster. But as an explanation of the current conflict such emphases take too little account of culture, in the broadest sense of that term.

Richard Jenkins, himself an anthropologist, goes the farthest in terms of a social scientific *mea culpa*. He asks if social scientific analytical models of reality are intrinsically more accurate than folk models (taking into account religion and culture) of the same reality. In short, are

5. Michael Farrell, *Northern Ireland: The Orange State* (London: Pluto, 1976).

6. Paul Bew, Peter Gibbon, Henry Patterson, *The State in Northern Ireland, 1921-72* (Manchester: Manchester University Press, 1979).

7. Peter Gibbon, *The Origins of Ulster Unionism* (Manchester: Manchester University Press, 1975); Henry Patterson, *Class Conflict and Sectarianism: The Protestant Working Class and the Belfast Labour Movement* (Belfast: Blackstaff, 1980).

8. Whyte, *Interpreting Northern Ireland*, 187.

historical and/or contemporary actors in society guilty of false consciousness if they insist that cultural concerns are of vital interest to them? Or, Jenkins asks, does the social scientist, like mother, know best? Jenkins, correctly in my view, insists that social actors' self-understanding should be accorded respect, and that social scientists are not necessarily better placed to make sense of a conflict situation than the immediate participants themselves.[9]

If the conflict in Northern Ireland is not fully or solely about class and economic conflict, and if we should take the self-description of the participants seriously, then why should we not use the political names they give themselves and ask, concurrently, if the conflict is not really best understood in political terms. There are various meanings of "nationalist" and "unionist." These are political terms, revealing a political historical consciousness and political objectives. Simply put, a nationalist is one who wants an Ireland united and independent from Britain. A unionist is one who wants to maintain the British link between Northern Ireland and the United Kingdom. In both views, it is agreed that the main conflict is between Britain and Ireland, with nationalists traditionally blaming Britain for Ireland's troubles and with unionists traditionally blaming Ireland for Britain's Ulster troubles. In the discussion to follow we will distinguish between traditional and contemporary nationalist and unionist definitions of the political problem of Northern Ireland. This helps us to see how far understanding has come in a relatively short while.

The traditional nationalist interpretation of the Northern Ireland problem turns on two notions: that the island of Ireland forms a natural national unit for whatever people reside thereon; that the problem of an Ireland divided against its natural self is to be laid to the door of Britain. This view is best articulated by Frank Gallagher in his *The Indivisible*

---

9. Richard Jenkins, "Northern Ireland: In What Sense Religion in Conflict?" in *The Sectarian Divide in Northern Ireland Today,* Richard Jenkins, Hastings Donnan, and Garham McFarlane (London: Royal Anthropological Institute, occasional paper no. 41, 1986), 4-5. While Jenkins does not mention the following work, it fits his concerns well: an egregious example of social scientific work that largely misses the point by insisting that class and status, rather than culture and religion, are vital is, Cecilia A. Karch, "Anglo-Saxon Ethnocentrism: Its Roots and Consequences in Northern Ireland and the Southern United States," in *Taking State Power: The Sources and Consequences of Political Challenge,* ed. John C. Leggett (New York: Harper and Row, 1973), 419-33.

Island,[10] in which it is insisted that Irish people, of any political stripe, never really wanted partition. He maintains that Northern Ireland was never viable in either political or economic terms, and that British subsidies alone keep the province going. This viewpoint is also articulated in the Irish constitution, in which that new nation asserted its right "to the unity and integrity of the national territory." These assertions, be it noted, took no note of the existence of, or the feelings of, the people who formed the majority in the six counties of northeast Ireland. However, the viewpoint of traditional nationalists has been challenged by people who are also undeniably nationalist, i.e., desiring a united Ireland, but who saw the division not between Ireland and Britain but rather between the peoples of Ireland themselves.[11] Since the onset of "the troubles" again in 1969, the revisionist historiography accelerated, most notably in the writings of such southern Irish political luminaries as Garret Fitzgerald and Conor Cruise O'Brien. Taken together, their works conclusively shift the focus for division in Ireland from British machination to Ulster Protestant reluctance.[12] By allowing for an objective reality for another "people" residing on the Irish island, the bedrock of traditional nationalist interpretation was eroded.

The traditional unionist interpretation of the Northern Ireland problem also turns on two notions: that there are two distinct peoples in Ireland; and that the problem resides in the refusal of nationalists to accord to the Protestants a political right of self-determination that the former claim for themselves. This view was best articulated in M. W. Heslinga's *The Irish Border as a Cultural Divide,*[13] which is the direct counterpart to Frank Gallagher's work, noted above. For Heslinga, and for most unionists, the real nation, and natural unit, is the British Isles, with the real affinities being east and west and the differences being north and south. In this view, Ireland has no historical or sociopsychological basis to claim that the island should be one state. Such views sustained unionist ideology for a long time, in which people in Ulster

10. Frank Gallagher, *The Indivisible Island: The History of the Partition of Ireland* (London: Gollancz, 1957).

11. Especially Donal Barrington, *Uniting Ireland* (Dublin: Tnairim, 1959), who wrote in conscious opposition to Gallagher.

12. Garret Fitzgerald, *Towards a New Ireland* (London: Charles Knight, 1972); Conor Cruise O'Brien, *States of Ireland* (London: Hutchinson, 1972).

13. M. W. Heslinga, *The Irish Border as a Cultural Divide* (Assen, the Netherlands: van Gorcum, 1962).

would chant slogans about a "Protestant parliament for a Protestant people." Yet, reality began to overtake such unionist perspectives when "the troubles" broke out anew in the late 1960s, most notably in the writings of the academic historian, A. T. Q. Stewart, who wrote trenchantly, that

> most people, if asked to define the chief symptoms of the Northern Ireland troubles, would say it is that the two communities cannot live together. The very essence of the Ulster question, however, is that they *do* live together, and have done for centuries. They share the same homeland and, like it or not, the two diametrically opposed political wills must coexist on the same narrow ground.[14]

Writers who portray unionist ideology, whether or not descriptively or normatively, began — by the late 1970s — to admit that in Ulster there resided a minority community that had rights and legitimate aspirations. Thus the tendencies of contemporary unionist writing was to converge, paradoxically, with that of contemporary nationalists, i.e., that the nationalists could now admit the legitimate existence of Protestant institutions and ideology and vice versa.

The seemingly unassailable point that there are two communities in Northern Ireland, and that the conflict is between them — not Britain and Ireland — is an astonishingly new interpretation. But, as well as new, it has now become the consensus interpretation of most observers. Traditional nationalist and unionist interpretations — i.e., blaming Britain or Ireland — despite their longevity are now quaintly passé. Writers articulating the internal-conflict interpretation may still and nevertheless be unionists or nationalists, but they are focusing, at long last, on the two communities themselves. Having said that, however, there is one last point to be considered in this context. In view of the concerns of this chapter — to what extent is religion at the heart of things in Ulster — we need to ask if politics is the main concern. In one of the best books on contemporary Ulster, Stewart's *The Narrow Ground*, we read the following:

> The fact is, however, that the quarrel is not about theology as such and remains, in its modern form, stubbornly a constitutional problem,

---

14. A. T. Q. Stewart, *The Narrow Ground: The Roots of Conflict in Ulster* (London: Faber and Faber, 1977), 180.

though religion is the shibboleth of the contending parties. Essentially the conflict in Ulster is not different from other conflicts in the modern world: it is about political power and who should wield it.[15]

Having seen that social class and economic conflict are necessary but not sufficient causes for "the troubles" we need to answer Stewart's point about politics. Is the conflict about politics, like other modern conflicts, and is religion merely "the shibboleth of the contending parties"? We have previously agreed that social scientists do not necessarily know better than participants themselves, so we should look at what they say. In answer to Stewart's concern we should grant immediately that, of course, the conflict in Ulster is "about political power and who should wield it." But, such a statement does not answer the significant question about the meaning of politics, i.e., wielding political power to do what?

Herein is a significant interpretive difficulty. The Catholic-nationalist group sees the conflict in political terms. Their politics is about requiring the state to meet the legitimate needs and aspirations of the minority community in Ulster, whether or not within an all-Ireland context or in a United Kingdom context. The Protestant-unionist group is not of so single a mind,[16] and they attend church less frequently than Catholics, thus making categorical judgements about them problematic. Yet, while there are some Protestants who view the conflict in political terms many, if not most, see the conflict in religious terms. For them religion is vastly more than shibboleth, and vital to their worldview and to the actions that spring therefrom.

At this point the critical reader will want to ask: can one really and seriously say that religion, as commonly defined, is at the heart of "the troubles," at least for Protestants? This invites the subsequent question of: what do we mean by religion, as commonly defined? Religion, one supposes, for most people, is either a matter of private psychological comfort or of institutional allegiance, involving adherence to doctrines or theological positions. But, is this enough of a definition of religion?

John Hickey's work helps us here in talking about explicit religious beliefs and their social importance. What Hickey contributes to the

15. Ibid.
16. Fred Boal, John A. Campbell, and David N. Livingstone, "The Protestant Mosaic: A Majority of Minorities," in *The Northern Ireland Question: Myth and Reality*, Patrick J. Roche and Brian Barton, eds. (Aldershot, England: Avebury, 1991), 99-129.

discussion is the insight that social scientists and historians express a disinclination to believe that there is a "concept of commitment, or the ensuing fact that people are capable of ordering their actions on the basis of commitment."[17] Commitment to religious belief—apart from social origins and effects—is not the stock-in-trade of academic analysis. Hickey sees the historic roots of the Reformation as still operative in Northern Ireland.

> The forces that are provoking that "problem" find part of their roots in the religious tradition that has influenced Europe and America at least since the sixteenth century. The peculiarity about Northern Ireland is that the conflict which took place in the remainder of Europe and in the United States some centuries ago is taking place in this province *now*. The other societies have found some means of dealing with that problem and producing a "modus vivendi" for the conflicting groups. Northern Ireland has not.[18]

Hickey details the pattern of perceptions among Protestants—especially of the Reformed, Calvinist Protestants of Ulster—about the Roman Catholic Church. While these worldview assumptions may be said to describe more of the pre-Vatican II Catholic Church, and therefore be out-of-date, they nevertheless represent the deeply-held views of many, if not most, Ulster Protestants. The argument proceeds as follows: The mission of the Catholic Church may be to convert the world but, within that, a central purpose is to protect the *depositum fidei*. This means that the organizational structure of the Church must remain separate from the State. So, while the Church may claim to intervene in activities that are the moral functions of the State, it cannot accept the reverse, that political leaders be allowed to intervene in the affairs of the Church. Thus, the Roman Catholic Church could never become an "established" church, like the Church of England, because secular political leaders, whether a hereditary monarchy or an elected parliament, could never be accorded directive and controlling power over the Church. To Protestants, this is all wrong. They see religion as functioning to bring Christians together to form a "holy city," a city created by the voluntary association of like-minded persons who find the warrant for

17. John Hickey, *Religion and the Northern Ireland Problem* (Dublin: Gill and Macmillan, 1984), 80.

18. Ibid. (emphasis is Hickey's).

187

their authority not in the church but in the Bible. As Hickey concludes: The religious divide in Northern Ireland is not based purely on the symbolic membership of a group with different political ideologies but is rooted in different interpretations of the Christian faith, which, in turn, help to form attitudes as to what "society" and its institutions should be about.[19] Historians David Hempton and Myrtle Hill agree: "Any attempt to unravel the complexities of the Irish Protestant psychology must take as its starting point the overriding sense of moral responsibility with which evangelicals were imbued, and which blurred the distinctions between religious and political activities. For evangelical contempt for the Roman Catholic Church emanated not only from its doctrinal 'heresies' but from their social and political consequences."[20]

It is in this context that one can begin to understand the desire of Ulster Protestants to maintain the State of Northern Ireland, because it is, for them, their last line of defense in a logical argument that had begun with a different Christian worldview. For Protestants, the theological notion of covenant is both deeply ingrained in their religious thinking and easily transferable to social contract thinking. Like their Calvinist coreligionists in South Africa, the Protestants of Ulster are fond of writing covenants that combine religion and politics in nationalistic context.[21] Indeed, on the fiftieth anniversary of the founding of the Northern Irish state, some 334,000 men and women signed their names to the Ulster Covenant. It stressed that the forces trying to undermine the government of Northern Ireland were ". . . subversive of our civil and religious freedom . . ." thus requiring them to ". . . hereby pledge ourselves in solemn covenant throughout this our time of threatened calamity to stand by one another in defending our cherished position of citizenship in the United Kingdom."[22]

19. Ibid., 87.

20. David Hempton and Myrtle Hill, *Evangelical Protestantism in Ulster Society, 1740-1890* (London: Routledge, 1992), 81.

21. The comparison between Calvinism and political ideology in Ulster and South Africa is suggested in Robert C. Crawford, *Loyal to King Billy: A Portrait of the Ulster Protestants* (New York: St. Martin's Press, 1987), 106-17. A more highly-developed and well-articulated rendering of this comparison, and on the idea of religio-social covenant, to which we shall return, is Donald Harman Akenson, *God's People: Covenant and Land in South Africa, Israel and Ulster* (Ithaca and London: Cornell University Press, 1992).

22. Quoted in Hickey, *Religion and the Northern Ireland Problem*, 88.

John Whyte, the best overall, recent interpreter of the Northern Irish scene, does not like Hickey's viewpoints, and calls them "extreme."[23] But what is "extreme" in them seems to be that Hickey takes religion very seriously. Whyte wonders why religion can cause strife in Ireland whereas the terms "Protestant" and "Catholic" in other countries "mark a purely religious difference."[24] Whyte seems to have misunderstood what it means to say "purely religious." Religion is never sealed off from its social context; in fact, the very sort of Protestants we are studying here — mainly Presbyterians — found their religious ideology in conjoining religion and culture, and they eschew attempts to make religion solely a private matter. The viewpoint argued here is that it is unimaginative, even sterile, to try to distinguish between the discrete domains of religion and politics. As aptly stated by anthropologist Richard Jenkins, "Religion often concerns itself with issues that are apparently political, and politics may equally be self-consciously religious."[25] Just so in the case of Ulster, where Protestant politics and Protestant religion are not only interconnected but spring from a single worldview.

Frank Wright, a political scientist, helps the discussion at this point with his subtle and nuanced analysis of Protestant ideology. While he does not discuss the ideology's origins, he notes its affects and effects by laying down a gauntlet to conventional social science in writing that, in Northern Ireland, "Ideology tends to structure experience rather than the other way around."[26] This ideology is, importantly, an autonomous one, in that it lives in a self-fulfilling world of its own, relatively untouched by empirical reality. So, when Catholics are openly hostile, Protestants say that the real face is showing; when Catholics are cooperative and ecumenical, Protestants wonder what ulterior purpose the Catholics are trying duplicitously to pursue. At the bottom of this attitude is a foundational belief about the nature of Protestantism and of Catholicism. In sum, it is a version of the Whig theory of history, that God (or, as Jefferson said, "Nature's god") wants the right to triumph in the end. In this view of things, the right means the continual expansion of liberty and the conquest of tyranny. The internal mechanism of this progressive

---

23. Whyte, *Interpreting Northern Ireland,* 104.
24. Ibid., 105.
25. Jenkins, "Northern Ireland: In What Sense Religion in Conflict?" 9.
26. Frank Wright, "Protestant Ideology and Politics in Ulster," *European Journal of Sociology* 14 (1974): 213.

development is religion, and that Protestantism will always be on the side of liberty and Catholicism on the side of tyranny.

Protestantism in Ulster, however, is not a monolithic social force. A useful distinction, if not pressed too far, between Protestants has been offered by Owen Dudley Edwards. For Edwards, there are at least two types of Protestants, the "confident" who tend to ignore Catholics and the "fearful" who are hyperconscious of the Catholic presence in their midst.[27]

The Rev. Dr. Ian R. K. Paisley is the most faithful representation of this fearful ideology in contemporary Northern Ireland. He was born in County Tyrone in 1926 and was raised in the staunchly unionist town of Ballymena in Co. Antrim. After some Bible school training he was ordained in 1946 in an independent church. His career is another example of the transatlantic connection. Paisley's honorary doctorate was given by Bob Jones University, in South Carolina, a university known as the most militant fundamentalist university in America. In 1951, Paisley founded the first congregation of the Free Presbyterian Church, a small denomination of which he has been the sole moderator. While the denomination itself is quite small, the sociopolitical ramifications of "Paisleyism" is Ulster-wide. It will do no good to try to dismiss Paisley, as some scholars have, by calling him a "fanatic," his rallies "stunts," his rhetoric "ranting hyperbole," "neanderthal," "laughingly recondite," even "antediluvian."[28] Far better to see Paisley as many Protestant people in Northern Ireland see him, as a legitimate political leader with religiously-informed views that many Ulster people share but would not state so boldly in public.[29]

In one of his own publications Paisley put forward, in 1966, the essence of Protestant religiopolitical ideology,

Liberty is the very essence of Bible Protestantism. Tyranny is the very essence of Popery. Where Protestantism flourishes Liberty flames. Where Popery reigns Tyranny rules.... As Liberty and Tyranny have no common meeting place, so Protestantism and Popery cannot be

27. Owen Dudley Edwards, *The Sins of Our Fathers* (Dublin: Gill and Macmillan, 1970), 64.

28. Tom Gallagher, "Religion, Reaction and Revolt in Northern Ireland: The Impact of Paisleyism in Ulster," *Journal of Church and State* 23 (Autumn 1981): 423-44.

29. The book by Steve Bruce, *God Save Ulster*, noted above, is a model of careful yet diffident scholarship on this controversial leader.

reconciled. Popery is tyrannical in every sphere of life. . . . On the other hand Protestantism is the torch-bearer of Liberty. Protestantism, at a stroke, cuts down all the shackles of superstition and priestcraft. The soul is free to commune with its Maker. There is one mediator between God and man — the man Jesus Christ. . . . The Protestant's home is his castle. He brooks no interference from Pope, priest, pastor, preacher or prelate. . . . No one can control the Protestant's education or the books which he shall read. He is free born and trembles not at priestly threats or the Papal curse. . . . At the ballot box the Protestant exercises complete liberty. . . . In our province the battle lines between Papal Tyranny and Protestant liberty are joined.[30]

Well does Frank Wright conclude that in Ulster, religion and politics are inextricably bound, so that the continued crisis of political legitimacy is a "battle between two religious systems carried on in the fields of politics."[31] Despite the disinclination of some scholars to accept this point,[32] there has been ample qualitative and quantitative research to demonstrate that evangelical political ideology is formative (one does not say determinative) in Protestant thinking well beyond the merest numerical confines of the evangelical wing of Protestantism as such, as David Taylor and Martha Abele MacIver have shown.[33] Precisely because the state of Northern Ireland has endured the contesting of legitimacy since its founding, the social ramifications of evangelical ideology are shared by most Protestants (card-carrying evangelicals or not) because it affords them a secure sociopolitical identity in a confusing and

30. From *The Protestant Telegraph,* May 28, 1966, quoted in Wright, "Protestant Ideology," 224.

31. Ibid., 223.

32. Especially John Whyte, *Interpreting Northern Ireland,* 108, and Ian McAllister, "The Devil, Miracles and the Afterlife: The Political Sociology of Religion in Northern Ireland," *British Journal of Sociology* 33 (1982): 330-47; "Political Attitudes, Partisanship and Social Structures in Northern Ireland," *Economic and Social Review* 14 (1983): 185-202.

33. David Taylor, "Ian Paisley and the Ideology of Ulster Protestantism," in *Culture and Ideology in Ireland,* Chris Curtain, Mary Kelley, and Liam O'Dowd, eds. (Galway: Galway University Press, 1984), 59-78; "The Lord's Battle: Paisleyism in Northern Ireland," in *Religious Movements,* Rodney Stark, ed. (New York: Paragon House, 1985), 241-78. Martha Abele MacIver, "A Clash of Symbols in Northern Ireland: Divisions Between Extremist and Moderate Protestant Elites," *Review of Religious Research* 30 (1989): 360-74.

conflictual situation. It should be emphasized, moreover, that religion's formative role is not merely functional, that is, derivative mainly from a desire for political cohesion. It is that, to be sure; but political ideas are generated by religious beliefs. In MacIver's sensitive and illumining inquiry into the beliefs of Protestant political elites, she noted the different views of the three political groupings among Protestants: Democratic Unionist (DUP), Official Unionist (OUP), and Alliance. The last was included for completeness, not because it is politically effective or much representative of Ulster Protestantism. The conclusion of her unique work indicates a strong symbolic convergence between conservative religious beliefs and conservative political views. The evangelical movement, in gospel halls and in Presbyterian, Anglican, and Methodist churches, has had a disproportionate share in shaping Unionist ideology and practice.

The evangelical movement is a multinational phenomenon that emerged in all Protestant denominations in the English-speaking world. From approximately 1740 onwards, this Anglo-American, pan-Protestant movement was to become both a revitalizing force within Protestantism and a major critic of "established" religion, whether socially or intellectually. Its signature was the desire to convert others to the Christian faith. Therefore it believed deeply in direct evangelism, both on an individual and communal basis. Since established church leaders often were either opposed or apathetic to evangelical zeal, evangelical leaders and laity alike prayed for what they called "revival," a communal turning of many people to the paths of righteousness.

Evangelicalism is a fairly broad movement that encompasses several types of churchmanship (from Anglican to Pentecostal) and varying perspectives on the relationship of Christianity to culture. At the far right of evangelicalism one finds fundamentalism, at once a part of the broader evangelical movement and its most severe critic. It is the fundamentalist faction within evangelicalism that gives the larger movement most of its bombastic firepower.

It is curious that this term — fundamentalist — has gained such wide usage in Ulster because it is of American origin. Specifically it refers to a set of religious doctrines and attitudes put forward early in this century in a series of pamphlets — *The Fundamentals* — by an organization called The World's Christian Fundamentalist Association, of Minneapolis, Minnesota. The movement that drew inspiration and cohesion from *The Fundamentals* was, and is, a militantly anti-modern movement among evangelical Protestants. It draws its theoretical and theological foundations largely, though not exclusively, from Calvinism, and its affect and élan from the Methodist and Baptist revivalist tradition, the hallmark of American Protestantism.[34]

George Marsden, in a path-breaking article, compared American fundamentalism with its cousin, British evangelicalism. While the two shared a tendency toward biblical literalism and a conversionist zeal, they differed markedly in one significant respect. British evangelicalism seemed to understand the role of history in religiocultural development, whereas American fundamentalists had a view of history that was distinctly anti-modern.[35] Thus, the fundamentalist's religion is construed in terms of defending a heritage. This heritage often reflected the secular American self-definition of America being a unique place, exceptional in the world's history, in which Europeans might begin again.[36] If one can combine the notion of a religious covenant (the Calvinist God who purposes his inscrutable will) with a Whig theory of history about the constant expansion of liberty (and Methodist-Baptist free will), one has a very potent force indeed. This explicit conjunction of religious and political ideology is the essence of what Robert Bellah called "civil religion."[37] While fundamentalists in America are not the only upholders of civil religion, they are the most consistent of its contemporary defenders.

We cannot here fully rehearse, but can note, the historiographical sea change on fundamentalism and evangelicalism that has occurred over the past twenty years.[38] Prior to about 1970, religion was largely ignored

34. The most outstanding scholarly interpreter of fundamentalism in the United States is George M. Marsden, whose *Fundamentalism and American Culture* (New York: Oxford University Press, 1981) is the definitive study.

35. "Fundamentalism as an American Phenomenon: A Comparison with English Evangelicalism," *Church History* 46 (June 1977): 215-32.

36. I have explored some of the perpectival issues surrounding the claim of American exceptionalism in "Viewing America: A Christian Perspective," *Fides et Historia* 17 (1984): 56-67.

37. Robert Bellah, "Civil Religion in America," *Daedalus* 96 (Winter 1967): 1-21.

38. The fruits of the new work have been discussed with care and insight by Leonard J. Sweet, "Wise as Serpents, Innocent as Doves: The New Evangelical Historiography," *Journal of the American Academy of Religion* 56 (1988): 397-416; and by Douglas A. Sweeney, "The Essential Dialectic: The Historiography of the Early Neo-Evangelical Movement and the Observer-Participant Dilemma," *Church History* 60 (March 1991): 70-84.

by historians outside the confines of what was then called "historical theology" or "church history." When mainstream historians discussed religion at all (especially conservative Protestantism), they painted a picture of regressive protest to the developing consensus of American values.[39] Fundamentalism (and to an extent, evangelicalism also) was often portrayed as anti-intellectual (though in reality it was much concerned with ideas), as rural and possibly Southern (though in reality its ideas were generated in the urban North) and simplistic (though in reality a simple and straightforward idea that accorded with the Bible was thought to be "truth" to the fundamentalist believer).

Ernest R. Sandeen was the first scholar to begin the revision on fundamentalism. Rather than allowing religion, especially fundamentalism, to be defined as merely reactive to social change, Sandeen persuasively portrayed fundamentalism as a genuine religious movement. But as valuable as Sandeen's pioneer work was, he applied too narrow a scope to his work, insisting that fundamentalism be defined "partly, if not largely, as one aspect of the history of millenarianism."[40] He was challenged in this respect by George Marsden. The two exchanged views in a journal, and those comments would give shape to the historical debate for years to come.[41] Marsden's main concern was not to doubt fundamentalism's basic religious character but to correct Sandeen's having given too little of fundamentalism's social context, and to show the way in which the movement at once rejected and reflected American culture. Marsden's more fully-orbed views, now widely accepted by historians and social scientists, see this religious movement as a social, political, intellectual, and "American" phenomena.[42]

Sandeen's work was cut short by his untimely death and scholars of religion are the worse for his inability to build on his seminal work. Yet in one of his last articles he was showing signs of incorporating

39. Richard Hofstadter's *Anti-Intellectualism in American Life* (New York: Alfred Knopf, 1963) is a notable example.

40. *The Roots of Fundamentalism: British and American Millenarianism, 1800-1930* (Chicago: University of Chicago Press, 1970), xix.

41. George M. Marsden, "Defining Fundamentalism," *Christian Scholar's Review* 1 (Winter 1971): 141-51; Ernest R. Sandeen, "Defining Fundamentalism: A Reply to Professor Marsden," *Christian Scholar's Review* 1 (Spring 1972): 227-32 (to which Marsden added a short reply, 232-33).

42. These interpretive possibilities are carefully laid out in Marsden, *Fundamentalism and American Culture*, 199-228.

cultural perspectives into his work. He was inquiring into an authentic conservative tradition in America that was religiously based. He noted the rapid advance of "modernization" and with it the secularization and alienation that ineluctably follow. In pointing people back to basics, "the process of rapid, technologically induced change seems destined to succeed where poets and historians have previously failed. By stripping every sector of American society to its bare essentials, to its irreducible commitments, this giant change machine is defining the American character."[43] Sandeen saw the epitome of the modern person as one able to adapt to all changes and to commit to nothing permanent, with values only functionally suited to adaptation. On the other hand he saw an authentically conservative "American" as a person with something to remember and to protect, i.e., both the central truths of the Christian faith and the American culture in which they had been so important for many years.

Returning our focus to Ulster, we need to ask if "real" fundamentalism can exist outside the United States. The leading historian of Irish Presbyterianism, R. F. G. Holmes, while noting the deep influence of American-style fundamentalism on Ulster's religious and political life, rightly observes that the research is not conclusive as to whether fundamentalism was native to Ulster or imported there.[44] George Marsden, while otherwise insisting that fundamentalism is an American phenomenon, dropped a tantalizing footnote to the effect that the one possible exception to the rule might be Ulster.[45] Further, if it be true that the genius of American fundamentalism is its direct continuity with nineteenth-century revivalism, then Ulster could fit the definition because of the impact of revivalism in nineteenth-century Ulster. As Peter Brooke has shown, a coherent Presbyterian culture gave way, after the revival of 1859, to a less coherent but more inclusive Protestant and evangelical culture.[46] Moreover, Sandeen's suggestion about the role of modernization, with its alienating secularization, seems also to be true for the Protestants of Ulster. If modern changes strip away other forms

43. "Fundamentalism and American Identity," *Annals of the American Academy of Political and Social Sciences* 387 (January 1970): 65.
44. R. F. G. Holmes, *Our Irish Presbyterian Heritage* (Belfast: Presbyterian Church in Ireland, 1985), 152-53.
45. G. M. Marsden, "Fundamentalism as an American Phenomenon," 216.
46. Peter Brooke, *Ulster Presbyterianism: The Historical Perspective* (New York: St. Martin's Press, 1987).

of sociocultural identity, it may drive people back to basics, and cause them to reassert their identities based in memory; to remember again what, in another connection, Abraham Lincoln called "the mystic chords of union."

The idea of "the covenant" is important to discuss at this point. Above, on the way to another point, we observed the potency of conjoining the Calvinist idea of the covenant with the Whig theory of history. This was the essence of evangelical "civil religion," that is, a belief that God has a special arrangement with a specific people, and that people's historic role is to stand for righteousness in society to enable the conquest of liberty and the defeat of tyranny. It is beyond dispute that such a belief lies at the heart of the American myth, that empowering story the Americans deeply believe about themselves.[47] As Bernard Bailyn and Nathan Hatch have shown, religion and politics were so intertwined in the minds of the (especially New England) revolutionaries that the defense of political and religious liberty — the Whig theory — was one.[48]

In contemporary Ulster, Ian Paisley is the most important, and divisive, leader in both religion and politics. His ideas about politics and culture are accepted, even cherished, by Protestants in Northern Ireland well beyond the merest confines of the fundamentalist sects. He spoke for a majority of Ulster people in 1985, just after Margaret Thatcher and Garret Fitzgerald had concluded the Anglo-Irish Agreement. No better statement about the importance of the religiopolitical covenant can be imagined than Paisley's diatribe against Margaret Thatcher.

> God has a people in this province. There are more born-again people in Ulster to the square mile than anywhere else in the world. This little province has had the peculiar preservation of divine Providence. You only have to read the history of Ulster to see that time after time when it seemed humanly impossible to extricate Ulster from seeming disaster, that God intervened. Why? God has a purpose for this province, and this plant of Protestantism sown here in the north-eastern

47. Best articulated, e.g., in Ernest Tuveson, *Redeemer Nation* (Chicago: University of Chicago Press, 1968).

48. Bernard Bailyn, *The Ideological Origins of the American Revolution* (Cambridge: Harvard University Press, 1967); Nathan O. Hatch, *The Sacred Cause of Liberty: Republican Thought and the Millennium in Revolutionary New England* (New Haven: Yale University Press, 1977).

part of this island. The enemy has tried to root it out, but it still grows today, and I believe, like a grain of mustard seed, its future is going to be mightier yet. God Who made her mighty will make her mightier yet in His Divine will.[49]

The critical reader of the above will want to ask how representative such a statement might be of Ulster Protestants in general, i.e., those outside of, or on the fringes of, fundamentalist evangelicalism. The insightful, recent work of Donald H. Akenson helps us here. In a brilliantly-conceived study of religiously-based covenantal politics in South Africa, Israel, and Ulster, Akenson reminds us of the social importance of "Scripture" in certain cultures. The covenant that Yahweh made with Israel of old has been appropriated to the modern societies named who also claim that they are special in God's sight: one Jewish nation appropriating its own scripture, and two nations informed by Calvinist ideology insisting that they are the modern fulfillment of the same scripture.

On September 28, 1912, virtually the entire adult male Protestant population of Ulster signed a document entitled "Ulster's Solemn League and Covenant." The political situation was at a knife-edge. It appeared that the Home Rule Bill for Ireland would soon pass the House of Commons in London, and become law. The General Assembly of the Presbyterian Church in Ireland passed a resolution outlining the general Protestant case for the Union and against political control from Dublin. In the autumn, when Protestant leaders composed "The League and Covenant" they were aware of committing a possible treasonous act in appealing directly to the King over the heads of Parliament. They referred to the Home Rule Bill as a "conspiracy," while declaring their loyalty to the Crown.[50] (See a copy of "The League and Covenant" on p. 198.)

Well does Akenson conclude: "That this document, which is the nodal point around which all subsequent Ulster history revolves, was a distinctly Presbyterian artifact is yet another indication of the real (but frequently unrecognized) cultural hegemony that the Ulster-Scots held over the entire Protestant population of the north of Ireland."[51] Alvin

---

49. Quoted in Bruce, *God Save Ulster*, 269-70.

50. Akenson, *God's People*, 185-89.

51. Ibid., 186. On the same point, see also R. F. G. Holmes, "Ulster Presbyterians and Irish Nationalism," in *Religion and National Identity*, Stuart Mews, ed. (Oxford: Basil Blackwell, 1982), 535-48.

Ulster's
Solemn League and Covenant.

Being convinced in our consciences that Home Rule would be disastrous to the material well-being of Ulster as well as of the whole of Ireland, subversive of our civil and religious freedom, destructive of our citizenship and perilous to the unity of the Empire, we, whose names are underwritten, men of Ulster, loyal subjects of His Gracious Majesty King George V., humbly relying on the God whom our fathers in days of stress and trial confidently trusted, do hereby pledge ourselves in solemn Covenant throughout this our time of threatened calamity to stand by one another in defending for ourselves and our children our cherished position of equal citizenship in the United Kingdom and in using all means which may be found necessary to defeat the present conspiracy to set up a Home Rule Parliament in Ireland. ¶ And in the event of such a Parliament being forced upon us we further solemnly and mutually pledge ourselves to refuse to recognise its authority. ¶ In sure confidence that God will defend the right we hereto subscribe our names. ¶ And further, we individually declare that we have not already signed this Covenant.

The above was signed by me at _____
"Ulster Day," Saturday, 28th September, 1912.

God Save the King.

Jackson makes a very valuable point in the same vein. He suggests that the events in Ulster prior to the First World War, and centering on September 28, 1912, "have served as a creation myth for Unionism in the twentieth century — as a kind of Orange Genesis."[52] Fundamentalism in Ulster, then, seems to conform to the typology of American fundamentalism, in both religious and political senses, i.e., by bringing the two together. But before we can say conclusively that Ulster fits the typology, we need to examine one more point, the sense of a cultural crisis.

American fundamentalism was a long time germinating but came to full flower in the years following the First World War. As Marsden has shown, fundamentalists believed America to be at the brink of crisis.[53] A number of things were believed to be under attack, which, taken together, questioned the moral warrant of Protestant cultural leadership. In politics, while Protestants never had total dominance, they exercised a hegemonic role that only rarely had been effectively challenged. With the political mobilization of the "new" immigrants from southern and eastern Europe under the leadership of the Catholic Irish, the "old" outsiders, the Democratic party was seen to be a threat to the "natural" state of politics under Protestant control. Further, the realm of public morals was being threatened, at least as far as evangelical piety was concerned. Prohibiting alcohol and enforcing sabbath observance were highly charged symbolic issues for most Protestants. Right from the beginning of the evangelical hegemony a critical issue turned on who had the power to define the social meaning of drink.[54] Moreover, the education of children was slipping away from the intellectual control of Protestants. Post-Darwinian ideas, along with so-called "progressive" methods, seemed to threaten the learning of civic virtue, always the powerful, if hidden, agenda of the public schools.

In trying to understand the rise of fundamentalism one must place the question in appropriate historical context. Now, by looking into

52. Alvin Jackson, "Unionist Myths, 1912-1985," *Past and Present* 136 (1992): 164-85.
53. Marsden, *Fundamentalism and American Culture*, 11-21; and more fully developed in the same author's *Understanding Fundamentalism and Evangelicalism* (Grand Rapids: William B. Eerdmans, 1991), 9-61.
54. Paul Johnson, *A Shopkeeper's Millennium: Society and Revivals in Rochester, New York, 1815-1837* (New York: Hill and Wang, 1978).

context one does not try to reduce fundamentalism's essentially religious character. However, it is not enough to state that fundamentalists are extremely conservative Protestants; such folk had been around for a long time and had not come forth in this special and separate (and separatist) movement. It took a special moment of a heightened sense of crisis, even hysteria, for a special movement of religiously-based militancy to arise. Militancy is crucial to their outlook. As Marsden observes, "Fundamentalists are not just religious conservatives, they are conservatives who are willing to take a stand and to fight."[55]

If the sense of a social crisis is necessary for a kind of fundamentalist militancy to arise among conservative Protestants, then Ulster seems to fit the pattern well. Ulster Protestants faced perceived threats similar to their American coreligionists: they were accustomed to hegemonic leadership in Ulster society and they resented the prospect of its loss; they worried about (what they called) the moral fiber of the society; theological liberalism in the churches and educational modernism in the schools were also viewed as singularly bad trends. The unique situation in Ulster, of course, was the proposed political changes within the United Kingdom that Home Rule would bring. They did not wish to become part of an Irish nation because they already had a nation toward which they felt deep loyalty. Moreover, in the great carnage of the First World War, they had proven that loyalty to Britain in the persons of the thousands of Ulstermen who had given their lives in the killing fields of France on behalf of crown and country. For the parliament of the United Kingdom to disown them after that sort of sacrifice was incredible to Ulster Protestants. The Home Rule Bill, whose implementation was postponed until after the war, seemed to many Ulster Protestants not only to be a conspiracy against them but a mean and spiteful one at that. Ulster people said "no" in the decisive winter of 1920-21, and many continue to say "no" to the time of this writing. It is often said that Ulster Protestants have a "siege" mentality, an allegation about which most Ulster men and women would be unembarrassed. They believe themselves to be committing everything they are and possess to a righteous cause. As David Miller has demonstrated, the intellectual origins of Ulster unionism in Scottish Presbyterian contract thinking cannot be ignored.[56]

55. Marsden, *Understanding Fundamentalism*, 1.
56. David Miller, *Queen's Rebels* (Dublin: Gill and Macmillan, 1978), 5.

Sociologist Steve Bruce has recently discussed what he calls the fallacies of "liberal" and "ecumenical" thinking in and about Ulster. Liberals, he suggests, generally believe that conflict is based on mutual misunderstanding, and that conflict resolution would follow if groups would redefine their goals. Ecumenicals, on the one hand, make a virtue out of accepting differences between religious groups. But, ecumenicals also insist that such differences need not be threatening to any "tradition," and that both sides should try to learn from each other. Bruce points out, however, that the real constitutional aspirations of the two communities are deeply-held and passionately believed in, and that liberal and ecumenical pronouncements seem — to ordinary people — to be out of touch with reality. The fact is that the equally legitimate aspirations of the two communities cannot be simultaneously fulfilled. At the same time there is a deep conviction on the Protestant side that their desires to remain British will, one day, be swept aside in some final negotiation between Dublin and London, thus deepening the Protestant sense of cultural anxiety.[57]

We have above noted the easy confluence of the notion of theological covenant and of social contract thinking. Arthur Aughey's recent review of Ulster thought in the 1980s, following the Anglo-Irish Agreement, is excellent. Ulster unionism "is at one and the same time completely loyal and completely rebellious. It prostrates itself before the Union Jack and every sympathetic utterance of royal and politician alike and takes to the street with an almost anarchic fervor at the slightest hint of its absolute values being 'compromised.'"[58] Thus the ambiguous nature of the state in Northern Ireland was, and is, the continued cause and sustenance of the sort of social crisis that brings conservative Protestants into a condition of wary militancy. In sum, fundamentalism may well be an American phenomenon, but it is not solely or uniquely so. For the reasons given above, we can suggest that the typology also fits Ulster quite well. Indeed, because of the peculiar circumstances in Northern Ireland, a province lacking consensus about its political legitimacy, militant fundamentalists achieved a social and political role denied their comrades in America.

57. Steve Bruce, *The Edge of the Union: The Ulster Loyalist Political Vision* (Oxford: Oxford University Press, 1994), 122-53.
58. Arthur Aughey, *Under Siege: Ulster Unionism and the Anglo-Irish Agreement* (New York: St. Martin's Press, 1989), 21.

III. Applications for Teaching History

Teaching History, the Gospel, and the Postmodern Self

JERRY L. SUMMERS

Ten years ago when postmodernism was a new concept to me, a mentor remarked offhand that I had already "missed the post-modern wave." Perhaps he was right, but the continuing interest in postmodernism and a condition called postmodernity suggests otherwise. Whether postmodernism is a covering term for such critical approaches as poststructuralism or deconstructionism, or for skeptical attitudes toward the modern world and worldview, the term's greatest problem is its ambiguity in meaning and usage. Nonetheless, its agenda reveals much about the confusion, frustration, and alienation people experience in the modern, or postmodern, West. Most recently associated with the globalization of business and economics, culture and politics, any of which still must be considered modern, postmodernism actually could be considered a longtime critical component of modernism and modernity itself.[1]

As a Christian historian I want to examine the implications of a

---

1. Clive Beck, "Postmodernism, Pedagogy, and Philosophy of Education," PES Yearbook, 1996; [www page]. Urbana: University of Illinois, June 15, 1996 [cited October 27, 1997]. Available from http://www.ed.uiuc.edu/COE/EPS/PES-Year-book/93_docs/BECK.HTM; Terry Eagleton, *The Illusions of Postmodernism* (Oxford, UK: Blackwell, 1996), 62-63; Douglas Kellner, "Globalization and the Postmodern Turn," [Douglas Kellner www page], May 17, 1997 [cited October 27, 1997]. Available from http://www.gseis.ucla.edu/courses/ed253a/dk/globpm.htm.

postmodern worldview for teaching history. If postmodern issues are valid at all, then postmodern perspectives influence historical perspective and should be considered in the integration of faith and learning. The problems of the so-called "postmodern self" suggest the need for a fresh understanding of persons using an authentic approach to history and Christian theological insights.

Historiography and Deconstructionism

Postmodernism and deconstructionism, by raising questions about objectivity and representation, have shaken old presuppositions about historical scholarship. The much-disputed "paradigm shift" that has affected science and all intellectual disciplines, including history, and the supposed growth in relativism are notable trends. Specifically, the New History and history after the "linguistic turn" included the deconstructionist impulse to broaden and democratize historiography by putting history more into the hands of previously ignored or excluded ethnic or minority groups.[2]

In its challenge to historiography on the issue of representation, deconstructionism has denied "the factuality that grounds the authority of history itself." Robert F. Berkhofer described the paradigm of the "Great Story" or "a postulation of the paradigm of normal historical practice" as a reconstruction of the past from evidence and a literary, synthetic representation of the past. Deconstructionists have tended to

---

2. Gertrude Himmelfarb, *The New History and the Old* (Cambridge & London: Belknap, 1987), 1-3; Peter Novick, *That Noble Dream: The "Objectivity Question" and the American Historical Profession* (Cambridge, UK, & New York: Cambridge University Press, 1988), 522-37, 543-45; Pauline M. Rosenau, *Postmodernism and the Social Sciences* (Princeton: Princeton University Press, 1992), 9-10. Lawrence W. Levine, "The Unpredictable Past: Reflections on Recent American Historiography," *American Historical Review* 94 (June 1989): 675, 671-79, passim; Michael Zuckerman, "Myth and Method: The Current Crises in American Historical Writing," *History Teacher* 17 (February 1984): 225, 219-45, passim; Joan Wallach Scott, "History in Crisis? The Others' Side of the Story," *American Historical Review* 94 (June 1989): 686-91; T. C. Patterson, "Post-structuralism, Post-modernism: Implications for Historians," *Social History* 14 (January 1989): 83, 86; Geoff Eley and Keith Nield, "Why Does Social History Ignore Politics?" *Social History* 5 (1980): 249-71; F. R. Ankersmit, "Historiography and Postmodernism," *History and Theory* 28 (1989): 139.

emphasize that the literary, possibly fictional, identity of history exists at the expense of "factual authority." But Berkhofer asserts that it's not time to relativize history or dismiss its objectivity and grasp of true facts. Regardless of one's politics or culture, one relies implicitly on the "Great Story" principle to do history. All histories belong to a greater, comprehensive history. No one view has greater intrinsic legitimacy over other positions, and no one historian can claim to know everything, although some might write as if they did. There is some difficulty if we assume the limitations and inequality of all viewpoints, but all human viewpoints should be open for discussion regardless of their level of objectivity or accuracy. No human viewpoint exists completely separate from all other viewpoints. Although perhaps I have oversimplified it here, that seems to be Berkhofer's point.[3]

Postmodern Curriculum Theory

A mélange of postmodern theories and critiques are now applied to the matter of curriculum development and pedagogy, particularly in the schools; that's no news given the growth of multicultural education and the debates over the proper cultural canon. The critical pedagogues propose alternatives to modern educational theories and practices, as in the limited selection of examples that follow.

As the first example involving a poststructuralist approach, Cleo Cherryholmes disparages the modern, liberal educational establishment in which professionals conform their teaching practices to the dominant "discourses-practices" so that they are, as Michel Foucault charged, "individuals caught up and proficient in discursive and non-discursive practices of their time who participate in discourses without origins or authors and over which they have little control." For example, the ambiguous term "educational excellence" has been the focus of contentious

---

3. Robert F. Berkhofer, "The Challenge of Poetics to (Normal) Historical Practice," *Poetics Today* 9 (1988): 435-40, 444-45, 448; *Beyond the Great Story* (Cambridge, MA, & London: Belknap, 1995), 2-16, 224-27; Nancy F. Partner, "Historicity in an Age of Reality-Fictions," in *A New Philosophy of History*, ed. Frank Ankersmit and Hans Kellner (Chicago: University of Chicago Press, 1995), 21-24, 30-31, 33, 39; and Murray Murphey, *Philosophical Foundations of Historical Knowledge* (Albany: SUNY Press, 1994), 264-68.

debates over educational reform in American higher education, debates which by some accounts have been a power struggle.[4]

William B. Stanley promotes the importance of "textuality" in life and knowing how to use "counterhegemonic praxis." Instead of transcendental human values, the "interpretive competence" achieved by developing *phronesis* or practical judgment should be the goal of critical pedagogy; students should have "the basic competence necessary for linguistic interpretation, as well as political and social action." This competence results from the shared effort to understand human needs in the multicultural context. Through *phronesis,* education would allow human beings to develop utopian community together, but not through the traditional methods. The "insights of postmodern and poststructural theory have made clear that we can no longer apply totalizing critiques, metanarratives, or any other appeals to objective knowledge or transcendental values."[5]

William E. Doll, Jr., seeks to replace the modern worldview and the dominant cosmological paradigm with one derived from a new understanding of the universe. His proposed postmodern, transformative curriculum theory abandons the Newtonian and Cartesian assumptions underlying modernity and modern educational theories. The "open system" curriculum is process-oriented and transformative; human beings as living systems are open systems, so "educational development would occur best when based on the type of system that characterizes being human." Biological, living systems provide an appropriate model for human development; therefore Doll turns to biological hierarchy theory. He focuses on the contradictory yet complementary features of brain function, the "chaotic" operations of billions of cells which are simultaneous with the operation of complex cell patterns in complex structures. The brain function metaphor suggests a new "Curriculum Matrix"

4. Cleo H. Cherryholmes, *Power and Criticism: Poststructural Investigations in Education* (New York & London: Teachers College Press, 1988), 13-14, 33-36, 35-37; citing Michel Foucault, *The Archaeology of Knowledge* (New York: Harper Colophon Books, 1972), 117; *Language, Counter-Memory, Practice* (Ithaca, NY: Cornell University Press, 1980), 200. D. W. Rossides, "Knee-Jerk Formalism: The Higher Education Reports," *Journal of Higher Education* 58 (1987): 404-29; C. Adelman, "War and Peace Among the Words: Rhetoric, Style, and Propaganda in Response to National Reports," *Journal of Higher Education* 58 (1987): 371-403.
5. William B. Stanley, *Curriculum for Utopia: Social Reconstructionism and Critical Pedagogy in the Postmodern Era* (Albany: SUNY Press, 1992), xiv, 189, 210, 215, 220.

which is constructive, nonlinear, and postmodern in a way analogous to the idea of the mind as a tool that constructs meaning.[6]

Lastly, Patrick Slattery provides a holistic approach in which the postmodern curriculum will be a "theological text," and education will incorporate theological and spiritual perspectives. He would minimize or eliminate the scientific, technical curriculum methodologies which scorn religious concerns and enshrine "materialistic atheism in the Newtonian worldview."[7] Let's consider this:

> Postmodern curriculum promotes the exploration of this mystery of eternity and the return of theology to its authentic place as queen of the sciences, not in the premodern sense of an authoritarian monarch to be feared or in the modern sense of an antique barren goddess to be displayed in a museum, but rather as the postmodern benevolent and nurturing Sophia, goddess of eternal wisdom.[8]

The postmodern curriculum will be a process, not a program to be completed, a personal and communal experience, not a methodological, technical course. Theology is "an autobiographical process, a cosmological dialogue, and a search for personal and universal harmony." The "text" is "a phenomenological encounter between word and reader." The curriculum will be a theological text with which to commune with "Sophia" and the sacred, with "self-immersion into myth, mysticism, cosmology, eternity, and the holy center of life." Slattery believes the postmodern curriculum as theological text will provide liberation. I want to propose how a Christian theological perspective amenable to Christian experience ultimately offers more.[9]

---

6. William E. Doll, Jr., "Foundations for a Post-Modern Curriculum" (Washington, DC: ERIC Documents Reproduction Service, 20-24 April 1987), 5-6. Reprinted in "Foundations for a Post-Modern Curriculum," *Journal of Curriculum Studies* 21 (1989): 242-44; "Prigogyne: A New Sense of Order, A New Curriculum," *Theory into Practice* 25 (Winter 1986): 10-16; *A Post-Modern Perspective on Curriculum* (New York & London: Teachers College Press, 1993), 1-4, 57-58, 61-62, 65-66, 161-62.

7. Patrick Slattery, *Curriculum Development in the Postmodern Era* (New York & London: Garland, 1995), 67-68, 71-72.

8. Ibid., 74-75.

9. Ibid., 77, 80-81, 91. Slattery's point about the postmodern curriculum as theological text suggests much about the need for colleges and universities to reconsider the way they serve, especially the private, denominational schools. For a view to refocusing the scripturally-based mission and seeking new ways to attract

JERRY L. SUMMERS

The Postmodern Self and the Challenge for Learning

Critical pedagogical theorists assume the reality of a new, or postmodern, situation, and in that situation a revised, postmodern "self" or "subject." No one definition of the postmodern self dominates, although from a psychological perspective there has been some concern for a more holistic, non-reductive approach to studying individuals than has been true for much of modern psychology.[10]

Holistic conceptions of personhood and the postmodern self undergird attempts to redefine and describe postmodern students, their approaches to and expectations of life. One view notes the irony of providing the traditional curriculum for postmodern students, who supposedly seek to know through opinion and experience and not from recognized authority, to establish meaning in terms acceptable to their peer group, and to keep an "ironic distance" from those matters they regard as authoritarian or elitist. These students feel trapped in the present consumerist culture. Tim McCracken writes that the self is redefined in the "transpersonal age," so that truth is a social construct rather than the "transcendental truth available only to those who have been initiated into the elite."[11]

Henry Giroux has observed that today's youth dwell tensely on the border between the highly structured, technologized, modern world and the "postmodern world of hybridized identities, electronic technologies, local cultural practices, and pluralized public spaces." Because society produces one's social identity, the postmodern society redefines one's humanity. Rapid global change has influenced a generation of

---

students and deliver education cooperatively with the churches, see William E. Hull, "Southern Baptist Higher Education: Prospect," *The Southern Baptist Educator* 61:1 (September 1996): 8-9.

10. Steiner Kvale, "Postmodern Psychology: A Contradictio in Adjecto?" *The Humanistic Psychologist* 18 (Spring 1990): 42-47; cf. S. Koch, "Epilogue," in *Psychology: A Study of a Modern Science,* ed. S. Koch, vol. 3 (New York: McGraw-Hill, 1959), 729-88.

11. Tim McCracken, "Double Coding: Some Characteristic Differences between Modernism and Postmodernism and the Implications for Honors Education" (Washington, DC: ERIC Documents Reproduction Service, 18 May 1987), 4-6, microfiche; "Between Language and Silence: Postpedagogy's Middle Way: Part I The Text" (Washington, DC: ERIC Documents Reproduction Service, 16 May 1989), 12-13, microfiche.

students for whom postmodern pedagogy can best meet their educational needs. As for postmodern youth, be they "baby busters," "slackers," "Generation X," or "border youth," their prospects in adulthood seem less promising than for the previous generation. That may be true if one accepts that the complex, imbalanced postmodern world suppresses personal identity, provides little security, lacks firm boundaries, and confounds relationships among persons in an era of globalization.[12]

Giroux addresses the difficulties of youths who cannot relate to or respect modern responses to life's challenges and who are uncertain about everything. Despite the contributions of modernity in "the language of public life, democratic struggle, and the imperatives of liberty, equality, and justice," a postmodern pedagogy will help reconcile such a critical modernism to the new conditions of life and identity that confront today's youth.[13]

Toward a Christian Transformative Response

Postmodernistic issues may be inconsequential, given the ubiquity of cross-cultural influences and the irrelevance of essentially Western postmodernism in many parts of the world. But for now it seems sensible to listen to the postmodernist critics and to engage their viewpoints creatively and positively, for they do, after all, comment on matters of universal concern. If Christian educational institutions are to promote personal and social change for the good and prepare students for service during a time of "globalization," then there can be no substitute for studies that build intellect and judgment while clarifying vocation.[14]

---

12. Henry A. Giroux, "Slacking Off: Border Youth and Postmodern Education," *JAC* 14:2 (Fall 1994), 2-4, 7; [www page]. Tampa: University of South Florida, December 15, 1994. [cited March 21, 1996]. Available from http://nosferatu.cas.usf.edu/JAC/archive/gir142.html.

13. Ibid., 11-12.

14. Postmodernism as a set of responses to specifically Western cultural problems may make no sense outside the West: Richard B. Cunningham, "Theologizing in a Global Context: Changing Contours," *Review and Expositor* 94:3 (Summer 1997): 351-62. Consider the "post-postmodern take" on higher education which deemphasizes theory and knowledge and recognizes the benefits when students focus on application. Students could integrate theoretical knowledge with interdisciplinary study experiences, community involvement, "outside learning," and practical in-

A Christian transformative curriculum may bring the best understandings of Christian theology and community to bear on problems such as our diminished ability to conduct rational debates about the things that promote a civil society, and the difficulties people have with our society's increasingly artificial and antihuman features. It may promote understanding through practical experiences and international study. The history curriculum, if conceived and implemented with an awareness of these matters, can add much to an interdisciplinary university curriculum. The standards for historical research and teaching will not vanish just because the scope of historical scholarship has broadened so extravagantly. Moreover, the broadening of historical studies continues to correct the long-term historical failure to recognize the United States of America as a multicultural country, and it will help us all to understand global multiculturalism. Besides, a more democratic historical practice should appeal to Christians who believe the ground at the foot of the Cross is level. A multiculturally and pluralistically sensitive curriculum will help to prepare students to build productive relationships in the global, truly multicultural context, if only because it is realistic. If preparation increases opportunity, then graduates will have more choices, successes, and influence in building relationships that change lives.[15]

The alienation of the postmodern self and social segregation attract concern, whether from postmodernists, multiculturalists, critical pedagogues, or Christian churches. The loss of community, and worse, as Charles Taylor has asserted, the decline of "the politics of democratic will-formation" and of political identity, makes coping more difficult for everyone. That observation, combined with the late Christopher Lasch's controversial description of the new elites, gives disturbing insight into the way political and economic elites can use power to mutate and dominate individuals and nations. The various "privileged communities" of the creative and super-competent elites relate to overlapping and

volvement in the arts. Many institutions already do this with great benefit to their students. About post-postmodernism or neopragmatism, see John E. Wills, Jr., "The Post-Postmodern University," *Change* (March/April 1995): 59-62.

15. Anthony C. Thiselton, *Interpreting God and the Postmodern Self* (Grand Rapids: Eerdmans, 1995), 131-35. Thiselton acknowledges the postmodernist arguments about the manipulative dominance of power structures, but objects to the idea that "*all* truth-claims are bids for power" (135). For a discussion on the new possibilities afforded historians and their students, see Lawrence W. Levine, *The Opening of the American Mind: Canons, Culture, History* (Boston: Beacon, 1996), 142-46.

interchangeable "circles of power — finance, government, art, entertainment." The connection corresponds strongly to the "structures and spheres of power" that Foucault identified, and constitutes a mundane but powerful example of the Apostle Paul's "rulers" and "authorities" and "cosmic powers of this present darkness."[16]

What does this imply for how Christian higher education institutions prepare students? We pursue the life of the mind and spirit while we receive students from varied backgrounds. They complete college degrees and attain a new social status. Will these students have adopted the attitudes and lifestyles not of elitists but of servants? Only the servants will be able to do anything to temper the effects of fragmentation and alienation in our world. Only the servants will consistently choose to influence people through sacrificial living rather than through the selfish and dehumanizing use of knowledge and power.[17]

The rarified arguments of postmodernists or poststructuralists may amount to valid criticisms of power structures or systems of dominance, the assumptions and objectives of power-elites and of interest groups. But such investigations possibly are inappropriate for undergraduates who are striving to master basic scholarship. However, teachers can at

16. Charles Taylor, *The Ethics of Authenticity* (Cambridge, MA, & London: Harvard University Press, 1991), 118-19; Christopher Lasch, *The Revolt of the Elites and the Betrayal of Democracy* (New York & London: W. W. Norton, 1995), 29-38. Lasch cites Robert Reich, *The Work of Nations* (New York: Alfred A. Knopf, 1992). Thiselton (132) cites David Lyon, *Postmodernity* (Buckingham, UK: Open University Press, 1994), who identifies the inseparability of social, philosophical, literary, and political matters. François Lyotard decried the "totalism" of technocracy, and how the "system seems to be a vanguard machine dragging humanity after it, dehumanizing it in order to rehumanize it at a different level of normative capacity." *The Postmodern Condition: A Report on Knowledge,* trans. Geoffrey Bennington and Brian Massumi (Minneapolis: University of Minnesota Press, 1985), 62-63. Similarly, in C. S. Lewis: "What is now common to all men is a mere abstract universal, and H. C. F. [highest common factor], and Man's conquest of himself means simply the rule of the Conditioners over the conditioned human material, the world of post-humanity which, some knowingly and some unknowingly, nearly all men in all nations are at present labouring to produce." *The Abolition of Man* (New York: Macmillan, 1972), 84-86; Ephesians 6:12 (NRSV).

17. Social responsibility, moral meaning, purposeful competence, and a vision for life that makes sense are among the themes Steven Garber discusses in *Fabric of Faithfulness: Weaving Together Belief and Behavior During the University Years* (Downers Grove, IL: InterVarsity, 1997). He emphasizes the call to servanthood, regarding higher education as more than training for a career or a "passport to privilege" (69).

least lead students to read from various perspectives and to survey the "voicings" of various individuals and people groups. For undergraduate history survey classes a basic and well-proven approach is to read and discuss the distinctive texts of world cultural traditions, including those of the Western tradition. It is a foray into foundationalism, but I have been delighted to see students enthusiastic about their first insights into the value assumptions of other historical cultures.

Surely a good general knowledge of one's own cultural traditions gives a proper foundation for multicultural comparisons. Visitors to the United States from other cultures consistently demonstrate little or no inclination to discuss their own cultures from a Western perspective first! The teaching task includes the challenging but delightful work of recognizing, describing, and analyzing global multiculturalism in order to understand its influence on us all. For example, there is no escaping the ubiquity of media influences that pervade and connect cultures. On a recent trip to China, I was able to tune into such a horror as the "Ren and Stimpy Show" or to "Oprah" at four in the afternoon on microwave broadcasts from Hong Kong television. I can only imagine what the Chinese thought.

Christians Doing History

What brings value to the history classroom is surely a component of the servant's attitude in *agape* love, the dynamic other-interestedness[18] of the teacher whose faith pervades historical research and reflection, and the classroom presentations and discussions. The student should find one value-added quality in the teacher-student relationship wherein studying together is a redemptive, grace-filled activity which may even activate faith. It is a witness of the dynamic presence of the divine Spirit in the life of the teacher, prompting or affirming that presence in the life of the student, and vice versa.

The quality of dynamic other-interestedness in teaching also models an attitude of openness and patient, sustained inquiry into historical issues that affect current experience. This is analogous to building interpersonal relationships: in making friends one interacts, builds trust, and comes to grips with those features of the other's past that comprise

18. 1 John 4:19.

and commend the person who is "friend" today. We seek the kind of meaningful relationship that will overcome the travails of the postmodern self or of the modern self (I think we can choose either) and its faults and wounds. Postmodernists and "postmoderns" still seek a satisfying historical model of the self, one to show how to transcend the challenges of postmodernity. We Christians think we have found just that for every era — indeed, a touchstone, a paragon who, though cloaked with mystery, presents the clearest, most desirable model of fulfilled humanity. Historical study yields fruit as we are able to seek to know more about historical figures before and since Jesus of Nazareth. Despite the comparatively fine detail we have about many more recent figures, we understand them incompletely, as we do even ourselves. Historically speaking, we gain insight about the past as time passes, but we also must learn to accept the benefits of experience in the present we share with others. The continual expectation of crisis comes partly because we fail to use the power of servanthood; the overwhelmed, postmodern self needs overwhelming love, and servanthood that meets personal need.

Thus I return to the teaching and learning relationship, recognizing my limitations and those of other limited individuals. But the common desire to learn also prompts cooperation. I want to communicate what I can of my understanding of history, and my students typically believe history will increase their understanding of the world and life. They enter a class assuming differences of role and authority between themselves and the teacher: I am to tell them what to do, and how. I struggle to convince them that I do not have all the agenda, and that we have objectives to reach together. Perhaps I have the advantage of a more sophisticated historical understanding, but collectively and repeatedly they teach me my limits. Our common commitment to history increases my understanding.

Adult interdependence is a valid goal of higher education. My experiences with ill-prepared, unconfident students suggest that I have not mastered whatever may contribute to personal development in my students. Their (and my) personal growth depends to some degree on the nature of the relationship I seek to build with them. I want students to know I have their lifelong well-being at heart, and I think I gain strength by striving to blend personal interest, graciousness, and tough-minded caring in order to encourage character and self-confidence in my students. I'm not sure what influence I have. Nonetheless, if the aim of Christian education is to facilitate changed minds, then authentic personal relationship must meld with scholarly discipline to engender hope. In this way I believe the liberation of Christ surpasses the valued, ideal, modern agenda in education, because Christian liberal education aims to prepare persons to know themselves better in relation to God, and to serve others in diverse settings. And so, it is a strong species of hope for Christ-like transformation which the Christian may consider the only satisfactory hope for the postmodern self.[19]

My Christian students want to be servants. Their view of history must relate to and come from the sense of vocation they have as people of God. They trust, hope, and believe their obedience will make a difference, even though servanthood inevitably involves suffering. That suffering may come as the product of adopting a lifestyle consciously contrary to the schemes of modernity or postmodernity. Suffering results also from quitting comfortable, customary cultural patterns and surpassing old horizons. The Christian struggle to reform one's conception of education means exchanging old intellectual and spiritual assumptions for a firm sense of purposeful vocation, by no means an easy assignment.[20]

Anthony Thiselton has discussed the temporal vocation of persons: while they live in the time given to them as God's people they make a difference because they live in hope and can convey it to others. One's vocation fulfilled within God's frame of values will not harmonize with the helpless "situatedness" of the postmodern self. Instead, there is a new horizon, a broader world full of hope, that takes shape from the Trinitarian model of love as the basis of selfhood. The dynamic other-interestedness of *agape* is the very stuff of the mutuality of the Trinity enveloped in the Holy Spirit's power.[21] Christian theology explains how persons can be fully persons and reconciled to others only in loving relationships. That also will not harmonize with the failures of human history, that is, the continual subversion and corruption of humanity that

---

19. Thiselton, 145, citing Jürgen Moltmann, *Theology of Hope* (London: SCM, 1967), 103, 36, 41. Moltmann, writing on theological concepts: "They illuminate reality by displaying its future. Their knowledge is grounded not in the will to dominate, but in love to the future of things . . . engaged in a process of movement [they] call forth practical movement and change." Also, "They do not seek to make a mental picture of existing reality, but to lead existing reality towards the promised and hoped-for transformation" (Moltmann, 36, 18).

20. Ibid., 147, 149.

21. Ibid., 151, 156; citing Wolfhart Pannenberg, *Systematic Theology*, vol. 1 (Edinburgh: T & T Clark, & Grand Rapids: Eerdmans, 1991), 426-27.

has happened whenever persons have demeaned themselves by demeaning others.

The postmodern self has a complex problem. Perhaps "human nature" does not change, but we can see how persons develop under the influence of social, cultural, and historical factors. By leading students to examine the social "self" historically we may understand how the circumstances of birth, environment, and experience always have shaped individuals. Of course such agenda figure in multicultural studies and education. History shows the need for creativity and clear understanding to meet the dehumanizing challenges which we always have with us. However, the confident message of the faithful and a liberating hope is this: that the model of properly centered humanity in Jesus Christ and the theological comprehension of divine love in the Triune God remain powerful resources in the present. There is something to commend the gospel concept of rebirth as a new creation, "reconstituted self-identity," as an alternative to the constituted, situated, and alienated postmodern self.[22]

Scripture Interprets the Self

The Christian historian, recognizing the broader evidences and counterevidences for proper human values in history, may doubt the postmodern metanarrative of the systematization of the will to power and propose an alternative view. Thiselton, in his chapter, "Textual Reading Interprets the Self," discusses how the encounter with texts affects selfhood and self-identity. First, one may learn about the author of a text. Second, the biblical text is said to transform the selfhood of the reader. Third, a text may reveal what is otherwise hidden in one's self as the text makes of the self an object of understanding. Fourth, interpretations may reveal more about the interpreters than the texts they interpret. Fifth, also particularly concerning the biblical text, as scripture interprets the self, the "possibilities for future change and growth" become evident.[23] These hermeneutical or interpretive principles, as they apply to the examination of any text, apply also to historical texts.

If understanding is our goal, then we must respect narrative texts as purveyors of truths that supersede our individual and group perspec-

22. Ibid., 160-61.
23. Ibid., 63-66.

tives: the process of "hearing out" anyone's historical text may require a willingness to submit to the writer's claims in a way analogous to the way one may need to respond to the "claims" of the Word of God on one's life. That is, if one wants to know the other through the text.[24]

As to the problem of persons entering dialogue, to engage carefully, respectfully, with the ideas of another is a way to be personally transparent and encourage the same of the other. This attractive principle can help to begin relationships and build friendships, although one will not want to be uncritically blind to certain of the other's ideas. Perhaps no benefit comes by attempting dialogue with a hostile critic or cultured despiser of the faith; however, the Christian bears the first responsibility to initiate the kind of relationship that can change a life.

As this issue relates to historiography and historical interpretation, it is valid to examine the motivations and commitments of those who doubt the coherence and truth of conventional history, especially if they have no satisfactory alternative. Their presuppositions may result from their association with a particular social, cultural, or political group, and to the degree their assertions prompt the decline of civil, reciprocal discussion, we must ask why they deserve a hearing.

On this point, given the debates on diversity and representation in the historical profession, and to the extent there are many new attempts to present and represent the stories of groups absent in conventional histories, many groups of people claim the right to be heard and to be recognized through mutually respectful dialogue. Multiculturalism joins here with the problems of the postmodern self; that is, multicultural expression amid globalization is more and more the true context of any solution to or explanation for the postmodern self. Because biblical interpretation is most important for self-understanding and identity in the Christian tradition, is it any surprise that alienated individuals and groups seek to be recognized as legitimate and important by ensuring that their stories are written or otherwise recorded?[25] May I suggest that historical, textual self-expressions constitute attempts to define the lives of people groups in some transcendent, purposeful way, just as biblical texts and

24. Ibid., 65, citing Rudolf Bultmann, "The Problem of Hermeneutics," in *Essays Philosophical and Theological* (London: SCM, 1955), 242-45. Thiselton compares Bultmann's assertions at that point to the historical hermeneutics of Dilthey and Heidegger.
25. Ibid.

the traditions of interpretation and application convey the continuity and community of living faith?

The Christian theistic tradition is powerful after all. The Ephesian letter speaks of barriers breached between God and humankind through Christ. Therefore, the multiple voicings of a multiculturalist history are in a sense compatible with the concept of human liberty in the Spirit of God. This remains the superlative challenge, else why would postmodernists and multiculturalists pursue the humanizing agenda of recognition and participation in affirming community? Consider for example the critical pedagogues in their quests for holism, transcendence, and community through educational change. The divine Spirit seeks various avenues to make people hungry and thirsty for dignity and harmony, and the gospel allows no ultimate satisfaction apart from Jesus Christ and the community he promises. Features of community exist in our pluralistic world, although no community achieves perfection or becomes a "utopia." In the Protestantized, then secularized, West, that is a monumental problem for the churches and for Christian institutions of higher education.

Teachers and students who think faithfully can benefit from the challenging and enriching interrogation of history. Christian historical thinking assumes that we recollect how God decisively and uniquely entered history by choosing a body and by working out the details of human salvation amid an ethnic society set in the pluralized world of the Roman empire. The theological and historical ramifications of the incarnation justify our struggles in time and among cultures to live and serve convincingly as Christians. Contrary to the many contemporary, theoretical, or sophistic approaches, that insight must encourage the simultaneous engagement of spirit and intellect. It is "storied," narrative food for the soul, for it honors both inquiring mind and yearning spirit, expressing the richness of divine purpose and accomplishment through human experience across time, despite the thwarting of divine purposes in human circumstances.

Doing Justice in History:
Using Narrative Frames Responsibly

G. MARCILLE FREDERICK

Does Micah's injunction to "do justice, love kindness, and walk humbly with your God" (6:8) have any bearing on a Christian's historical work? I believe that it does. We do justice when we give all the historical actors their due, not privileging those who had the most power, or for whom we have more data. Loving kindness means exercising compassion towards our historical subjects. They were no more limited by their location and biases than we are. They were creating lives as they went; we need to re-create those lives with a minimum of moralizing. To walk humbly is to recognize that even hindsight is not fully accurate and that our accounts are never definitive.

In this chapter, I will look at how pedagogy in survey courses can serve both students and the subjects of study — those women and men whose lives we trace, and those events and things we describe. I will do so with some help from an unexpected source, the intellectual historian Hayden White. White began his career in the late 1950s as a historian of medieval Arabic thought, but he soon began to concentrate on historiography, specifically on how story forms shape their contents. He was heavily influenced in this by anthropological and folklore approaches, which emphasized a story's commonalities with other similar tales, rather than a story's uniqueness. For example, instead of reading *The Adventures of Huckleberry Finn* for its adventures or for what it could tell us about Samuel Clemens or nineteenth-century American black/white relations, these approaches note its structural similarities to other adventure stories, whether these be in the narrative shape, use of dialogue, or its types of protagonists. These similarities to other novels, the common stock of literary forms and devices from which Clemens drew to construct *The Adventures of Huckleberry Finn,* shape the literary content of the story as much (if not more) than Clemens' inventiveness.

Such an approach would seem at first to be the antithesis of historical work, which approaches the past looking for its specific context and its unique features. White argued that while this specificity did exist in the past, historical accounts nevertheless fell into typical narrative patterns. Eventually, following the structuralism of Claude Lévi-Strauss,[1] White argued that our minds organize material by applying narrative structures (which exist in the mind) to the data at hand. He identified these structures with the four classical rhetorical tropes (metaphor, metonymy, synecdoche, irony). Based on these are four modes of emplotment (Romance, Comedy, Tragedy, Satire). When we create stories, we fit the available data into one of these forms. For White, the order is in the mind, not in the events the mind traces.[2]

How can White's theory help us as Christian historians? His work can help us do justice in two ways. First, White emphasizes the multiplicity of possible narratives that can be generated by one set of data. Doing justice to, say, Western civilization is then telling *one* story, not trying to tell all of them. We are responsible for the story we tell, not for all of the stories we cannot possibly include. Second, by realizing that we must make choices in our telling, that we do not have access to a God's-eye view of history, we are freed, in my judgment, to "walk humbly," rejecting the temptation to view our dated, located, limited storytelling as *the* story.[3]

I will draw on one piece of White's complex historiographical theory, i.e., narrative emplotment. I emphasize this because I believe historians deal with narratives in at least two ways. Some of us still write them. Others

---

1. Hayden White, *Metahistory: The Historical Imagination in Nineteenth-century Europe* (Baltimore: The Johns Hopkins University Press, 1973), 30-31.
2. One can see the influence of a Kantian intellectual framework, in which one cannot get to "things in themselves" (the past and *its* order in this case), but instead the mind creates its own order. I owe this point to Robert Sweetman. See Immanuel Kant, *Kritik der reinen Vernunft,* 2nd ed. (1787), translated as *The Critique of Pure Reason* (many English editions available). See White, *Metahistory,* 6-7.
3. While there are many possible stories, there are not an infinite number. Nor are they all of equal value. White, *Metahistory,* 31.

of us use them more implicitly, in our periodization or in how we define our subject specialty. For example, the periodization of ancient, medieval, and modern history has the implicit shape of a comic narrative: from the greatness of the ancients through the dark ages in the middle (distinguished only by being "between" the other two periods) to the progressive moderns. This periodization begins to appear (and take hold) in the fourteenth century. The Italian humanists who created it were trying to create historical space for their own city-states over against the claims of the Holy Roman Emperors. Both the emperors and the humanists claimed to be the rightful heirs of the Roman empire. For the emperors, this meant asserting a continuity, while for the humanists it meant a discontinuity.[4] This shape also contains judgments about the three periods and emphasizes the discontinuities between them. I will have more to say about narrative shapes and the judgments implicit in them later.

White argues that stories provide meaning by being of certain types. The historical narrative explains past structures "by representing them." That is, the story's meaning is to be found in its shape. "Emplotment is the way by which a sequence of events fashioned into a story is gradually revealed to be a story of a particular kind."[5] The historian makes an argument, as it were, by putting the story in a familiar shape (Romance, Tragedy, Comedy, Satire).[6] We recognize the type of story we're hearing, and thus understand the historical matter.[7] The Romance involves

4. Ernst Breisach, *Historiography: Ancient, Medieval and Modern* (Chicago: University of Chicago Press, 1983), 159-60, 181.

5. White, *Metahistory*, 2, 7.

6. White calls these "archetypal" shapes (*Metahistory*, 8). Readers and listeners as well as writers tend to transform stories into familiar shapes. Edmund Blair Bolles gives the example of a First Nations story which memory theorist Frederick Bartlett told to some non-Aboriginal experimental subjects. The story featured a battle and a number of unusual details, including ghost warriors. Bartlett asked his listeners to retell the story to him after fifteen minutes, and again after four and six months. With each retelling the story became shorter and lost more of its First Nations character. The listeners gradually transformed "a baffling yet moving story into something comprehensible but dull." *Remembering and Forgetting: An Inquiry into the Nature of Memory* (New York: Walker and Company, 1988), 68.

7. White suggests that there may be three additional types: Epic, Fairy Tale, and Detective story, but he does not elaborate on this (*Metahistory*, p. 8, n. 6). I think his decision to link the four tropes with (four) modes of emplotment pushed him to exclude these and other possible types. White is not clear on how the tropes and forms of emplotment are linked. *Metahistory*, 29-38.

"the hero's transcendence of the world of experience," the triumph of something good over something bad, especially if that triumph involves beating the odds, breaking through traditional boundaries, doing the miraculous. Satire is the opposite theme — there is no redemption; it is "a drama dominated by the apprehension that man is ultimately a captive of the world rather than its master." The other two plot types, Comedy and Tragedy, involve partial transcendence of the world, but in two different ways. "In Comedy, hope is held out for the temporary triumph of man over his world by the prospect of occasional *reconciliations* of the forces at play in the social and natural worlds." These reconciliations are symbolized by the festivities which terminate the narrative. Though the party will eventually be over, things are in balance for the moment. In Tragedy, there is only the sober realization that one cannot beat the system. The protagonist and audience gain, however, in their understanding of how the system works.[8]

White further asserts that the same set of facts can serve as a basis for a plot in each of the four modes.[9] Let me illustrate this by telling four slightly different — and admittedly simple — stories. They differ in their sense of what is significant. Although each story could contain all of the facts, the formal design of each pushes for the inclusion of some and not others. Here's a Romance: It seemed impossible for me to get to church on time — the alarm clock failed to go off, I had a run in my hose, my Bible had gone missing. Worse, the streetcars only run every twenty minutes on Sunday. As I left the house, I saw the streetcar round the corner just ahead of me. But God knew I needed to get to church. A friend who usually goes to church by a different route came by and gave me a ride. Here's a Satire: It was almost impossible for me to get to church on time — the alarm clock failed to go off, I had a run in my hose, my Bible had gone missing. Worse, the streetcars only run every twenty minutes on Sunday. As I left the house, I saw the streetcar round the corner just ahead of me. A friend who usually goes to church by a different route came by and gave me a ride. As we rode along, I had to listen to my friend's quarreling, screaming children. I got to church with a headache. And we were still late. Now a Comedy: It was almost

8. White, *Metahistory*, 8-11.
9. "The same event can serve as a different kind of element of many different historical stories, depending on the role it is assigned in . . . the set to which it belongs" (White, *Metahistory*, 8).

impossible for me to get to church on time — the alarm clock failed to go off, I had a run in my hose, my Bible had gone missing. Worse, the streetcars only run every twenty minutes on Sunday. As I left the house, I saw the streetcar round the corner just ahead of me. The friend who came by and gave me a ride also had some quarreling, screaming children along. I got to church with a headache. And we were still late. But I wasn't as late as I would have been if my friend hadn't come along. As a Tragedy: It was almost impossible for me to get to church on time — the alarm clock failed to go off, I had a run in my hose, my Bible had gone missing. Worse, the streetcars only run every twenty minutes on Sunday. As I left the house, I saw the streetcar round the corner just ahead of me. I was late despite getting an unexpected ride from a friend. As a result of all this, I resolved to go to bed earlier on Saturdays and to lay my clothes and Bible out ahead of time.

I found, as I wrote these stories, that the formal design of each pushes for the inclusion of some story elements as against others. The narrative form in which we choose to cast our story impinges upon what we can see in the historical landscape. There is an interplay between what I see in the facts and what the story form I select would emphasize. If I am attentive to God's role, then I will tend to leave out the screaming kids and the fact that I was late anyway. It's not that they didn't happen, but they are insignificant next to God's activity. Moreover, they clutter the narrative. If I am struck by my story's similarity to the "can't win" nature of Satire, the more significant the impediments to my getting to church on time appear. If God shows up in this story at all, it's with an ironic twist. I set out to tell the "late-for-church" story emphasizing different things, deliberately trying to fit each plot type. While I (following White) think that historians seldom consciously choose such plots, we may be quick to spot subconsciously the plot potential of many historical matters. If we like underdogs, we may more easily transform our historical matter into a Romance narrative. If we are attracted to the mysterious movements of God (or Reason, or Progress, or whatever) we may find ourselves writing Comedies. There is no necessity that we do so: there is no narrative form just sitting there in the dust of our historical data, waiting to be brushed off and displayed.[10]

10. White, *Metahistory*, 7, 430. " . . . The historian confronts a veritable chaos of events . . . out of which [she or] he must choose the elements of the story [she or] he would tell" (p. 6, n. 5).

White claims that "a given historian is forced to emplot the whole set of stories making up his [or her] narrative in one comprehensive or *archetypal* story form."[11] While I agree that the narrative form is not inherent in the data, I do not accept White's contention that a historian is forced to write in one of these four narrative forms. First, his choice of four tropes (and these four), and their linking with the narrative forms of Romance, Tragedy, Comedy, and Satire, seems to me limiting and arbitrary. Other lists of rhetorical tropes include many more types.[12] Second, while White's model claims that the tropes (and their attendant story forms) are structures of the mind, they came about historically. Rather than revealing some kind of universal structures of the mind, I suggest that these story forms are a brief catalog of ancient Greek dramatic styles. White himself suggests that the detective story might be a possible narrative form. If it derives from some mind structure, White needs to explain why the detective story does not appear until the nineteenth century.[13] There is another sense in which White's story forms are not universal. They are all stereotypically masculine, emphasizing the hero (often a loner against overwhelming forces) in an agonistic, confrontational mode. All of the forms of emplotment, as White describes them, involve winners and losers, not partners and cooperation. For example, in the Comedic form, there are "occasional reconciliations" of forces; why not "occasional conflict" instead? I wonder if the need for dramatic tension peculiar to these plotted narratives works against the inclusion of more slow-moving, or less conflictual, situations. For example, do the common experiences of childrearing and patterns of socialization pale (in a dramatic sense) next to the vibrant colors of armed conflict? I also wonder about the cross-cultural applicability of these plot types.

11. White, *Metahistory*, 8.

12. F. W. Lancaster, *Vocabulary Control for Information Retrieval*, 2nd ed. (Washington, D.C.: Information Resources Press, 1986), 46-47, has eleven types. Bede identified thirteen tropes in his *De schematibus et tropis* (700 or 701). See the translation by Gussie Hecht Tannenhaus, "Bede's *De schematibus et tropis* — a translation," *Quarterly Journal of Speech* 48:3 (October 1962): 237-53. For more background on rhetorical tropes, see James J. Murphy, *Rhetoric in the Middle Ages: A History of Rhetorical Theory from Saint Augustine to the Renaissance* (Berkeley: University of California Press, 1974).

13. For more on the history of the detective novel, see Alma Elizabeth Murch, *The Development of the Detective Novel*, rev. ed. (London: P. Owen, 1968).

Hayden White grounds the multiplicity of narrative forms in the multiplicity of tropes, which he maintains are the structures of historical consciousness. White insists on this pluriformity of stories because he wants historians to be free to shape the past. For him, if humans cannot shape the past, we cannot be free to shape the future.[14] I do not think that we need such an expansive view of our own freedom to shape the past in order to shape the future, nor do I find such a view desirable. Moreover, I think White, in affirming our construction work in/on history, fails to take proper account of the materials with which we make those constructions. For example, the language we use when we write history has a history of its own, a bundle of connotations we have to be aware of. While "the War of the Rebellion," "the war of Northern aggression," "the War Between the States," and "the American Civil War" all refer to the military and social conflict that took place in the United States[15] between 1861-1865, these phrases manifestly do not mean the same thing. We cannot use any of these phrases without calling up a host of (perhaps unintended) meanings. Words and historical evidence have a concreteness and individuality that we must respect. We cannot make them into anything we choose.

While these criticisms have their place, I do not think that they undermine White's larger point.[16] If there is a multiplicity of stories to be told, we are freed from the need to attempt a History with a capital "H" (or THE Renaissance, or *Western Civilization: the Real story*). Our work is shaped and limited not only by our data and our biases, but by the narrative forms we choose. Much as we might like to tell several stories at once, we invariably end up giving more weight to one than the others. Each narrative frame reveals different nuances in the data, just as changing the frame on a painting brings out different shadings and colors.

While I do not think that we are forced to use the common narrative forms White describes, I observe we have done so in survey courses. Surveys are perhaps prone to simple narrative construction because their purposes include giving our students a taste of everything, and (more

14. White, *Metahistory*, 433.
15. Those sympathic to the Confederate cause would say "between the United States and the Confederacy" rather than "in the United States."
16. I have developed these and other criticisms of White in my M.Phil.F. thesis, "Hayden White on Historical Narrative: A Critique" (Institute for Christian Studies, Toronto, 1992).

importantly) trying to set a larger context for the more focused courses.[17] In Western civilization and American history survey courses, our orienting stories are usually in the shape of Romances. The typical story describes the rise of democracy (usually thought of in terms of expanding the voting franchise), from the Greeks and Romans through its decline in the late Empire and the Middle Ages to its implicit revival in the Renaissance and Reformation, and its triumph with the successive franchisement of black men, European immigrants, women, and eighteen-year-olds. Sometimes the story includes freedom as a strong component, which is often also conceived of in political terms or in an economic progression from slavery and feudalism to mercantilism to capitalism.[18] Even if our experience, or that of the group we are studying, suggests otherwise, the form of the survey pushes us to devalue the data that doesn't fit the form, or to make that data serve the form. I have come to realize that though I work in nineteenth century American social history, my orienting grid is still the political chronology — Lincoln, Johnson, Grant, Hayes — that I learned in grade school. I have not yet found a series of period markers that work as well as these successive administrations. It is also difficult to reorient myself in historical time — it is almost like learning a new language. The late nineteenth-century U.S. is still gilded, still populated with robber barons, although I see more of "the masses yearning to breathe free" than I once did. I realized that the grid's placement of "the little people" on the edge of history, an inert mass which could be pushed around at the financiers' whim, didn't square with the historical record. This "faceless mass" organized strikes,

17. Western civilization courses have also had other purposes, as Carolyn Lougee notes: "In cultural terms, the Western Civ ideal was homogenizing and normative: it socialized the young from whatever particularist background traditions to a uniform standard of thinking and behaving that ought to characterize America's expanding educated class." "Comment" on Gilbert Allardyce's "The Rise and Fall of the Western Civilization Course," *American Historical Review* 87:3 (June 1982): 727.

18. Jacques Le Goff, in his essay, "For an Extended Middle Ages," in *The Medieval Imagination* (Oxford: Blackwell, 1988), 18-23, has suggested some narrative shapes based not on politics and economics but on, e.g., technology (forms of transportation and communication). Lewis Mumford, in *The Technics of Civilization* (New York: Harcourt, Brace & World, 1934), has suggested a periodization based on the motive power used (human or animal strength, water, steam, internal combustion, electricity).

married, played, made eloquent pleas for justice, and lived lives full of passion and pain, despite abusive power and too little money.

Nor did my own experience of blue-collar life fit the cog-in-the-machine metaphor. There is richness in giving a cup of cold water, welcoming a child, visiting the sick — a richness Jay Gould could never match with his bundles of stock certificates. The problem, for me, is that the grid, while a useful scaffolding for the historical work in progress, also obscures the work. The political-economic grid places some experiences (e.g., industrialization and the accumulation of capital) in more prominent view than others (e.g., child-rearing and popular entertainment).[19] Changing technology in the steel mills meant, for Andrew Carnegie, an opportunity to grab market share. For a puddler at one of the small Pittsburgh mills, swallowed up as steel production centralized and became capital-intensive, it was the loss of a craft, a skill, a livelihood. Fitting the deskilled and dispossessed workers' view of technological change into the narrative of the Gilded Age is like putting sin into theology — it has to be included, but it doesn't harmonize with the story. If the story's emphasis is on the outcome of industrialization, it's hard to keep the puddlers from becoming the inevitable fuel of technological progress, or the poor losers who didn't have Carnegie's foresight (alas) to see where history was going. Although Carnegie plays a more powerful role in industrialization than the mill puddler, often American history survey courses turn him, as well, into the servant of a larger process like industrialization or the triumph of corporate capitalism.

Sometimes the shape of the accepted periodization forces you to choose the experiences of one group over another. Joan Kelly has argued that women did not have a Renaissance.[20] Reappropriation of Greek and Roman thought did not lead to more political and social freedom for women, but its opposite. Is it possible to do justice to women's experience without throwing over the periodization, without doing away with the Renaissance? Many colleges have dealt with the (male-) gendered nature

19. The American Social History Project Staff's *Who Built America? Working People and the Nation's Economy, Politics, Culture and Society* (New York: Pantheon, 1990-92) offers an alternative periodization of American history based on workers' experience.

20. See her essay, "Did Women Have a Renaissance?", originally published in *Becoming Visible: Women in European History* (Boston: Houghton Mifflin, 1977), reprinted in *Women, History and Theory: The Essays of Joan Kelly* (Chicago: University of Chicago Press, 1984), 19-50.

of the accepted periodization by creating another stream of courses in women's history, with an alternative period grid. This approach creates as many problems as it solves. First, it leaves intact in the regular (usually required) survey courses the notion that "the main story" is the story of men. "Separate but equal" courses on women's and men's experiences, especially when women's history courses are not required, can leave women on the margins of the "real" story being told in the regular survey courses. Second, this approach does not integrate women's and men's experience, creating a segregation in the courses that does not exist in reality. Third, this approach forces the students who take the women's history courses to try to fit these two periodizations (women's history and the other one) together. Adding courses with an alternative periodization avoids the hard thinking about whether we can create new periodizations that will work for all groups when their experiences seem to call for divergent periodizations. We do not then have to face the possibility that such a periodization may be impossible. Fourth, this approach may seem to work as long as there are only two groups (women and men) to consider. But what about when the groupings divide into, say, black and white women and men? Rich and poor women and men? The possibilities for splitting groups into smaller and smaller bits based on their differing experiences may be nearly infinite. Will we then create a nearly infinite number of courses and periodizations?

Another approach has been to keep the traditional periodization but to stuff more points of view into it.[21] Take a topic each week and rotate it like a diamond: the French Revolution from the points of view, respectively, of king, nobles, church, Parisian peasants, Edmund Burke, Groen van Prinsterer, Karl Marx, and so on. The next week: sailing vessels, eating habits, or interchangeable parts. Indeed, the way to deal with history's complexities is to balance topics and points of view. Do we have enough women? ethnic groups? class distinctions? political, social, economic, religious topics? This approach creates a different problem: how does the periodization relate to the topical themes? We leave students awash in details, cynical about all methodologies, chary of all points of view. We lose the diamond of history in its facets. What we gain, besides an appreciation of complexity, is a fund of anecdotes or moral tales. We give up trying to tell a story at all.

21. Which is not so different from the proposal to create a nearly infinite number of courses and periodizations.

I believe that we cannot think historically without some kind of grid, some larger narrative, with all the oversimplifications and blind spots that entails. I would prefer not to speak of "metanarrative," because I do not believe these grids function inherently as a means of rational totalization and oppression. That is, these narratives do not claim to comprehend and explain the whole, nor are they primarily rational and logical in character. Rather, they are founding stories, taken on faith (or habit) and not exhaustive stories.[22] We also need, I think, some kind of spatial grid, a geographical sense of where we are. It is no accident that the primary field identifications of historians are time period and geographic location.[23] What Hayden White has helped us to see is that there is more than one possible grid, and that all grids are both partial (fragmenting) and holistic (synthesizing). But how do we decide which story to tell? For whom is the story we are telling tragic, or ironic? For whom is it a Comedy or Romance? Even if we are sympathetic to the steel mill puddler, he becomes at best a tragic episode or subtheme in the larger Romance of Western Civilization. The only way to give him his due has been to invert the story. Some have taught the now ironically titled "Western Civilization" as a Tragedy, with the loss of aboriginal and folk cultures the centerpiece of the tale. History is, I submit, more of a mixed bag than either of these possibilities allows.

I would like to affirm even more strongly than historians' different points of view "imposed from without" (as it were) the possibilities of different points of view "from within." For example, what if the missed streetcar story focused not on me, but on the friend who gave me a lift? It might then still include my tale of woe, as I tell my friend about my errant alarm clock. In another tale, the streetcar driver slows down and looks for that lady who is always in a rush, carries a Bible, and usually has a run in her stocking, and the driver hopes that she isn't home sick.

22. See Robert Sweetman, "Of Tall Tales and Small Subversive Stories: Postmodern 'Fragmatics' and the Christian Historian," *Fides et Historia* 28:2 (1996): 50-68. Jean-François Lyotard's *The Postmodern Condition: A Report on Knowledge* (Minneapolis: University of Minnesota Press, 1984) provides the initial articulation of the concept of metanarrative.

23. I am indebted to Ruth Rempel for this suggestion. I do not know of any work on "metageography" that parallels work on "metanarrative." Martin W. Lewis and Kären E. Wigen's *The Myth of Continents: A Critique of Metageography* (Berkeley: University of California Press, 1997), which I have not yet seen, sounds promising in this regard.

Or I might appear in the story only as a missed fare, part of a pattern of decreasing ridership the streetcar company is worried about.

Historians doing construction work don't start from scratch. The matters we narrate didn't just happen to the folks involved. They had dreams and plans. They acted, as well as were acted upon. Their past actions affect us even as our storytelling "acts on" them. We, as historians, bring our formal tools (including narrative forms), and our points of view (sometimes formalized, as in Marxism, and sometimes implicit, as in racism). Our subjects, likewise, bring their doings, makings, constructions, interpretations. Paying attention to what the folks involved thought, or how the action affected them, enables us to include groups previously left out of even Hayden White's tropological stories. Our subjects have different points of view from each other and from us. Their views are intrinsic to our tale, internal to the historical matter. No single plot (or plot type) is big enough to hold all of our subjects' intrinsic points of view (let alone all the points of view the historical community may hold). White allows that there may be — indeed, should be — a variety of plots that historians make about a single historical matter. But he does not consider that the points of view of any of the "characters" in the plot might have any effect on the tale told. Also, by insisting that a narrative historical work contains only one main plot, he closes off the possibility of intrinsic voices in the story that interfere with or subvert the main plot. If we use stories to make sense of our individual and corporate lives, where we think we are headed in the story may become a kind of self-fulfilling prophecy. We will consciously or unconsciously shape our futures to reflect the story form we believe we are "in." For example, I might view my present life as a Comedy. After several difficult years, I am engaged to be married, at which time there will be an "occasional reconciliation of the forces at play" (to use White's phrase) in the wedding. After that, life goes on. Because I view this as a Comedy, I trust I will not be surprised if there are still difficult times after the wedding. The "reconciliation of forces" is "occasional," neither permanent nor inevitable. However, I could view this move to marriage as a Romance, with its overtones of final triumph. If so, I might be shocked when "the honeymoon is over." We can stick to our stock stories, shaped around Comedies, Tragedies, Satires, and Romances, bearing in mind the limits of each. But there is another way we can deal with the mill puddler. Individuals and groups participate in more than one story. We can take the puddler as a person, identify him not just by his craft, but by his religion, his social circles, his eating habits, his family, and his religion. Industrialization, while critical to many things in his life, was not the only thing in it, perhaps not even the most important thing to him. Even within the narrower story of his work the puddler is both victim and agent, disempowered and active, oppressed and triumphant. We can craft stories in which our "characters" play several roles. Our assessment of individuals or groups might then look like a biography of an actor's life, a discussion of the many roles that person or group played, a linking together of the many roles within the same subject. We can still ask the question: why this role, and not another? How did this person or group come to take this role? The metaphor of "role" provides us with both agency and its limits. Some roles are never offered, or are inappropriate. Some roles are declined, or reshaped. Those involved take up their callings, respond to opportunities and difficulties.

Since we can't tell all the stories, we have to decide which persons to track, which tales to tell. Here, I submit, is where a Christian historian can make choices in favor of those things we believe are most critical to faith: love, hope, joy, peace, endurance, compassion, and so on. Even when we are studying evil persons and horrible situations, we can bear witness to the truth. We can have an eye out for how all things are working together for good. We can put our energy into studying and bearing witness to the kinds of people Jesus spent his time with: the ordinary, the sick, the outcast, the searching.

If we cannot include multiple points of view simply by cramming more into our Romances, Satires, Comedies, or Tragedies, neither should we confuse our students and ourselves by constantly shifting external or internal points of view. I suggest we take as our beginning the point of view of a group of historical actors, watch what they do and what happens to them. We focus on one facet of the diamond for awhile, and let its reflection illuminate the entire structure of the course. If women had no Renaissance, what are we going to do in our course devoted to that time period and geographic area? Maybe we stick for a semester with what *did* happen to women, and let that illuminate the rest. Next year we do the course through the experiences of a different group. This year the mill puddler and friends, next year Carnegie, Frick, Gould, and Vanderbilt. Each year we admit that we don't have the tools to tell *the* story, but we can tell *a* story, a true story, about the past. Admitting to ourselves and our students that our vision is partial can have the paradoxical effect that we see more, and see better. When we are aware of our limits, we can pay better attention to what is inside of our field of vision. Our inclusions and exclusions become conscious and deliberate. When we tune in to one voice, we hear it more distinctly, but are aware of the welter of voices just down the dial, the static which contains voices we cannot make out.

But now we return to the question with which I began: is this just? My own sympathies lie with the mill puddler, not the robber baron. The robber baron not only reaped the financial benefits of his oppression of others, but he has reaped the historical benefits too. Historians have deemed him more worthy, his tale more worth telling, than the mill puddler's. But there is no intrinsic reason why this is so. Contemporary Roman historical writing contained no references to Jesus, an itinerant preacher in a remote part of the empire. Yet we deem Jesus' story of the utmost importance. We claim, in faith, that the City of God will outlast "the eternal city" of Rome. We then have a responsibility to try to counteract the pervasive stock cultural story, in which Carnegie and the rich have historically (in both senses) received more attention. We have this responsibility for three reasons. First, by ignoring "marginal," previously silenced voices, we perpetuate the wrong done to those people during their lifetimes. They lived lives as vibrant, as full, and as important, as those of the wealthy and powerful. In following Christ, we too must lift up the lowly to the center of the story and fill the hungry with good things. If we tell our students, directly or indirectly, that power and wealth are what matters in history, what are we telling them about their own lives? What gods are we encouraging them to serve? But if we bring forward the poor and serve those who cannot return our service, this means also sending the rich away empty of textual centrality, bringing down the powerful into the footnotes, scattering the proud here and there in the text. Second, because the dominant cultural story favors the powerful and wealthy, we need not worry that they will receive their due. The mass media, political rhetoric, and popular culture are like a continuing rerun of *Lifestyles of the Rich and Famous.* Presenting an alternative story is going against the stream. Our students may have never before considered that there is any story but one, one that emphasizes the politically, economically, and socially powerful. They may not have considered how that story (probably) excludes them and their ancestors. Third, we must study those who have not been studied before, "not because some politically correct dogma mandates it, or because we want to provide a 'feel good' therapy [for that group], but because we have to study [them] in order to understand our society and culture" of which they are a part.[24] How can we even give Andrew Carnegie his due without including his thousands of employees? In doing justice to the mill puddler, or women, or any other group, we are doing justice to the subject of history as a whole, history in all its "splendid messiness."[25] This is our calling; for a historian, there is none greater.

24. Lawrence Levine, *The Opening of the American Mind: Canons, Culture, and History* (Boston: Beacon Press, 1996), 156.

25. Simon Schama, "Clio Has a Problem," *New York Times Magazine*, 8 September 1991, 32.

Christianity, History, and Multiculturalism

EDWIN J. VAN KLEY

Among the more common politically correct terms used on American college and university campuses these days is multiculturalism. A long and cumbersome word, it seems to be misused frequently enough to render its precise meaning uncertain. Adjectivally it is applied to people, to families, to courses, and programs of studies. Administrators and university advancement offices talk about the desirability of a multicultural student body and faculty. By that they seem to mean that it would be desirable to have students and faculty from differing ethnic and cultural backgrounds in the hope that the cultures they represent will become part of the institution's intellectual and social world and will help students better to understand themselves and that world. The same ideal no doubt motivates what are not always accurately called multicultural programs. But whatever reservations we may have about the use of the term, the ideal behind the clunky word will not go away, and we must, both as historians and as Christians, reckon with it. If I may risk a minimalist definition of that ideal, I think it embraces not only an acceptance of a variety of cultures but also an attempt to understand and respect cultural traditions other than our own in order better to understand our neighbors in this racially and culturally diverse nation and on this shrinking planet. Furthermore we often come to a richer understanding of ourselves, mirror fashion, in comparison with other cultures. We may bumble a bit in our attempts to implement this ideal, but in the academy there appears to be rather wide acceptance of it. Certainly our colleges and universities, however much or little they presently embody the ideal, must prepare the next generation to live in this multicultural global village.

Christians face the same imperatives. Increasingly Christian churches in this land are ethnically and culturally mixed, and in the wider world the church has established itself in and acclimated itself to every variety of human culture. Understanding of and respect for each other's traditions and cultures is necessary if Christians are to tell the good news and do Christ's work together in an increasingly small world. Furthermore, Christians also have known all along that humankind is one: created by God, descended from Adam, redeemed in Jesus Christ. We used to sing about it in Sunday school: "red and yellow, black and white, all are precious in his sight." Many churches symbolize the unity of the Christian church across the ages and the miles by celebrating an annual worldwide communion Sunday. Christian scholars and teachers, therefore, should be among the more ardent proponents of multicultural ideals and goals in their academic institutions.

But these multicultural ideals and goals are not easy to achieve; some would say impossible. Edward Said in his *Orientalism* has effectively contended that what might have appeared to be Western multicultural-ism regarding the Near East during the past two centuries, not only foreign-office expertise but also scholarly studies of the Islamic world and its representation in art, literature, and music, grew out of and was conditioned by positions of power, by Western imperialism, and by a clear sense of Western cultural superiority. According to Said, what appears to be scholarly or artistic interest in Near Eastern or Islamic culture is really just another way of dominating, manipulating, and re-structuring it.[1] A "Review Symposium" on Said's book in the *Journal of Asian Studies* of March 1980 shows several participants in general agree-ment with Said as they applied his insights to their respective Asian fields.[2]

Perhaps Said is correct regarding much of the "orientalist" or Asianist scholarship of the past two centuries, regarding Western under-

1. Edward Said, *Orientalism* (New York: Pantheon Books, 1978).
2. Robert A. Kapp, Michael Dalby, David Kopf, and Richard A. Minear, "Re-view Symposium: Edward Said's *Orientalism,*" *The Journal of Asian Studies* 34:3 (May 1980), 481-577.

standing of the "other" in an age of Western cultural domination of the planet. The West, however, did not always dominate the planet, and a study of Western history in its global context prior to its nineteenth and twentieth century triumph discloses a startlingly different relationship between the West and the world's other high cultures which might provide useful lessons in multiculturalism for today's students. The study of global history thus might aid us in achieving and teaching multicultural goals.

By about 500 B.C. the globe supported four major centers of civilization: China, India, the Near East, and the West, if we consider Greek culture antecedent to what eventually became the West. Of the four the West was probably the least impressive. This was certainly the case after the fall of the Roman Empire in the fifth century A.D. From roughly 500 B.C. to A.D. 1500 the four centers of civilization coexisted in a kind of cultural balance. During these millennia each center continued to develop its peculiar cultural style, and each continued to spread its culture and often its control to the peoples and lands on its periphery. While the inhabitants of each center were aware of the others, sometimes traded with them, and occasionally borrowed from them, the contacts were sufficiently thin so that no one center threatened the existence, independence, or culture of the others.[3] During this long period, that is, through most of civilized human history, there was no question of Western superiority. No visiting professor from a Martian university would likely have predicted the eventual triumph of the West.

Most of what was known in the West about the other centers of civilization during the millennia of cultural balance evoked admiration, not a sense of superiority. The Greeks, for example, knew that India was very large, extremely hot, fabulously rich, and the source of much gold and precious stones. Greek writers also reported some negative aspects of Indian culture such as *suttee* and polygamy, and some outlandish things such as gold-digging ants, dog-headed people, and people with feet large enough to serve as parasols when supine. The Romans knew that India was the source of spices and that the much coveted silk came from China, which they called *Serica* as well as *Sinae*. With the rise of the Mongol empire in the thirteenth century direct overland travel between the West

3. The above macrohistorical scheme comes primarily from William H. McNeill, *The Rise of the West: A History of the Human Community* (Chicago: University of Chicago Press, 1963).

(Europe) and China became possible. A surprising number of papal or royal envoys, missionaries, and merchants traveled there, several of whom wrote reports of what they did and saw. Marco Polo's was not only the most popular but also the most comprehensive and reliable; in fact no better account of China was available in the West before the middle of the sixteenth century. Marco Polo considered China to be the largest, most populous, wealthiest, and strongest land in the thirteenth-century world.

During the long era of cultural balance (500 B.C. to A.D. 1500) many important scientific and technological innovations appear to have migrated to the West from the other centers of civilization, more often from China than from the others. The migration of technology was usually gradual, involving one or more intermediaries, the innovations usually being established in the West without any clear ideas about their origins; indeed without much interest in their origins. Much of the basic technology that enabled the Europeans to sail directly to Asia in about A.D. 1500 and later to begin their march towards global domination, was known earlier in the Asian centers and only later adopted or separately invented in Europe. The list is exceedingly long, but among the more important for Europe's post-1500 expansion were Indian-Arabic mathematics, gunpowder, printing, the magnetic compass, and the stern-post rudder. Without these there would have been no European expansion.[4]

While it had lagged well behind the other centers of civilization through most of civilized history, by 1500 the West's marine and military technology had begun to equal that of the Near East, India, and China and was obviously superior to that of the peripheral areas such as Africa, Southeast Asia, and the Americas. While by itself not very impressive, Vasco da Gama's voyage to India's Malabar Coast in 1498 established direct maritime contact between the West (Europe) and Asia and also inaugurated a new era in the relationships between the four major centers of civilization on the globe. Soon after 1500 the Europeans, beginning with the Portuguese and later followed by the Dutch and English, began to dominate the seas of Asia. As they did so, however, they moved along well-established sea-lanes, visited bustling seaports, and fit into a complex trading world which had been developed earlier by Muslim mer-

4. See Donald F. Lach, *Asia in the Making of Europe*, Vol. I: *The Century of Discovery*, Bk. 1 (Chicago: University of Chicago Press, 1965), 1-86, and Vol. II: *A Century of Wonder*, Bk. 3 (Chicago: University of Chicago Press, 1977), 395-400.

chants and which stretched from eastern Africa to the Philippines.[5] That they were able eventually to dominate this commercial world was due not to their superior ships and armies, but to the fact that the great Muslim empires of the sixteenth century — the Safavid Persian, the Ottoman Turkish, and the Mughul in northern India — seem to have been too busy consolidating their newly won empires to contest the Western intrusion. These powers as well as the Southeast and East Asian empires of Siam, Vietnam, China, and Japan had all as a matter of governmental policy turned away from the sea to their land empires and to land taxes as the source of their wealth and power. Had any of these resisted the European incursion the story might have had a very different ending. But they did not. The Mughul emperors, for example, usually allowed Europeans to trade freely in their ports, frequently without duties. Apart from the illegal Portuguese settlement at Macao, Europeans were not permitted to trade in China at all, and the Dutch attempt to force a commercial opening of China in 1622 was pathetically unsuccessful.[6] Only small Muslim commercial port-city states like Makassar on Celebes, Aceh on Sumatra, and Banten on Java, resisted the Dutch, and even these were not easily or quickly defeated.[7] Between 1500 and the middle of the eighteenth century the Europeans were able to carve out empires in peripheral areas such as the Americas, the Pacific Islands, and insular Southeast Asia, but they did not threaten the major centers of civilization in Asia. There they traded on sufferance, if at all. Fitting the history of Europe, and even that of France, England, or the United States, into that global context would go a long way towards dispelling notions of innate Western superiority.

Direct maritime contact with Asia almost immediately brought greatly increased quantities and varieties of Asian products to Europe; some familiar, like pepper and fine spices, and others, like Chinese porcelain and tea, new to Europeans. Some produced astonishing effects

5. On Islam's role in world history see Marshall G. S. Hodgson, *The Venture of Islam: Conscience and History in a World Civilization* (3 vols.; Chicago: University of Chicago Press, 1974).

6. See John E. Wills, Jr., *Pepper, Guns and Parleys: The Dutch East India Company and China, 1622-81* (Cambridge, MA: Harvard University Press, 1974), 21-23. For details see W. P. Groeneveldt, *De Nederlanders in China* (The Hague: Martinus Nijhoff, 1898).

7. See, for example, Bernard H. M. Vlekke, *Nusantara: A History of the East Indian Archipelago* (Cambridge, MA: Harvard University Press, 1945), 158-84.

in European society and industry.[8] Soon descriptions of the places and peoples who produced the products accompanied the products to European marketplaces.

At first, during the sixteenth century, the publications seem designed to inform other Asia-bound fleets about the conditions of trade or to elicit support for the newly founded Christian missions. Before long, however, the travel tales and descriptions became popular in their own right and profitable to publish.[9] During the seventeenth century what had been a fairly impressive stream of literature about Asia became a flood. Hundreds of books about the various parts of Asia, written by missionaries, merchants, mariners, physicians, soldiers, and independent travelers, were published during the period: at least twenty five major descriptions of South Asia, another fifteen describing mainland Southeast Asia, about twenty on insular Southeast Asia, and sixty or more on East Asia. In addition to these major independent accounts there were scores of published Jesuit letterbooks, derivative accounts, travel books containing brief descriptions of many Asian places, pamphlets, and newssheets. Finally there were composite encyclopedic descriptions, scholarly studies on Asian medicine, botany, religion, and history, and translations of important Chinese and Sanskrit works into European languages. These publications, varying in size from small pamphlets to lavishly illustrated tea-table volumes, were reprinted, republished, pirated, translated into most European languages, and collected in large multivolume compilations of travel literature. Press runs ranged from about 250 to 1,000 copies, and five to ten editions were not uncommon. In sum, the image of Asia was channeled to Europe in a huge corpus of publications which was widely distributed in all European lands and languages. Few literate Europeans could have been completely untouched by it, and it

8. Consider the social effects of tea in the Netherlands, for example; or the establishment of the Delft porcelain industry in imitation of Ming porcelain; or the technological innovations triggered by British attempts to compete with Indian calicoes which we customarily regard as the beginning of the industrial revolution. Regarding tea drinking see E. Van Kley, "The Effect of the Discoveries on Seventeenth-Century Dutch Popular Culture," *Terrae incognitae* 8 (1976): 36-39; on porcelain, H. E. van Gelder, "Oud-Nederlandsch aardewerk," *De gids* 88:4 (April 1924): 1-18; and on Indian calicoes, Dietmar Rothermund, *Europa und Asien im Zeitalter des Merkantilismus* (Darmstadt, 1978).

9. For a comprehensive survey of the sixteenth-century travel literature, see Lach, *Making of Europe,* Vol. I.

would be surprising indeed if its effects could not have been seen in contemporary European literature, art, learning, and culture.[10]

This vast corpus of sixteenth- and seventeenth-century European literature about Asia does not convincingly illustrate Said's "orientalism" and thus, like viewing Western history in global context, provides insights into multiculturalism from our own, Western, history. In the first place it does not support Said's thesis because, compared to the high cultures and great empires of Asia, European cultural and material achievements were not obviously superior, and Europeans were quite incapable of imposing their will on most of the newly discovered Asian peoples. To be sure, intemperate, uninformed, or hasty judgments on the part of Europeans frequently stereotyped Asians and their societies. Certain fixed formulations emerged from both the texts and the illustrations published in Europe. Hindus, for example, were thought to be obsessed by caste and the worship of a multitude of monstrous gods, Muslims by extreme judicial severity, Chinese by undue attention to ceremony and convention, Japanese by a calloused indifference towards suffering and death, Jains by an excessive respect for lower forms of life, Buddhists by an uncritical tolerance of all religious beliefs and sects, and all Asians by annoying and sometimes repulsive social habits and dietary customs. Indian *suttee* and Chinese footbinding were rarely applauded. Dutch writers almost invariably described Javans, Sumatrans, Amboinese, and Bandanese as lazy, dishonest, violent, and treacherous, probably because in many Southeast Asian places these peoples were subject to Dutch rule. Dutch reporters were not similarly biased about the Asians they did not attempt to govern, and they admired the successful and powerful Asians — Chinese, Indian, Japanese, and Siamese — as much as did other Europeans.

But while these and other hostile stereotypes reflected the prejudices of European and Christian commentators about a foreign and sometimes exotic scene, they must not be considered in isolation. They were balanced, perhaps over-balanced, by expressions of sincere admiration for the achievements of Asia's great civilizations. For example, most European writers admired Asian craftsmen and their products — Indian textiles and

10. For the European literature on Asia published during the seventeenth century and the images of the various parts of Asia which may have been derived from it see Donald F. Lach and Edwin J. Van Kley, *Asia in the Making of Europe*, Vol. III: *A Century of Advance*, Bks. 1-4 (Chicago: University of Chicago Press, 1993).

jewelry; Sumatran, Javan, or Makassarese boats; Sumatran or Javanese krisses; Japanese swords; Chinese porcelain, silk, and lacquerware. They frequently described Asian craftsmen as more skilled than their European counterparts, not only in what they traditionally produced but also in imitating European products. European attempts to imitate Asian products — for example, Indian cotton cloth and Chinese porcelain — were not very successful. Nevertheless, clumsy attempts to reproduce Ming porcelain resulted in a new industry in Delft, and the attempt to compete with Indian calicoes may have engendered the innovations in British textile manufacturing which we associate with the Industrial Revolution. Curiously, despite the fact that by the first third of the seventeenth century European ships controlled Asia's seas, almost all European observers admired Asian ships and boats, fairly convincing evidence that European control of Asian seas in the seventeenth century resulted more from the indifference of Asia's great powers than from superior European technology. On land, networks of roads with regularly spaced hostels for official and other travelers in countries like China, Siam, Japan, and the Mughul Empire evoked regular admiration.

Most European observers were overwhelmed by the huge populations of Asian states and by the numerous large cities. Remember that in the sixteenth and seventeenth centuries large populations were not considered intractable problems but signs of wealth and strength. In fact European observers almost unanimously admired the power and wealth of Asian courts and seemed never to weary of rehearsing the details of their luxury. It seems they also never tired of reporting population statistics for the Mughul Empire, Siam, China, and Japan, or the numbers of soldiers who could be quickly called up by these rulers and the taxes which could be raised from these numerous peoples. Europeans seemed just as impressed that Asian governments were able to keep such accurate statistics for their populations, armies, and revenues. No contemporary European state could have done so. China's was the most impressive population. European writers found it difficult to convey its immensity to their readers. They described huge cities, larger than any in Europe, within sight of each other. To better envision its population Father Martino Martini suggested that his readers regard China with its fifteen provinces, each larger than any European kingdom, surrounded as it is by the Great Wall, as one enormous city.[11]

11. Martino Martini, *Novus atlas sinensis* . . . (Amsterdam: Joannes Blaeu, 1655), 5.

Admiration for China, however, was not confined to its population. Beginning with Mendoza and the earliest sixteenth-century Jesuit reports, Europe's image of China was, if anything, too adulatory. The Jesuits and other writers extolled its abundant natural resources, skilled craftsmen, and brisk commerce which enabled the empire easily to support its huge population. They marvelled at its imperial palaces, fine bridges, the porcelain tower in Nanjing, and at China's most celebrated engineering feats: the Grand Canal and the Great Wall. Perhaps even more impressive than the emperor's powerful and sumptuous court was China's large, complex bureaucracy, staffed not by hereditary aristocrats but by scholars selected through competitive, written examinations for their command of Confucian philosophy, history, poetry, and even art. In the words of Johann Hoornbeek, a conservative Dutch theologian: "Here verily is a land where philosophers rule and rulers philosophize."[12] A huge corpus of official histories recorded an antiquity far higher than that of the Greeks, Romans, or Hebrews, replete with great philosophers and poets to rival the best of the Western tradition. Confucian philosophy, Chinese learning and education in general, the written language, and the huge number of published books also evoked adulatory descriptions. China was described to Europeans as a uniquely literary culture; for this and many other reasons it was regularly recommended as a model for Europe.

Obviously there were limits to the admiration of Asian religions. Those who described Asia to European readers were almost unanimous in their distaste for Islam, although increasingly during the seventeenth century they discerned differences between Indian and Southeast Asian Islam and the Near Eastern varieties. Merchants and sailors often depicted Asia's other religions as gross idolatry or devil worship. Even perceptive observers like the Jesuits painted mostly negative pictures of Japanese and Chinese Buddhism. On the other hand, Jesuits in Siam and Tibet, where Buddhism was the official religion, described Buddhism quite sympathetically. It appears that their stereotypes of Buddhism were formed as much by the attitudes of the local elites as by their Christian prejudices.[13] In

12. Johann Hoornbeek, *De conversione indorum & gentilium, libri duo* (Amsterdam: Johannem Janssonium, 1669), 44.

13. See E. Van Kley, "Buddhism in Early Jesuit Reports: The Parallel Cases of China and Tibet," in *International Symposium on Chinese-Western Cultural Interchange in Commemoration of the 400th Anniversary of the Arrival of Matteo Ricci, S.J. in China* (Taipei: [n.p.], 1983), 803-15.

China, the bureaucracy was officially Confucian, and officials often viewed Buddhism with disdain, a fact which the Jesuits in China incorporated into their mission strategy. Despite their understandable Christian bias, however, several European writers painstakingly struggled to understand the intricacies of sectarian Buddhism, Hinduism, and even popular Daoism; and they presented their findings with remarkably little antipathy and considerable respect.[14] Meanwhile the Jesuits in China were if anything too admiring of Confucianism, usually considering it to have evolved with admirably few adulterations from the ancient worship of the true God and sometimes not considering it to be a religion at all. Most writers also seemed to respect the personal behavior of the common believers in Asian religions. Hindus were praised for their courtesy, modesty, and compassion, and the public morality of the common believers also drew favorable comment. One Jesuit in China observed that despite the stories Confucians told about them he found most Buddhist priests to be sincere, pious, and chaste.[15] Many writers — remember the background of the European wars of religion — openly admired Hindu and Buddhist tolerance for other religions, although missionaries were frequently frustrated by it.

Despite what European writers considered idolatrous religions, and distasteful social or dietary practices, the image of Asian peoples which emerges from the sixteenth- and seventeenth-century literature was mostly positive. Among the positive stereotypes were the industry and frugality of Chinese peasants and craftsmen, the modesty and seclusion of Chinese and Japanese women. Asian women generally were admired for their chastity and fidelity. On the other hand, the exclusively male European observers reported with surprise and some admiration that several city-states of India and Southeast Asia were ruled by powerful queens; that some Southeast Asian male monarchs were personally served and guarded solely by women; that on India's Malabar Coast and in the Marianas Islands matrilineal systems of descent prevailed, where women also held property in their own right; that in Siam and Insulindia

14. See, for example, Philippus Baldaeus, *Afgoderye der Oost-Indische heydenen*, ed. A. J. de Jong (The Hague: Martinus Nijhoff, 1917); Abraham Rogerius, *De open-deure tot het verborgen heydendom* (Leiden: Francoys Hackes, 1651); and David Wright in Olfert Dapper, *Gedenkwaerdig bedryf der Nederlandsche Oost-indische Maetschappye op de kuste en in het keizerrijk van Taising of China* (2 vols.; Amsterdam: J. van Meurs, 1670), I:42-51.

15. Alvaro Semedo, *The History of the Great and Renowned Monarchy of China* (London: J. Crook, 1655), 89-90.

commerce and many agricultural tasks were considered women's work; and that in most parts of Insulindia women could initiate divorce, remarry, and inherit property.

Most observers considered Asian children better behaved than European children, despite the gentler discipline with which they were reportedly raised. Learning and literacy were judged to be held in higher esteem throughout Asia than in Europe. Despite the apparent absence of scientific principles, Asian medicine was generally respected and the European physicians who traveled in Asia seem to have learned more than they taught. Early sixteenth-century Jesuits judged the Japanese to be the "best people yet to be discovered": loyal, courageous, and white.[16] Many later observers, however, reported that other Asians did not admire white skin. But regardless of skin color, the personal conduct of ordinary people in the high civilizations of Asia was frequently seen as superior to that of Europeans and held up for emulation.

Many of the stereotypes, both positive and negative, and even many of the descriptions were borrowed from previous literature; frequently European travelers in Asia saw what they expected to see, all of which might be understood to support Said's thesis. The texts sometimes seem to take on a life of their own. But over time the stereotypes were frequently modified, qualified, and discarded in the face of new evidence. Even the most China-struck Jesuit writers also reported flaws in China's marvelous government: bureaucratic factionalism, greedy and rapacious officials, officials' abuse of power, and overly harsh punishments, for example. Likewise, despite their generally harsh judgment of Javan character, Dutch officials found individual Javans and even some general Javan characteristics admirable. They also judged the landscape to be spectacularly beautiful. Many European writers who explored the reasons for *suttee* and footbinding came to understand, if not approve, even these offensive practices.

How then can Christian historians — or any historians — elude what Said calls "orientalism" and achieve something approaching the ideal of multiculturalism in our thinking, teaching, research, and writing? First, simply by consistently taking a longer view; by always consciously fitting the smaller and more recent pieces of history we teach and write about into their universal, global context. They are, after all, small,

16. C. R. Boxer, *The Christian Century in Japan* (Berkeley: University of California Press, 1951), 74-77, 401-5.

usually recent chapters of the big story — the history of the human race. If we are able to keep the big story constantly in view as we work perhaps we will be less likely to universalize the small pieces; to mistake our backyards for the world and our times for all times. Second, and admittedly closer to my own backyard, to become more familiar with the West's own attitudes towards the other in the centuries before it dominated the globe and to discover that the smug "orientalism" about which Said rightly complains was not always our distinguishing characteristic. It is not an easy task. For many historians it means always seeing the entirety of American history — never mind the little pieces — as an offshoot of a much older and richer Western or European history which in turn during most of human history was the least impressive of the four major centers of civilization on the globe.

Finally we should realize and teach that the modern, secular, quantified, scientific, industrial Western culture which has come to dominate the globe during the past two centuries resulted from rapid and massive changes in Western culture beginning about 1600. This transmuted West, as Marshall Hodgson called it, has indeed suppressed or distorted all traditional cultures, including traditional Western culture.[17] It has indeed become cosmopolitan global culture and as such, whatever its original relationship to the traditional West, need not always be directed by Westerners.

17. Marshall G. S. Hodgson, *Rethinking World History: Essays on Europe, Islam, and World History*, ed. Edmund Burke III (Cambridge: Cambridge University Press, 1993), 44-71.

Contributors

MARGARET LAMBERTS BENDROTH is Associate Professor of History at Calvin College.

C. STEPHEN EVANS is Professor of Philosophy and Dean for Research and Scholarship at Calvin College.

G. MARCILLE FREDERICK is Librarian at the Institute for Christian Studies, Toronto.

D. G. HART is Professor of Church History and Director of the Montgomery Memorial Library at Westminster Theological Seminary.

BILL J. LEONARD is Dean of Wake Forest University Divinity School.

GEORGE M. MARSDEN is the Francis A. McAnaney Professor of History at the University of Notre Dame.

SHIRLEY A. MULLEN is Professor of History at Westmont College.

MARK A. NOLL is Professor of History and the McManis Professor of Christian Thought at Wheaton College.

RICHARD POINTER is Professor of History at Westmont College.

JERRY L. SUMMERS is the Sam B. Hall Professor of History at East Texas Baptist University.

CONTRIBUTORS

ROBERT P. SWIERENGA is Research Professor at the A. C. Van Raalte Institute at Hope College and Professor of History Emeritus at Kent State University.

EDWIN J. VAN KLEY is Professor of History Emeritus at Calvin College.

RONALD A. WELLS is Professor of History and Director of the Calvin Center for Christian Scholarship at Calvin College.